To V

Of Course I Said Yes!

Enjoy!

Arthur Barrow

Dedicated to my wife, Randi Barrow.

Copyright © 2016 by Arthur Barrow

Cydonian Music

Chapter One

I was not a prodigy, nor was I encouraged by family or friends to pursue a career in music, though there were some musical people in my family. I never had a mentor, and I did not even start playing the bass, my main performing instrument, until I was in my early twenties. What I did have was a good ear, a natural affinity for unusual harmonies and odd time signatures, and a lot of love and enthusiasm for music. This book tells the unlikely story of how I came to live the life of a professional musician and composer.

My earliest memory of music is hearing my father play Chopin nocturnes on the old baby grand piano in our living room. He would often play them for my brother, my sister, and me to calm us down and help us go to sleep after we had been put to bed for the night. Being put to sleep by my father playing lullabies on the piano is a truly lovely memory, and may be the reason why classical music is my favorite to this day.

He played pretty well, really. His dad had been a piano teacher, so my father and his siblings all took piano lessons as soon as they could sit at the keyboard. My grandfather was said to have been very strict, and would not allow any popular music to be played in the house. So none was played, at least while he was around. My dad said that the children had to hide their sheet music of popular songs and suffer the consequences if any was found by their father. My dad carried on that "tradition" by banning the playing of any rock records in the house when he was home. I never met my grandfather; he died when my dad was only about 16. Luckily, a cousin of mine saved some of his things which I now have, including a 100 year old leather bound copy of the Beethoven piano sonatas with his name inscribed on the front: Arthur Barrow.

Though my father played piano well, his real love was the organ, especially theater organ. My father grew up in Buffalo, New York, so I always thought of him as a New Yorker. His older brother was in seminary school in New York City in the 1920's. My father used to visit him there, and they would go see silent movies in the grand movie houses of the day. He loved hearing the "Mighty Wurlitzer" in the hands of the master musicians who provided live accompaniments to the films. His favorite part was before the movie began, when the organ console would rise up from the orchestra pit on a hydraulic lift and entertain the audience for a few dazzling minutes. My dad loved to tell us about the Wurlitzers, how some had real pianos, xylophones, and percussion playable from the organ console, as well as the "toy counter." That was an array of buttons connected to *real* fire bells and train whistles, suspended sheet metal for thunder, and a variety of other live sound effects. That is where the phrase "all the bells and whistles" comes from. It should come as no surprise that my other strong early memory of music was hearing my dad play his George Wright theater organ records, which were pretty amazing. I now have a lot of those recordings on CD's. His recorded versions of "Slaughter on 10th Avenue" and "Quiet Village" are second to none.

My father never made a living in music, but he was the assistant organist at St. Luke's, our Episcopal church in San Antonio. That meant he played at the dreaded 7:45 a.m. communion service with never more than a handful of people in attendance, half of whom were our family. Since he always liked to warm up beforehand, we arrived a*t 7:00* a.m. and had to wait 45 minutes before sitting and kneeling through the service! That is one of the reasons why I have a strong dislike for church to this day, but fortunately, it did not affect my love of organ music. He was also responsible for educating me about the natural harmonic series that is found in musical tone. He explained how the mixtures of those harmonic overtones are part of what creates different timbres, as in the way a flute sounds different from a clarinet. I know professional musicians today who have almost no understanding of this important and interesting subject, but my father was well versed in it.

I don't know if there is really a genetic component to musicality, but it turns out I do have musical forebears on both sides of my family. My first instrument was a plastic ukulele given to me by my maternal grandmother, who used to play ukulele and sing in her younger years. She said she once had a radio show in Corpus Christi called "Billy and Her Uke." (The poor woman's first name was William – the explanation was that her parents wanted a boy.) She did parodies of popular songs of the day, until she did one about the local sheriff which he did not find amusing. That was the end of her Corpus Christi radio career. So much for freedom of speech in old Texas. She also wrote original songs. I have a cassette tape of her singing some of them. They are very sweet and corny love songs.

My mother claimed not to care much about music, though she did have a favorite song, "Greensleeves." Yet when she was old and suffering from dementia, one day, from out of nowhere, she began singing "San Antonio Rose" in a lovely molto vibrato voice as we drove through the Texas hill country on a Sunday afternoon. I had never really heard her sing like that before.

I got that plastic uke when I was in second grade, and my brother and I both enjoyed playing it. Pretty soon we – mostly he – had written an original up-tempo instrumental chord tune on it which was about 20 seconds long. That was enough for me, so I took it to school for a class talent show. My main competition was a bright girl named Mary who had been taking piano lessons and played well for a second grader. She played her piece and received a nice round of applause. Then I whipped out my plastic uke and played our original tune (it never had a title). When I got to the snazzy ending, the room went wild. They loved it! It was my first taste of pleasing a crowd, and I liked it

It wasn't long until I started to learn how to play by ear. The first time I recall doing it was picking out the bass line to "Hit the Road, Jack" on our baby grand piano when I was nine years old. I was thrilled and encouraged that I could do it. Using my ear has proven to be very valuable to me in my musical life.

I have always loved riding a bike. I had a clunky one-speed, and I learned to do a few tricks on it. Sometimes, I could pull off a two-wheel drift on a street corner where there was a little sand. I could even ride it up stairs, I swear. Once or twice I took it up one of the two-story metal fire escape slides at the school, and rode it down, launching myself into the air for several seconds! I was fast, too. I knew a guy named Chris Geppert who went to St. Peter's, the nearby Catholic school. Chris showed up at the St. Peter's asphalt school playground one day with his brand new fifteen-speed German bike that his rich parents had bought him. It was a sweet ride, but he was a bit hefty. One day I challenged him to a race across the playground. I gave it all I had and rode like the wind, leaving him in the dust of my one-speed clunker. Chris grew up to be a well-known pop singer. More on him later.

In my third grade music class, the class project was for us to write a song together with the teacher. Ours was titled "Bicycle Bill." Someone came up with the first line, "Bicycle Bill was such a clown." I suggested "He could ride bikes upstairs and down" as the next line. The teacher said it was no good because no one could ride a bike up stairs. I protested that I could, and another kid chimed in with "I've seen him do it!" The teacher relented, and the line remained on the chalkboard - my first lyric, and it was based on real world experience.

Like his father before him, my dad insisted that all his kids take piano lessons. He made sure my older brother and sister stuck with them, and they both studied for long enough that they learned to read music pretty well. Some years later, it was my turn for lessons, but things worked out differently for me. The learning pieces I was given were so simple that I memorized them right away. When I went in for my lessons, I would play just fine, but I would be looking at my hands as I played from memory. The teacher wanted me to read the sheet music and even put a piece of cloth over my hands so I couldn't see them, but it didn't help. I didn't really like the lessons. I guess my parents gave up on making me take them, and so the lessons ended. I wish I had continued because I might be a better music reader now. Sight-reading has never been my strong point. I'm still working on it, though. I spend a half hour almost every day reading through Bach organ pieces, and I'm getting better.

Having an older brother and sister, I ended up with a lot of hand me downs, and I grew to resent that somewhat. It got to the point where if my brother had done something, I didn't want to do it. He was a boy scout, so I wouldn't join. He was an acolyte, or altar boy in church: not me. My sister sang in the church choir, and talked me into trying it one time. I hated it, especially the robes. My brother had played clarinet in the school band, and then later switched to sousaphone in high school. Since we still had his clarinet, my parents thought I should try playing it in the sixth grade school band. They even spent a couple of bucks having it refurbished. I went once or twice to the band class, but I soon decided it wasn't for me and quit. I did still like strumming on things, though.

Sometime in about 1962 our neighborhood got its first "beatnik." He was a very nice guy with a beard named John, I think, who played guitar pretty well. He heard me flail away on my uke, and thought I had potential. He encouraged me and suggested to my parents that they get me a 4-string tenor guitar because the chord fingering was the same as a ukulele. Amazingly, they bought me a nice Harmony tenor guitar for my eleventh birthday. I was thrilled.

By this time, I was getting into folk songs, specifically, the Kingston trio, mainly because we had one of their albums. Who knows why we owned it, but I liked it and learned quite a few of their songs by ear off that record. It was a great way for me to learn a lot of basic chords and develop my ear. I particularly liked the humorous ones like "Bad Man's Blunder" which is about the consequences of shootin' a deputy down. My parents liked to have friends over for cocktails. Often, after they had a few, my parents would ask me to get my guitar and entertain the guests, which I was happy to do. Those were fun times. (A few years later, when I was into Zappa, they asked me to perform at one of their parties. I said yes, as long as I could play whatever I wanted. I whipped out "Take Your Clothes Off When You Dance" and "What's the Ugliest Part of Your Body." To my great surprise, they were still quite entertained!)

By the time I got to junior high I had discovered something far more musically advanced than the folk songs I had been learning: surf music. My next-door neighbor had a Ventures album, and we loved it. "Pipeline," "Wipe Out," "Windy and Warm," and "Walk, Don't Run" were some of our favorites. Wow, these surf bands were playing "bar chords" and "leads," techniques of which I had no knowledge. It was then I knew I had to get an electric guitar. It would be my first 6-string.

I took the bus down Broadway to Mayfield Music, where I saw the guitar of my dreams, or at least the guitar I might have a chance to actually own because it was way cheaper than a Fender: an Alamo Fiesta. (Yes there really was a local music manufacturer named Alamo, like everything else in San Antonio.) It was a 2-pickup sunburst lightweight model with really awful action, but I didn't know about such things then. It was sure more fun to play than my tenor guitar. Being electric, of course I would need an amp. The cheapest one in the store was a Kent with a four-inch speaker, one knob, and about one watt of power, useful for practice only. Mr. Mayfield made me an offer: with the tenor guitar as a trade-in, I could get the Alamo and the Kent for $100.00. I set my heart on that combo.

There was only one problem: my father hated rock music and the electric guitar. He was not going to lift a finger or fork over a dime to help me buy it. I thought I might raise the money by mowing lawns in the neighborhood, but he said no. That would be too much wear and tear on his mower. I thought I might raise the cash by washing some neighbors' cars. To that, he conceded, even allowing me to use water from our yard hose. The wet stuff must have been almost free.

So, in the summer between seventh and eighth grade, I hustled around the neighborhood and talked people into letting me wash their cars for $1.50 apiece. The neighbors were pretty helpful, and after a couple of months, I had saved up about $70. That's a lot of car washing.

One hot summer night my parents had their friends the Wyatts over for a few drinks on the front porch. Miles Wyatt was a great, fun loving, successful commercial real estate guy who smoked cigars, drank, and played excellent boogie-woogie piano. I told him about saving up for the guitar, showing him the page in my notebook where I was keeping track of how much I needed to fulfill my dream. When he saw that I needed just $30, he pulled out his wallet and handed me three tens! I couldn't believe it! My father insisted that I pay it back, which I did, of course. I think my dad was a little embarrassed and/or shamed by the whole affair. My brother told me later that he had intended to help me out himself, but Mr. Wyatt beat him to it.

By the next day, I had my Alamo! I was so excited I slept with the thing. I was playing bar chords, learning leads, rocking out – the whole bit. What great fun. Within a month I was in my first band: The Deacons, comprised of drums and three electric guitars. We made one guy turn down his tone control and play the bass parts. We were getting more and more into surf music, even though San Antonio is a very long way from anywhere that one can surf. We just loved the way the guitars sounded, and it was fairly easy music to play and be learning some basics at the same time. I know from a tape I have from the time that my voice had not yet even changed, and I was already a working musician, sort of. Of course, I didn't have a decent amp, so I always had to borrow one or plug into the second channel of my bandmate's amp. I think we had a total of about three paying gigs. It didn't last long. The next band incarnation was The Townsmen. It, too, was short lived. Dickie, the drummer moved away, so it was time for something new.

In the ninth grade (1966–1967) the solution was The Restless Ones, named after the movie. I had never seen or heard of the film and had no idea what it was about. Our bass player, Jesse, suggested it and it stuck. In this band we had drums, two guitars and a bass, with me on lead guitar. By then bandmate Jim had put together a homemade strobe light in shop class that was pretty cool. It consisted of a round piece of wood about a foot and a half in diameter with a hole cut on one side, mounted on a fan motor that was attached to a box with a strong bulb in it. It worked pretty well, but it is a miracle the thing never caught fire. We all agreed that the strobe was enough to make us a "psychedelic" band. We got some paisley shirts and had some cards printed up that said, "The Restless Ones – For Your Psychedelic Entertainment." Yep, we were psychedelic high school freshmen.

We actually had quite a few paying gigs, including our big one: a high school dance way down in Del Rio, a border town. It paid the enormous sum of $125! Of course we had to pay for our own transportation and a motel out of that. Jim's dad, always the accommodating one, drove us down there and the whole band shared one cheap motel room. I remember playing The Electric Prunes' song "I Had Too Much to Dream Last Night" at that gig, so we were pretty psychedelic, all right. Our bass player got into trouble when he bought a switchblade in Mexico and got caught with it. The whole band got into trouble staying up late and making too much noise in our shared motel room. That band fell apart when we lost our drummer, Mike, whose dad made him quit due to poor grades.

I have a vague recollection of the first time I was ever on TV. I must have been around 14 or 15 years old when the father of a school chum of mine, who was some kind of a small time promoter, was trying to establish a local American Bandstand type of show in San Antonio and had gotten R.C. Cola as a sponsor. We auditioned for it and were hired to be the house band. The show was broadcast live from a gymnasium sized room with a stage at either end. We set up at one end and the guest band was at the other. For some reason, the director had me sit on the edge of the stage when we performed. I recall playing and singing lead on "In the Midnight Hour." I never actually knew the words to the song except for the first verse, so I just faked my way through it! Nobody seemed to notice. The only other thing I recall is that the guest band was a popular Texas psychedelic band, The 13th Floor Elevators, who played their hit, "You're Gonna Miss Me." They are credited with being one of the first psychedelic bands ever. I think that we did the show only once before the plug was pulled.

By the start of my sophomore year I had outgrown my Alamo guitar and was ready for something better. A guy I knew named Steve - who looked like Donovan and was an expert at doing light shows with an overhead projector and vegetable oil - had an almost new Fender Stratocaster that he wanted to sell because he decided he wanted a Telecaster instead. I think the Strat sold for about $250 new, and he was asking $175 for it. I had the money (that I had earned doing gigs, mind you) but my dad still had the say-so as to what I could spend it on. He said I could pay no more than $150 for the Strat. Steve said $165 was as low as he would go, so without telling my dad, I borrowed $15 from my bandmate Jim and got the guitar. I was thrilled all over again. The action on it felt like butter to me, and it had the rich Fender tone *and* a whammy bar. I was in love. This is the guitar that was destined to be *the* Stratocaster with a whammy bar. It was a secondhand guitar, and yes, we practiced in the garage by the Dodge, a green 1951 four door sedan. Not long after I bought it, Jimi Hendrix exploded onto the music scene and Steve wanted to buy it back from me, but I said, "No way!"

I remember clearly the first time I heard some Hendrix songs. There was a little canteen by the high school football field called the Mule Stall, the Mules being the name of our football team, where there would be dances with live music after the games. There was a good local band there one night called The Children who played versions of "Purple Haze," "Fire," and "Foxy Lady." I was so blown away by the songs that I asked the band about them after the set. One of them said, "That's Jimi Hendrix, man!" That was the first I heard of Hendrix, and his music was amazing even when played by a local San Antonio band! My next memory of him was hearing "Foxy Lady" on the car radio of our '56 Chevy. I didn't even realize at the time that the incredible sounds I was hearing were coming from a guitar. At first I thought it was some kind of electronic machine or something. When it finally dawned on me it was a guitar, I thought, "I don't know who this Jimi Hendrix guy is, but he sure has a hell of a good guitar player in his band!" Then when I found out Jimi *was* the guitar player *and* he was playing a Stratocaster just like mine, well, I was over the moon to say the least.

Buying the new guitar coincided with the birth of another band. This incarnation was called The Wisdom. We all know how wise high school sophomores are, right? This band had an organ player, who played a Gibson organ like Ray Manzarek's, and a lead singer who had a P.A., a first for any band I had been in. Up until that time, we plugged a mic into a guitar amp. I still did not yet have a decent amp, however. I had moved up to an old Fender Deluxe, but it never had enough power, so I was still borrowing amps. This band did a few gigs, some at the many military bases around San Antonio. Our biggest gig was going to College Station, Texas, home of the Aggies, to play a frat party. That band fizzled, too, of course, when bandmate Jim was sent off to a private military academy, also due to poor grades.

In 1967 The Doors' first album was released which featured the incredible masterpiece song "Light My Fire." I was an impressionable fifteen year-old and it quickly became my favorite song. It still is. Having a "favorite song" is a very teenage thing, of course, but I love everything about it: the fabulous melodic intro, the mysterious tonality of the verses, the extended solos, the lyrics, the vocal performance, and the dynamics are superb in every way. Who can resist the urge to sing along with the final "Try to set the night on fire!!!" I soon borrowed that first Doors album and listened to it many times. Though I bought very few records in order to save money for music equipment, from then on I bought every Doors album as soon as they were released up until the time Morrison died. I think The Doors were one of the most important bands from the sixties, and I am still a huge fan.

It was also about this time that I really began to appreciate the genius of The Beatles. I had a copy of *Sgt. Pepper's Lonely Hearts Club Band* and listened to it so often that I just about wore it out. In fact, I had heard it so many times that I could virtually "play it back" in my head by merely thinking about it and "hearing" it as if I was experiencing it on headphones. I would often "listen" to it mentally from top to bottom as I did my weekly lawn mowing task which took about forty minutes. It was exactly the right length of time so that the final chord of "A Day in the Life" would be dying out just as I was hacking the last blade of grass. I think this mental exercise may have helped me later in my music career when I needed to do a lot of memorization.

Somewhere in there I learned to play some very basic drums. Our drummer had shown me a few simple beats, and when he left his drums at our house for a while I had a chance to practice them. Another friend of mine had a band whose drummer couldn't make a couple of gigs. Their drummer let me borrow his drums to do the gigs, which were a lot of fun. I recall playing drums at the Fort Sam Houston army base for a bunch of G.I.'s. Having all those military bases in and around San Antonio was actually a good thing for musicians. The bases provided quite a bit of work for local bands, so this kind of gig was pretty common. But this time, for reasons I can't remember, we wore very phony looking Beatle wigs! I don't think we fooled anyone, though. What a weird scene. No doubt many of those poor army guys had been in Vietnam, and came back only to be entertained by a few kids in Beatle wigs. Such a deal.

It was about this time that my dad fulfilled a dream he'd had for decades. I even have a letter referring to it that he wrote to my mother when he was stationed in the Philippines during World War II. He finally bought a Hammond organ: a beautiful RT3, the flagship Hammond of 1959. He sold the family piano to help pay for it and to make room for it. He bought it from the new main organist at our church, a very enthusiastic woman named Madolyn who really brought some life to the music in the church. She was an amazing player, quite inspiring. The Hammond had been her practice organ, but she no longer needed it, so it was the perfect opportunity for my dad. The main part of the organ is the same as a B3. The difference is in the pedals: the RT3 has a two and a half octave concave pedal board so that you can play the complete classical repertoire, and an extra tone generating system for the pedals that includes the very low 32' sub-octave tone that can be added to the normal Hammond pedal sounds. In contrast, the Hammond B3 has only a flat two octave pedal board. I still have that organ at my studio and it gets a lot of use.

For Texans, our family had a fair amount of culture. We attended performances by the San Antonio Symphony Orchestra at the Municipal Auditorium several times, and my dad even took me to a classical guitar concert there by the great Carlos Montoya. But the best classical performance I saw in San Antonio was the utterly incredible Virgil Fox playing his new electronic Rodgers organ in the late 60's. Man, he blew the roof off the place! My dad and I both loved it.

It was also around this time that I went to my first live rock shows. At that same Municipal Auditorium I saw the Beach Boys with Chad and Jeremy (or was it Peter and Gordon?) and later The Jimi Hendrix Experience with The Soft Machine as the opening act. I thought they were both good, but Jimi was incredible. Things were pretty crude in those days, and they didn't even have a proper P.A. They just used the little built-in speakers in the ceiling that were meant for announcements. All you could really hear was the guitar and some distorted bass, but that was OK, since Jimi's guitar was what I came to hear.

I also saw Randy California and Spirit play there with the bald headed drummer who was Randy's stepfather, Ed Cassidy. The curtain opened to a wall of Acoustic brand amps and a deafening blast of tape feedback noise coming from an Echoplex, something I had never heard before. They then launched into their latest single "I Got a Line on You." They were really good, too. Twenty years down the road I would actually get a chance to record some music with them. I also saw Frank Zappa and the Mothers play at the same Municipal Auditorium with Flo and Eddie in 1970. More on all of that later.

My next band, in my junior year, was with a guy named Ralph who was a good organ player, but a very strange guy. He was smart with electronics, and convinced us that instead of getting jobs to save money for good equipment, we should build the amps from kits and make speaker cabinets in shop class. It was a dumb idea. It took forever, and the amps turned out to be unreliable, as we soon found out. The band was called "The Celebration of the Gnu" after the Jim Morrison poem "Celebration of the Lizard." We played a lot of Doors, Hendrix, and Cream. When we finally did do our "big gig" it was a disaster.

My high school hosted concert events called "pay assemblies." Once a month or so they would have local bands play in the school auditorium and charge 15 cents at the door. It occurred during what would normally be the useless "homeroom" period after lunch. A few weeks before we were to play one of these events,

Chris Geppert's band, Flash, had played one, replete with a stage full of expensive equipment, including drums, a B3 with a Leslie, a bunch of Kustom amps, (those funny looking padded things) a good P.A., and a fog machine to boot. They were good, and the kids loved them.

Soon after that it was our turn to do a pay assembly. I should preface this story by saying we were not among the "cool" people at that school, which was very clique-ish. We were nerds, way before it was cool. I thought this was going to be my big chance to show how we really *were* cool because we could do something all the kids loved: play some rock and roll!

We had decided that it would be clever to dress up weird, in tuxes and tails and such. Our bass player wore a cape. As luck would have it, there was a drama class in the auditorium during the period right before we were to play, so we got no sound check at all. When we were finally able to get set up and turn on our gear, we discovered, to our horror, that the homemade bass amp failed! Ralph scrambled and figured out a way to run the bass through his home made organ amp. It worked, but it sounded awful. It was time to go on.

The curtain opened and we started playing "Hot Smoke and Sassafras" by the Texas band Bubble Puppy. We had talked a couple of girls into being our "go-go" dancers for the big event and they were shakin' it on either side of the stage. We sounded bad and looked like fools. Pretty soon a guy from another band, someone I had known since first grade, started booing and throwing stuff at us. This caught on right away, and a room full of people, a lot of whom I had known since grade school, joined in with the booing and throwing. I don't recall how many songs we got through, but we were about to try to shock everyone by playing Steppenwolf's "Goddamn the Pusher Man." We had just started it when some kid backstage decided to pull the curtain on us as the crowd began to walk out, perhaps preventing a riot, who knows.

This was a devastating experience. My dream of our performance propelling us to the status of "cool" was shattered. I had never taken any psychedelic drugs at that point, but I thought to myself, *"This must be what a bad acid trip is like."* Good student that I was, I was never one to skip class, but after this there was no way I was going to the very strict and tough Mrs. Vordenbaum's

English class I had coming up after our disaster. I knew I couldn't face it, and I was willing to accept the consequences for skipping it. When I got to her class the next day, she looked very angry and asked why I had not been in class the day before. I explained what had happened, expecting to get whatever punishment I had coming. Instead, to my surprise, she seemed to understand. She softened and decided to let me off the hook. God bless you, Mrs. Vordenbaum, I'll never forget that act of mercy. The Celebration of the Gnu was my last try at a rock band in San Antonio. Poor Ralph later got into meth, went crazy, and decided he was Jesus. He called me a few times after I moved to L.A. ranting and raving. When I told Zappa about him he said, "It sounds like that guy should have his own talk show." Ralph later kidnapped a woman, and ended up in prison a couple of times. He finally killed himself.

Chapter Two

Not too long after the Celebration of the Gnu debacle, a few really good things happened to me.

First, I discovered how much I loved Bach. I had installed a headphone jack into the bottom of our Magnavox console stereo, and one night after my parents had gone to bed I put on one of my father's organ records by Virgil Fox too see what it would sound like on the phones. While listening to him play the "Little Fugue" in G minor I had one of those mind blowing experiences where I suddenly realized how incredible Bach's music is. It made me want to try to play the organ myself. Shortly before I finished my senior year, my parents surprised me by asking what I wanted for a high school graduation present. I was surprised because I didn't realize I was entitled to one. Now that my dad had the Hammond, I asked for organ lessons, and that's what I got.

It was pretty rough going at first. I had a lot of catching up to do. Starting on an instrument like that at age 18 without a background in piano is not common. But playing piano does little to prepare you for playing the pedals. The pedals are really a keyboard with wide enough spacing between the notes that they can be played with your feet. The pedals are usually used to play bass notes. The hardest part is achieving the coordination between your hands and your feet. They have to be completely independent, and that can be mind boggling, especially at first, but I loved it. I also learned what a big difference there is between appreciating music by listening to it versus playing it yourself. The difference is profound. A much deeper intimacy with the music is attained through learning to play all of the exact notes and understanding how they fit together. When you can get all the voices of a Bach fugue going there is no other sensation that can compare to it. It is about the closest one person can come to being a full orchestra, and that is a powerful feeling.

Once I began to get serious about organ playing, my father would sometimes let me borrow the key to the big new pipe organ at our church. The church itself was always left unlocked in those days, so I could just walk in with the key to the organ console and play to my heart's content. I would often take friends over there at night when no one else was around. I'd play Bach, or Zappa, or just jam around. It was a high privilege and a blast.

When I think of that church, I can't help but think about how important religion became to my brother, Edward, who had a hard time dealing with life due to a misdiagnosis of epilepsy. When he was about thirteen, he began having horrible, extremely painful seizures. He had to take heavy barbiturates to control them, which they did, but at a price. The high doses of phenobarbital made him groggy all the time and changed his personality from a normal bright boy to an angry rebellious teenager who made life miserable for the rest of the family. He and I shared a bedroom, and I remember waking up every morning to a big fight between him and my gentle mother who was trying to get him out bed to go to school. Though he had once been a straight A student, by then he hated school and was making mostly failing grades.

When he had a brain scan in the early 1980's, his condition was discovered to be an inoperable brain tumor, not epilepsy. At that point, his drug regimen was changed to something milder, and it was like having my brother back, at least for a short time.

In his early twenties, Edward had taken solace in the new "born again" evangelical church movement that had reached even our staid Episcopal faith. The church had begun to do "Folk Masses" with guitars and folk songs instead of traditional church music. My brother roped me into bringing my guitar and participating a couple of times. Incredibly, we even did a version of the Lord's Prayer to the tune of a song about a whorehouse: "House of the Rising Sun." Stupid idea, but I have to admit that the words did fit the tune pretty well. I should add that even though I don't care for evangelical movements, this one really did seem to help my brother, and for that I am grateful.

I also must thank my brother for being the first person to expose me to odd time signatures. I went to his upstairs apartment near Brackenridge Park one day, where he played Dave Brubeck for me. It was the first time I had heard anything like it. Edward showed me how to count the 5/4 in "Take Five" and the 7/4 in "Unsquare Dance." In a few years I would be playing in 13/8, 19/16, 21/16, and so on with Zappa, but that was my first taste of odd times.

I also discovered Stravinsky during this time. I took a music appreciation class which was mostly pretty dull, but did have its moments. The school had a powerful hi-fi record player in the auditorium. Occasionally, the teacher would move the class there to play us some recordings of classical music. One day towards the end of the semester, he played part of "The Rite of Spring" and I was blown away. I soon realized that my father owned a Reader's Digest collection of great classical music that contained not only "The Rite" but also Debussy's "Prelude to the Afternoon of a Fawn," which I also loved. I was officially exposed to "modern" music, and I liked it. I soon owned my first classical record: Stravinsky's "The Firebird," which is still one of my favorite pieces of music.

The other important thing for me at that time was that I discovered Frank Zappa. I had heard some of his stuff over the previous couple of years, but I never really got it. My next-door neighbor had a copy of *Absolutely Free*. I had seen the cover and heard a little of the music, but it was all just too weird for me, and it seemed kind of anti-American or something. I came from a very conservative, religious family, and I wasn't used to anything like The Mothers.

But then I borrowed a copy of *We're Only in It for the Money* and I found that I could relate to the words as a teenager increasingly alienated from my parents and now my peers. I had big fights with my father about wanting to grow my hair long, for example, and he was absolutely *not* going to allow it. Through his songs, Frank enabled me to begin to see that there was more to life than what the other kids in school thought was worthwhile. It was OK to not be a jock or a BMOC. It was OK to be different. I'd lost whatever status I had in high school, and it didn't matter. And parents didn't have all the answers.

Then something else happened. The more I listened to Zappa, the more I started to realize there was some interesting music going on there. What the heck kind of chord is that? And what is this weird meter, and how did he make all those funny noises? I was becoming a fan. My outlook began to improve.

I then listened to some of Zappa's earlier records and I started to understand them better. Now the anti-American aspect seemed to change for me. It was about freedom – freedom from normalcy, from complacency, freedom to think for yourself. What could be more American than Freedom? I was pretty much alone in my Mothers love though. None of my friends liked them very much, but I believed that this music was saving my sanity and my life.

Thankfully, my high school days ended at the start of the summer of 1970. It was not a moment too soon.

I was excited when I saw that The Mothers were going to play in San Antonio on June 6th. Wow! I *had* to go check them out. I was not yet as big of a fan as I would soon become, but I was very curious. They were going to perform at the San Antonio Municipal Auditorium.

To my surprise, it wasn't the original Mothers at all. It was a whole new band with Mark Volman and Howard Kaylan (Flo and Eddie) from the Turtles on vocals. But it was still great. I remember the thrill of seeing Zappa HIMSELF live on stage for the first time. I knew it was really HIM because of that nose – I could see how huge it was from way back in the audience! I recall that Flo and Eddie had two mikes each: one that went straight through the P.A., and one that went through two big Leslie rotating speakers on either side of the stage for a special effect. Pretty cool, I thought. I liked the show, but I was not totally blown away the way I would be in the near future.

Not long after that I heard that The Mothers were coming to San Antonio again. This time they were going to play in a gym at Trinity University on October 8th, 1970. They opened with a satirical routine based on the old Richard Boone TV show "Have Gun – Will Travel" which was very funny. I can't recall much of the sketch, but I do remember that Frank would say, "then he gestured hypnotically and pulled out a card" while the band played the appropriate pulling out the card music from the TV show. The sketch ended with the TV theme song "The Ballad of Paladin," with the classic lyric "Paladin, Paladin, where do you roam?" It was very entertaining.

Before this concert, I had acquired a copy of the Zappa album *Hot Rats* which I loved, especially the great instrumental "Peaches en Regalia." Before the show I told myself not to expect them to play that tune, because it was obviously a track done in the studio with a lot of trickery, and no one would *ever* attempt to play something that complex live. Then, of course, they played it, and it was fantastic! It wasn't the same as the record: it was a live version. All the important parts were there but played with different sounds, along with Flo and Eddie singing some of the instrumental parts. It was my first moment of realization that Zappa's music was always in a state of flux, being re-invented for each new situation. Genius. For an encore they did the now famous "groupie routine" ending in a perfect version of "So Happy Together" with all of the wonderful polyphonic vocal parts at the end and everything! This time, I waited around after the show to get his autograph and try to talk with him. All I could think of to ask him was when they were coming back to San Antonio. He said, "We were just here!" That show was it for me – I was now a HUGE FAN. Zappa would dominate my musical life for years to come.

But there was something else very dark and unrelated to music that was going on at that time: the Vietnam War. The draft was in full swing, and by the time I turned 18, they were using a lottery system that assigned numbers to birthdays. The lower the number, the greater the chances of getting drafted. Mine was 83. Not good. They were going to come after me, but I didn't want to get drafted.

To my surprise, my republican father came to my assistance. As conservative as he was, he did not approve of the Vietnam war. He said it was not a real war since it had not been declared, but was rather what he called a "police action." I think he was so conservative that he figured if it really was an urgent threat, then the USA should just drop a few nuclear bombs on them, and not send our kids there to die in the jungle. Regardless, he didn't want me to have to go, and did what he could to help. I don't remember too many details, although I have a memory of him accompanying me to the draft board downtown to see what could be done. We may have looked into conscientious objector status.

There was still some kind of student deferment, so it was imperative that I stay in school, something I did not particularly want to do at that time. I was aimless, and did not have a clue what I wanted to do with my life. That September I had enrolled at San Antonio College (SAC), a two year community college, to try to keep the Army off my back, taking the usual basic courses and a music theory class.

By the time of the Zappa show in October, I had been feeling a bit ill for a while. I had a low-level achy feeling that wouldn't go away and I was running a slight temperature. I finally went to Dr. Calder, my father's friend and personal physician. He told me that I had mononucleosis, for which there was no cure other than bed rest.

I had to drop out of school, stay at home and do nothing. It was no fun. After a few weeks, I began to feel better, but if I got up and tried to do anything, I would feel sick again. This went on long enough that I did not enroll for the spring semester at SAC. I felt like I could have done it, but the doctor said it would be better if I didn't. Dr. Calder had lost his own son to cancer, and he kind of liked me, so I always wondered if he had me stay "sick" for longer than I really was since that would be an airtight deferment from Uncle Sam's draft.

    Eventually I got well enough that I could get up and do some fairly mild stuff like playing the guitar or organ a little. I was very surprised one day when my father showed up with an Ampex reel-to-reel tape recorder and a reel of tape! It didn't have a case; there was just the chasse, and it barely stood upright. I found out later that it probably came from a schoolroom where it was meant to be mounted in a cabinet for a language lab or something. I couldn't even figure out how to hook it up for a while (there was no manual) and I thought it was broken. I was very disappointed. But I finally got it to work, and although the transport was not too great, it sounded pretty good, and the best part was that it had "sound on sound" so I could overdub multiple instruments with it. It was my first step into recording, and I liked it. As I said, it was quite a surprise for my dad to buy a gift for me when it was not my birthday or Christmas. My mother told me later that she had shamed him into it. She said she told him, "You never do anything for that boy! Why don't you do something for him?" Yay, Mom!

    My mother was a very kind woman and did her best to help me through the illness. She even went to record stores for me and bought Zappa albums. It could not have been easy for a southern lady like her to go up to the counter and ask if the store had *Burnt Weenie Sandwich* or *Weasels Ripped my Flesh*, but she did. Yay, Mom again.

    Once I was well enough, I got a job driving a delivery truck for a flower shop. It was a fairly pleasant job that gave me time to think as I drove around the city. The people I worked for were nice, but I encountered a weird thing. The man who owned the shop loved to go out to lunch and eat a lot of Mexican food. But then, he would often come back from lunch and go into the restroom where he would make himself vomit so as to not gain weight! I had never heard of "binge and purge" before, and I found it extremely disgusting and strange. I still do.

I was soon able to start studying the organ again, but this time with a new, more inspiring teacher. My new teacher was Madolyn, the fabulous new organist at our church. I told her early on how much I loved Bach's "Little Fugue" in G minor, and that I looked forward to playing it some day. She said I could go ahead and start on it right away – why wait around if I was dying to have a go at it? And so I did. That was great advice, because it was a huge incentive to keep going, and do something other than the beginner's exercises I had been doing. I still enjoy playing that piece.

By this time I had gotten hold of a copy of *Switched on Bach*, the amazing album of Bach being "realized" on a Moog Synthesizer. I was very intrigued. It was the perfect thing to come along for me as I was getting more into Bach and technology at that time. A friend of mine, Will Alexander, found that a music store in town had an Arp 2600 synthesizer – not a Moog, but a cool synth nonetheless. We played with it in the store a couple of times, then Will surprised me one day by bringing it over to my house so we could experiment with it. Apparently, the people at the music store couldn't figure out how to work the thing and had heard that Will was a whiz with electronics. They asked him to take it for a week to learn how it operated so he could teach them about it. He left it with me overnight, so I stayed up late tinkering with the marvelous machine. After that, I was totally hooked on synthesizers. By the way, Will went on to have a stellar career as a keyboard technician for the likes of Keith Emerson, Yes, The Rolling Stones, No Doubt, and many more. He is considered to be one of the best in the business.

With the threat of the draft still looming, I knew I had to get back into school, but I didn't know where to go. I wasn't even sure what I should major in. To my father's credit, he always told me that the most important thing was to find something to do that I enjoyed. He said that was more important than becoming a doctor or a lawyer or something just because those professions paid well. He said, "You'll be spending the rest of your life doing it, so make sure it's something you like to do." I think that's still pretty good advice.

My first choice of schools was the University of Texas in Austin, where my sister Mary studied. Austin was groovy and cool compared to San Antonio, with their own burgeoning homegrown hippie scene. It was like a different world. I visited my sister there a few times, and I recall seeing a local psychedelic group called Shiva's Head Band at the famed Armadillo World Headquarters. There was no doubt that Austin was more my kind of town than San Antonio. When I told my father I wanted to attend school there, he said, "Absolutely not! They turned your sister into a communist, and I'm not going to have that happen to you!" (He was wrong about that. Austin turned Mary into a corporate lawyer, not a communist.)

This was actually a lucky turn of events. My friend Will had learned that North Texas State University in Denton (now called the University of North Texas) had an electronic music program with Moog synthesizers. It had a very well respected music school, including organ study, so it seemed like the best choice for me to study music and get a chance to use a Moog. Sometime before the start of the 1971 fall semester my father took me up to Denton to look around and audition on the organ. I had to demonstrate a basic level of proficiency to get into the music school. I played Bach's "Little Fugue" well enough that a kind and patient organ teacher, Mr. Dale Peters, allowed me into the program. He was to become my organ and harpsichord instructor while I was at North Texas. I think they needed to recruit more organ students into the program, because I was no great catch, believe me.

It's funny how things work out sometimes. It turns out Bob Moog, J.S. Bach, Frank Zappa, Communism, and Vietnam set the course for the rest of my life.

Chapter Three

So, off I went to Denton, Texas, 300 miles north of San Antonio, just above Dallas. I was 19, and it was the first time I had ever lived away from home. The dorm was pretty bleak, and the food was horrible, but at least it was air-conditioned, a first for me. I grew up in the heat of south Texas without it, and to be cool when it was hot outside was a real luxury.

Denton is in the heart of the Texas Bible belt, and it was in a "dry" county. This meant you couldn't buy alcohol in Denton except at "private clubs" where only beer and wine were served. There was one just off campus called the Final Exam which could be joined for $1 on the spot, so these "private clubs" weren't exactly exclusive. To buy hard liquor, you had to go to the next county. And of course there were churches, mostly Baptist, on just about every block, it seemed.

But I loved it there. After my painful high school times, it felt like a fresh start. No one in Denton had to know that my life long classmates had laughed and walked out on my band in that dreaded high school auditorium.

I took a full load including two private organ lessons a week with Mr. Peters, for which I was expected to practice at least two hours a day. I ate up all the theory and counterpoint classes (16th *and* 18th century, mind you) and I was exposed to something almost entirely new to me: jazz. There was a great jazz program at North Texas, and I met people who turned me on to John Coltrane, Miles Davis, Wayne Shorter, and all the rest. I had never heard of most of these musicians before. I was such an ignorant hick that one day in the cafeteria when I heard some guys talking about "Miles this" and "Miles that," I honestly thought they were talking about Buddy Miles, the Hendrix drummer. Luckily, I did not reveal my ignorance to them.

Within the first week or so of classes I saw a notice about an upcoming live electronic music concert at the music school recital hall. Back then "electronic music" meant serious experimental music using new abstract sounds, not the mechanical, hypnotic "electronic dance music" or EDM as it has come to be known. My friend Dave

Kuenstler, who had come up to Denton from San Antonio at the same time I did, went with me and we sat right in the front row.

It was a concert by my future composition teacher, Merrill Ellis. Merrill had worked with Robert Moog himself on the design of a portable synthesizer for live performance. Moog named it the E-II in honor of Mr. Ellis. That night Merrill had his impressive looking E-II on stage, and played a concert consisting of some live pieces, some tape pieces, and an excerpt from a larger work with a female vocalist. It was great! I knew then for sure I had come to the right place.

There was a catch, though. I had come to the school largely because of the electronic music labs with the Moog synthesizers. I soon found out that only composition majors had access to these labs. I had never written much of anything at that point, and had never really given composition much thought. Not one to be deterred, I signed up as a comp major anyway. As it turns out, I have written quite a lot of music since then, so this proved to be yet another bit of luck, a push in the right direction for me.

I had some excellent teachers at North Texas. There was Dr. Anderson, a physics professor who taught a required class in musical acoustics in one of those big old-fashioned theater style classrooms in the physics building. I enjoyed his class and did well in it. It was fairly easy for me because I had taken physics in high school and I had a head start on understanding the harmonic series, thanks to my dad and my organ study.

Dr. Anderson could be quite a showman. I recall one class where he was talking about how the density of air affects the pitch of a sound. Timing it perfectly at the very end of the class, he demonstrated this by turning his back to the class, inhaling helium (which is less dense than normal air) from a tank, then turning back around to us and saying in an outrageous sounding chipmunk voice, "And it makes your voice sound like this!" At that moment, the bell rang for the end of the class, and the entire room jumped to their feet and gave him huge applause, and a standing ovation. Now, that's what I call teaching.

Then there was William Gardner, my second year theory and ear training teacher. The first year theory students were taught by teaching assistants, and the best of those students got to be in Mr. Gardner's class the second year. This guy was a crack-up as well as being a great teacher. The theory class was Monday, Wednesday, and Friday at 8 a.m., and the sight singing and ear training classes were Tuesday and Thursday at 8 a.m. Most students would rather avoid early classes, but his were so good that they were always full and there were hardly ever any absences.

He was never in the class waiting for us to come in. He was quite theatrical, and made his entrance as if onto a stage just as the starting bell rang. Sometimes before he came in, he would peer through the little window in the door like he was spying on us until someone noticed him there. One time he came in wearing some silly new bright red patent leather shoes. He made his entrance; jumped up on his desk, pointed down and shouted, "Look at my new shoes!"

He didn't care much for the textbook we all had to buy, which was written by Robert Ottman, the head of the theory department. Ottman must have made a fortune on those books, as all North Texas music students were required to buy them. We hardly used the text at all – I still have mine, and it is like new – not a mark in it except for my name. Mr. Gardner taught theory his way, and looking at the Ottman textbook now, I am grateful he did!

He would put examples on the blackboard from the classical repertoire to analyze for the class. The theory classrooms were equipped with special blackboards that had music staves permanently painted on them. One day he was analyzing an example from a Brahms piece, and was talking about some rather clever thing Brahms had done. He said, "That Brahms, he knew his harmony. He sat right there in the back of the class, and I tell you, he knew his harmony!"

Mr. Gardner did not care for Stravinsky, though, which I thought was odd, because Igor sure knew his harmony, too. Asked about it in class one day, he said "Well, you can't really sing anything from 'The Rite of Spring' now can you?" A guy in the back raised his hand and sang the opening upper register bassoon melody, to which Mr. Gardner responded, "Stop smartin' off!" We all had a good laugh. He also said he didn't like the Beatles, but he did like Hendrix. I couldn't figure that out until I learned that his son was a rock guitar player and Mr. Gardner had transcribed some of Jimi's tunes for him.

He used funny little grade school rhymes and chants to help us remember the basic rules of theory like, "Don't double the leading tone! Don't double the leading tone!" or "Raise the leading tone in minor! Raise the leading tone in minor!" or, to the tune of "The Farmer in the Dell," he sang, "The seventh must go down! The seventh must go down! Heigh-Ho, the Dairy-o! The seventh must go down!" He even made the class chant out loud along with him. At exam time I would find myself reciting the chants in my head as I analyzed or harmonized the examples in the test, so I can say that his system really worked.

I was good with music theory, which is a lot like math. (Math had always been a strong subject for me from grade school through high school. In junior high I was placed in an advanced math program that put me in classes a year ahead of where I would normally be.) I did well in the ear training department since I'd been playing by ear all my life, but not so great with sight singing. Sight singing consists of having to be able to sing something by looking at the sheet music without referring to an instrument. I am not much of a singer anyway, and since I did not stick with the piano lessons early on, I was now paying the price. I was terrible at sight singing, and always felt intimidated by it. One day I had to sing in front of the class and I totally choked. Mr. Gardner frowned and said, "That was not too spectacular, Mr. Barrow." I never did get much better, I'm afraid. He could also occasionally give a compliment. I can't recall the context, but it had to be some kind of theory question that required figuring something out in your head on the spot. I responded correctly and he said, "Mr. Barrow has a good mental keyboard, I see." That set me all aglow.

The ear training part was my real forte. On exams I was always neck and neck with an "older" guy, (he was 30!) a guitar player named Jack, who sat right in front of me. For the ear training test, the students would sit at their desks with blank music staff paper. Mr. Gardner had the piano turned so the class could not see the keyboard. The starting note and the key of the piece were given by him to the class. He would then play the piece through slowly several times, and the students were to transcribe the melody *and* the chord changes without referring to any musical instrument. For the final exam, Mr. Gardner played the old classic popular song, "Deep Purple," which has a beautiful but complex melody and a lot of chord changes. I was the only one in the class who got it all 100% correct. My rival, Jack got a 99% because he missed one half-diminished chord. Hit the road, Jack! Actually he was a nice guy and we were friends.

I had a grad student composition teacher for a while named James Sellars who was another excellent teacher. His vast musical knowledge was an inspiration, and he turned me on to someone who became one of my favorite composers, Elliot Carter. He was from upper New York state, had studied at the New England Conservatory, and had the attending accent and old school ways. He even had his composition students come to his house for lessons and for dinners.

I sort of became friends with him, and went to his house one day to play him some of my music on his fabulous stereo. I wanted him to hear an organ fugue I had written before I studied with him. A fugue is a strict musical form popular in Bach's day which involves successive entrances of a melodic theme. I had recently recorded a version of my fugue in the electronic music lab using a Moog synthesizer. When I told Mr. Sellars I wanted to play him a recording of a fugue I had composed, he was surprised and said, "What do you know about fugues?" He must have assumed a hick kid from south Texas wouldn't know of such things. I said, "I play organ and have played a few Bach fugues already – I know what a fugue is." I had brought a joint with me and we smoked it before we listened to my tape. He was totally blown away and said it was brilliant, but then had second thoughts and said, "But now I don't know. Is it really good, or is it just the weed?" I had to laugh. Maybe it was or was not all that brilliant, but if it had been awful, no high was going to cloud his mind that much.

The time in Denton went by quickly. It was pretty much all music, all the time. When we weren't in class, we were playing music just for fun. As a music major, I had to take only a minimum of other subjects like English and history. The majority of my classes were in the music school and I breezed through most of those.

Just before the end of my sophomore year, I bought my first keyboard, a Hohner Clavinet. It is an electric clavichord, really. A clavichord is a stringed keyboard instrument that makes only a very quiet sound, and dates back at least to the time of Bach, who is said to have had one in his music composing room. The electric version is basically the same thing with a couple of magnetic pickups in it, solving the loudness problem. It makes that cool funky sound that you hear on Stevie Wonder's "Superstition."

I eventually became a composition student of Merrill Ellis, who headed up the electronic music labs. Through him I was able to become a teaching assistant and make a little money, minimum wage, as I recall, but that was OK. As a "research project" I did some soldering work in the shop there, and I also tutored students who were in the labs for the first time. I soon became Merrill's "roadie" in charge of his big Moog, the E-II, when he performed live. We took a road trip one time out west to Texas Tech for a concert in a gymnasium. When I got the E-II set up, it didn't work! Nothing! I'm no technician even now, and I sure wasn't one then. I knew of only one thing to try. I guessed that maybe a card of electronics had come loose from its plug-in slot during the ride, so I opened the thing up and re-seated all the cards. It worked! Whew. In addition to my roadie duties, Merrill had me bring my Stratocaster along to perform a guitar improvisation with him at the console of the mighty Moog E-II. It sure would be interesting to hear recordings of those performances, but I doubt if any exist.

With a lot of practice I made steady progress on the organ. I learned a few Bach Preludes and Fugues, and some lovely Brahms Chorale Preludes. My crowning achievement was learning and memorizing an organ piece often described as *fiendishly difficult*: The Prelude and Fugue in G minor by French organist/composer Marcel Dupree. The prelude has a lightning fast, relentless manual part and even calls for four note chords in the pedals.

Instrumentalists were required to perform a "jury" as a final exam. This meant playing something for the teaching staff of your instrument. For organists, the juries were held in the recital hall, which would be empty except for the instructors that made up the jury. I played the Dupree piece for the organ department, which consisted of my teacher and two others, all top notch players. I got through it without a train wreck, and was pleasantly surprised when one of the teachers, Dr. Brown, jumped to his feet applauding and gave me a one-professor standing ovation! I think my teacher and the other one were as surprised as I was at Dr. Brown's reaction.

I did various other jobs during my time in college, including a manual labor job working on the huge new airport that was being built nearby, now known as DFW. There was a big push to get the place up and running, so low-level workers like me regularly put in 10-hour days in the unrelenting Texas summer heat. At first I was on the crew pouring concrete for the runways; a massive operation that was brutally hard work. Luckily, I soon moved up to a better job, installing the templates that would hold the lights along the sides of the runways. So, the next time you are at DFW, look down at those lights and think of me sitting on the asphalt with a wrench and a level in a pool of sweat. I hope you won't find any that are out of alignment.

It was about this time that I began to play electric bass. I bought my first one, a new Fender Precision from Arnold and Morgan Music in Garland, Texas some time in 1974. I had always enjoyed myself when I picked a bass up and tried to play a little. It always felt comfortable in my hands, and I seemed to have a natural affinity for it. I also figured it would round out my skills and usefulness to play guitar, keyboards, *and* bass.

Although I was never in the North Texas jazz program, I played in my first jazz band during my Denton years. I met a piano player named Joe Rogers who was also a student of Merrill Ellis. Joe told Merrill he needed a bass player for a jazz group he had called "Master Cylinder," and Merrill recommended me. Amazingly, we had a regular gig at a jazz club in Fort Worth, of all places, a classic Texas cattle town. That was my first jazz gig, and my first gig on bass. It was a good way to get used to the bass chair and improve my reading ability. It turns out that reading one note at a time on bass is a lot easier than reading three staves of organ music, so I got along pretty well.

In my junior and senior years, I rented a three-bedroom house for $95 a month at 601 Texas Street. My roommate, Rick, was a Vietnam vet studying computer science and was also into music. He had a decent spinet piano, and I had my gear, so we decided to set up the spare room as a music room. The houses in that neighborhood were quite close together, however. An elderly woman lived next door who did not like to be disturbed. We'd heard that egg cartons would work as sound insulators, so we collected enough to cover the walls and ceiling. Unfortunately, we soon learned that egg cartons don't do much in the way of soundproofing.

One night I had some friends up from San Antonio for a jam who'd brought some good weed along with them. (In those days, getting busted could land you in prison for a long time. Don't forget, this was Texas.) It was a great jam; we were grooving our asses off and having a blast. But evidently, I had failed to remember to lock the front door. After we had played for a half hour or so, I looked up and saw that the door to the music room was slowly opening, and in walked two Denton cops. Petrified, we stopped playing and awaited our fates. One of the cops picked up and examined the huge "bong" pipe that was sitting by the door as the other began to speak. "Guys, we're so sorry, but we are going to have to ask you stop playing. The lady next door called and complained. We really hate to do it, because you guys sound fantastic!" They said goodbye, put down the bong, and left! Another act of mercy. Thank you, to those Denton cops wherever you are, and belated apologies to the lady next door.

I also played in a couple of rock cover bands, trying to make a few bucks. I can't recall the name of the band, but one night we had a high school dance gig in a town nearby. We had even worked up a version of Zappa's "Dirty Love" just for fun and to see if any of the adults in charge would notice and get upset. We got no flack. They either didn't notice or didn't care.

It had been raining quite a bit that week, and because the area around Denton is pretty flat, a lot of standing water had accumulated. The singer in the band, Tommy Sherrill, had a nice VW van that we used to cart our equipment. He lived outside of town and knew a lot of the back roads that he liked to use for shortcuts. After the gig, the two of us were going down one of those back roads in the dark, when the pavement seemed to disappear into a lake straight ahead of us. We stopped and discussed what to do. I was of the opinion that we should probably turn back and find another route. But it was his van, and he decided we should keep going, feeling pretty sure it would be just a few inches deep at most. He was wrong. As we drove, the water got deeper and deeper, but for some reason, he just kept plowing into it. I knew we were in trouble when I saw the headlights slip below water level, heard the engine die, and watched the water start to come in through every door in the van. We scrambled to get the more important gear like my guitar and amp top off of the floor and stashed up higher. We could see a light in what appeared to be a farmhouse about a hundred yards up ahead. We had no choice but to get out of the van and wade waist deep through the water to the farmhouse and ask for help, hoping not to meet any water moccasins along the way. Luckily, the farmhouse was above the water level, and the farmer came to the door. He said yes, he had a tractor with a chain, and agreed to pull the van out of the water, which he did, but for a price. As I recall, it just about equaled what we had earned at the gig that night.

Other than what I needed to learn for a few cover bands, I had mostly stopped listening to pop or rock music. I was exploring newfound realms of serious 20th century music and jazz, and I was getting ever more into Zappa. Part of the reason for this was that a lot of my 60's heroes were gone. The Beatles had broken up, and Hendrix and Morrison were dead. Mainstream rock music in the early 70's got very commercial, with the Bad Company or Allman Brothers types of bands that never appealed to me. I had discovered music that I found to be much more interesting. I did not have a TV or a radio (except in the car) so there is a gap of about four years where I am unfamiliar with a lot of the popular songs that other people know, although I do recall hearing "American Pie" blasting from just about every room that wasn't occupied by a music major in my dorm, Clark Hall. And there was a jukebox in the cafeteria where I heard "Roundabout" by Yes quite a few times, which was a lot better than "American Pie," as far as I was concerned.

Because I now worked at the electronic music labs, I had keys and access to the two that were available to students for electronic music composition. This meant I could go in and work with the Moogs and other gear at night and on weekends if no one else was there. I spent many hours in those studios having a lot of fun and learning more about recording and electronics. I also had keys to the small organ practice rooms and access to the bigger organs in the Main Auditorium and the Recital Hall, so I spent a lot of time at those consoles, too. What a lucky young man I was!

I took a class in contemporary music that I thought would be easy, but the teacher was pretty tough. We had to do a term paper, so a meeting was set up with each student to discuss the topic. I had two ideas: one was to do a paper on Stockhausen's "Telemusik," which I loved, or a paper on Zappa. My professor said I could do it on Zappa if I really wanted to, but he would probably give me an F. I wisely did my paper on "Telemusik," and the teacher loved it. I got an A-, and he even said he was going to put it on file in the library as an example of a good paper for other students to see. How things change. Dr. Klein, the current head of the composition department at North Texas, has been teaching a *class* on Zappa for a few years. I have done three residencies there involving Zappa related lectures and performances, as well as one at the University of South Dakota.

During my time in Denton I was buying all the Zappa albums I could find. I was becoming more and more of a fan with each new release, and it was exciting to find out that some of the musicians Zappa was using had been students at North Texas, like Bruce Fowler and Sal Marquez. How cool was that?

The school brought some good music to the campus. I saw the Earl Scruggs Revue there and thoroughly enjoyed it – that guy could really play the banjo. He was pickin' and I was grinnin'! I was privileged to hear the Paul Winter Consort as well. The university orchestra often put on concerts. I experienced a live performance of "The Rite of Spring" for the first time in the North Texas Recital Hall, now called Voertman Hall.

An eccentric woman named Dika Newlin was a professor at North Texas at that time. She had been a genius child prodigy and became a student of Arnold Schoenberg at UCLA in the 1940's. She was often seen around campus in a Beethoven sweatshirt, which was not the kind of attire favored by most of the faculty. Among other (mostly bizarre) things she did was to mount a performance of Schoenberg's "Pierrot Lunaire," a very involved composition I had never heard before. More typical of her activities was her performance of a composition she called "Tape Music" in which she unraveled a roll of duct tape for the screeching sound it made, then had an assistant, my freshman theory teacher, wrap her body up with tape.

I also had the privilege of going to my first Weather Report concert at North Texas, which was really an eye opener. For one thing, Alfonso Johnson played fretless electric bass, something I had not heard before. This was before Jaco Pastorius was in the band. I loved the sound. I was blown away by his "Cucumber Slumber" with all that slippin' and slidin'. I was also surprised by Joe Zawinul. On the WR records I had heard, he never did anything very flashy in the chops department. But he sat down at the acoustic piano in this concert and did an extended solo, in which he let us all know that he had plenty of chops indeed, thank you very much. I thought it was admirable that he had the self-control to save the showy stuff for live performance. And I can't forget to mention that I heard Wayne Shorter in person for the first time, who was indescribably great.

I went to Zappa concerts whenever I could. I saw him at least twice at the Armadillo in Austin, making the long drive just for the show. I hung around after one of the shows and asked Frank if any of his orchestral scores would ever be made available. That seemed to get his attention, but he was a bit vague in his reply. At the time, I was waiting to receive a copy of the Frank Zappa songbook I had ordered. It took forever to arrive, but when it did, I was happy to see that some orchestral excerpts were included. Interestingly, they were after the end of the regular songbook section and on a different kind of paper. I always wondered if my question had influenced the decision to include them at the last minute, but it never occurred to me to ask him when I had the chance.

The Zappa shows I saw in the early 1970's were all great, but the one in Dallas in 1974, I think, was the most mind blowing of all. At the beginning of the show, Frank introduced the first song by saying that for some reason this particular song had been getting some airplay around the Dallas area, so they were going to open the show with it. It was "Montana," one of my favorites, so things got off to a good start. They played "Inca Roads," too. This was the first time I had ever heard it, as it had not yet been released on a record. I couldn't believe how incredibly cool it was. It is still one of my favorite Zappa songs.

Then they played something way beyond my wildest expectations; an arrangement that I later found out was called "Dog/Meat." It was the "Dog Breath Variations" and "Uncle Meat" segued together. Being music that I thought would be impossible to play live, this was reminiscent of hearing the Flo and Eddie band play "Peaches" in 1970. This incredible ensemble had Ruth Underwood on percussion, George Duke on keys and vocals, Bruce Fowler on trombone, Tom Fowler on bass, Napoleon Murphy Brock on vocals, and both Ralph Humphrey and Chester Thompson on drums. What a band! Ruth's performance was the most astonishing thing I had ever seen or heard. At that moment, I had one of those rare ecstatic musical experiences in which I was completely carried away by the music, like a kind of nirvana. It was a peak experience that has remained unequaled in my life. I was so blown away by Ruth in particular that I went up to the stage as people were leaving and saw her packing some things up. I shouted to her something about how great she was. I think she heard me.

I would be finishing my senior year at North Texas in 1975, and came to realize that four years of academia was enough for me, as much as I had loved it. Now I knew what I wanted to do when I finished school. I wanted to play with the Zappa band. I figured bass was my best shot, because Frank played guitar, and I knew I would never be as good on keys as someone like George Duke, so I started focusing heavily on my bass playing.

There was still one more thing to do in Denton before I could graduate, which was to prepare and give a senior recital of my compositions. My friend, David Anderson, (son of the great musical acoustics professor I mentioned, Dr. Anderson) agreed to do a joint recital with me. We were both students of Merrill Ellis and very much into electronic music.

I really should have been composing nice woodwind septets and the like, but instead I had been spending my time on electronic music tape pieces and writing challenging music for electric rock band instruments. I had also written a twelve-tone piece for two marimbas with four players. I figured that since I had composed all of this music, it was still composing, no matter what kind of instruments I was writing for, so it should be acceptable. On April 10th, 1975, we put on our concert: *Music from the Peculiar Minds of David Anderson and Arthur Barrow* at the United Ministries Center just off campus. David was getting a reputation as a clever composer and was very good about getting posters printed and doing the whole promotion thing. We had quite a good turnout and the audience seemed to love the show.

By May, I was done with college, had graduated, and was ready to move on. I found out much later that Dr. Mailman, the head of the composition department, had attended our senior recital and was not at all happy about my compositions. He thought there should have been more writing for traditional instruments, and he probably had a point. Supposedly, he contemplated not allowing me to graduate, but changed his mind when he saw that I had a near perfect grade point average. I think he decided it would be easier just to get rid of me. I graduated cum laude.

The first in a series of Zappa related coincidences happened at about that time. After finishing final exams, I went down to San

Antonio for a few days. On my way back to Denton I was passing through Austin on May 20th, 1975 at the very moment Zappa was performing at the Armadillo World Headquarters. For some reason, I had decided not to try to catch the show, but I did have an eerie feeling knowing he was playing just a short distance from I-35 as I was passing through town. That show turned out to be part of the *Bongo Fury* album. These coincidences were destined to continue.

My plans for the future were beginning to take shape. An old friend from San Antonio, Phil Glosserman, had recently moved to L.A., right in the heart of Hollywood. I'd known Phil since the third grade, by which time he was already studying snare drum. He had boldly moved to California to pursue a career as a professional drummer, an idea that was still somewhat feasible at that time in Los Angeles. Phil had played drums in some successful bands in high school, notably with Chris Geppert's band, Flash.

I hadn't talked to Phil for a while, but he and I had been in touch a little in the early 70's. Like me, he was a Zappa fan, and when he found out I was finishing college, he urged me to join him in L.A. and give the music biz a go myself. I thought that sounded like it could be a good idea, especially since I now had the goal of playing with Zappa, and Frank was based in Los Angeles. Phil invited me to come for a visit and check the place out.

On May 25th, I cashed in a generous graduation present from my parents and took a flight to California. Los Angeles was like heaven, visually like the Garden of Eden to my eyes, with lush vegetation and beauty, especially compared to the flat, gray prairie of the Texas Bible belt. There was even ivy growing along the side of the freeways! I fell in love right away. Phil showed me around when I got there. We drove west on Sunset to the sea, through Beverly Hills and past UCLA. It was like a wonder-world. Instead of being flat and hot, there were hills and valleys and mountains, and the weather was great. Instead of Baptist churches on every block, there were recording studios and movie studios. And best of all, Zappa was here – he lived here, he recorded here, his band was based here. I could almost feel his presence in the air. A lot of the Zappa mythology landmarks were here, too. Phil's apartment in Hollywood was just a block from the Ralph's on Sunset. Just a few blocks west from there was the corner of Sunset Boulevard and Crescent Heights, where Zappa had noticed vast quantities of Plastic

People. Best of all, just up the street from there was Laurel Canyon where Zappa himself lived.

I was hooked. I decided I was going to make the leap and move to L.A., but I needed to line up a place to live when I returned permanently with all my stuff. The rents were pretty steep compared to Denton, so I rented the only place I could afford: a tiny bachelor apartment for $65 a month in Hollywood on Lexington, just north of Santa Monica between Vine and Gower. It was not a great neighborhood, but not terrible.

I got back to Denton, said goodbye to all my friends, and told them my plan was to move to L.A. and play in Frank Zappa's band. They probably thought I was crazy. Regardless of what they thought, my mind was made up and I was ready to head for L.A. But first I had to make a stop in South Texas.

I packed up my meager possessions – guitar, bass, Clavinet, amp, small stereo, my few records, a chest of drawers I had bought in Denton for $4 at a garage sale, and my clothes, then headed down to San Antonio to say goodbye to my parents. They had been kind enough to give me the old family car, a green 1963 Dodge 330, a four door sedan, with bench seats, an oval steering wheel, and a push-button automatic transmission. I could fit everything I owned into the back seat and trunk.

I spent some time in San Antonio visiting with family and friends until it was time to go. That day was June 1st, 1975. I have to admit my heart was in my throat as I climbed into the old green Dodge in front of the house in Alamo Heights where I had grown up. My mother and father stood at the end of the sidewalk and waved to me as I drove off. This was different from going away to college for four years. We all knew I was probably moving to California to stay. I wasn't going to be coming back home after college like most of their friends' children would do. There was no future for me in San Antonio, Texas. I turned around and waved back to them and headed off to find my way onto I-10 West. We all had tears in our eyes. I knew at that moment they really loved me, and I knew I really loved them, too. I still miss them.

Chapter Four

Trekking across Texas really drives home how huge the state is. San Antonio is in the middle of the state, but it takes a whole day on the highway just to get to the westernmost edge at El Paso. I made it slightly past El Paso and spent the night at a motel in New Mexico somewhere. Luckily, my stuff was still in the Dodge when I woke up the next morning.

The second day was brutal, going across the desert where the highway is straight for so many miles that it seems to disappear into a point ahead of you for long periods of time. I made it through New Mexico, Arizona, and the mountains in California. At least the navigation was easy. Get on I-10 in San Antonio and take it all the way to Los Angeles. My friend Phil had suggested I sleep at his apartment that first night before moving into my own place the next day. He told me to just stay on I-10 until I got to La Brea, get off and go north to Sunset.

As I came down and down through the mountains east of the city, I got my first taste of how bad the smog was. (It's a lot better now.) I could see that I was driving down into this murky, brown ooze of an atmosphere and thinking, Oh, God, this is where I'm moving? I had a serious moment of doubt, but drove on.

When I got to San Bernardino, it seemed to me that I must be in the city, so I started looking for the La Brea exit, not realizing that San Bernardino was still about 90 miles away from Los Angeles! Perhaps because I was getting very tired and was looking so hard for the La Brea exit, I managed to miss a turn and suddenly I was not on I-10 anymore, lost in the middle of a big downtown interchange. I got off the freeway as soon as I could, and found a parking lot to turn around in. I looked up and the sign said "San Antonio Winery." It was kind of a Twilight Zone moment: had I driven all that time just to end up back in San Antonio? Luckily, I found my way back onto I-10 and finally to Phil's pad, where I slept very well.

The next day I moved into my tiny place, found a phone booth and called my folks in Texas to let them know I was OK. It would take a few days to get a phone hooked up at my place. There was not a lot of moving in to do. The only furniture in the apartment was a bed and a lamp. I had my little chest of drawers, some clothes, my musical gear, and that was about it. The bathroom consisted of a stand up shower and a toilet. The only sink was at the "kitchen" end of the room, where there was also a refrigerator and a small gas stove. I set up my Clavinet and stereo and was ready to go. I was writing a lot of unusual instrumental music for electric instruments at that time and I was on a roll. I composed several pieces in that little room in Hollywood.

I went through quite a culture shock at first. I had gone from spending four years in a small north Texas town in the Bible belt straight into the heart of Hollywood. It was pretty wild back then. Houses of ill repute were numerous, having names like the "Institute of Oral Love," with girls hanging around the door without much hanging on them. I wore blue jeans, T-shirts, and Red Wing hiking boots in a land of flashy rock stars wearing gold lame and ridiculous elevator shoes. No two points in Denton were more than five minutes away; in L.A. every trip seemed to take at least a half hour, if not an hour. It was quite a contrast. On my first day, as I was cruising down Sunset near Hollywood High School, I spotted a Rolls Royce with plates that read JALEM. I wanted to see who was behind the wheel, so I pulled up next to it on the left in my Dodge. Just as I looked over to see who it was, the driver of the Rolls looked over at me with a smile and a wave: it was Jack Lemon! Yes, Hollywood and Denton were very different places, indeed.

There was a surprise waiting for me a little further down Sunset. At the time I moved to Los Angeles, there was a big promotional push for the Average White Band going on. As I was driving west on Sunset toward the strip, right there, on a very prominent billboard on the right just past Laurel Canyon Blvd., were displayed in huge letters the band's logo, AWB, which happen to be my initials! I laughed and thought it must be a good "sign." What a nice way to welcome me to town.

Another perfect thing happened for me: my (still) favorite Zappa album was released on June 25th, 1975: the fabulous *One Size Fits All*, with the new song I had heard at that great show in Dallas, "Inca Roads." Before it was released, I had heard that it was coming out soon, so I'd been calling Tower Records every day. I bought it as soon as it was available, and when I put it on my turntable and listened, I was blown away all over again. I would not have thought it possible at the time, but it made me even more of a fan than I had been before.

Phil and I did a lot together during that time, playing music and writing a couple of silly songs. We also went out often to hear music. There was a club on La Brea very near to where Phil lived where a jazz singer named Maxine Weldon performed. I had never heard of her, but we found out that Ralph Humphrey, who had played with Zappa, was playing drums for her. We went to the club and I thoroughly enjoyed seeing and hearing up close one of my favorite drummers, one I had only seen from a distance. We also went down to the Lighthouse in Hermosa Beach to hear George Duke with Chester Thompson on drums and Tom Fowler on bass. Among other things they performed Zappa's fabulous "Echidna's Arf," one of my favorite Zappa instrumental tunes. It was another great opportunity to see these respected and amazing musicians up close.

Phil and I went to the September 17th, 1975 performance of Zappa music conducted by Michael Zearott at Royce Hall on the UCLA campus. Frank was there, of course, and spoke to the audience a bit. It was fantastic! It was the first and almost only time I got to hear any of Frank's orchestral works live. I say almost, because Phil was so taken by the first concert that he wanted to go again the next night for the September 18th concert. When I said I would love to go, too, but couldn't really afford it, Phil bought both of us tickets – what a friend! Thanks, Phil. Both shows were excellent, and I was especially thrilled to hear "Strictly Genteel," one of my favorites.

Something that really stands out in my memory was when at the end of one of the concerts, Frank "orchestrated" on the spot a two chord vamp, the C# minor to D progression from "Black Napkins," assigning whole notes on various instruments to make the chords. He then brought Bruce Fowler out from the brass section to the front of the stage to do a solo over the orchestra. I can't think of a better testament to Frank's opinion of Bruce's musicianship than that. Frank could have easily played a guitar solo, but decided to let Bruce shine instead. Good call, Frank.

There was a musician's supply shop in Hollywood called Alpheus Music. I thought it was pretty cool when I discovered that Alpheus was close to where I lived. When I was still in Denton, I had been sending the onion skin masters of my scores to them to be reproduced by the ammonia process called Ozalid. Merrill Ellis had recommended Alpheus as the best place to have copies made. It was a busy place that did a lot of music reproduction for the film industry. I often went there to buy blank staff paper and other composing materials.

One day I looked at a shelf with some items for sale and saw a lovely leather music folder that had printed on it:

ABNUCEALS EMUUKA
ELECTRIC SYMPHONY ORCHESTRA
OBOE II

I couldn't believe my eyes and bought it right away. That was what Frank called the orchestra he used on *Lumpy Gravy*. I think it had to have been from one of Zappa's L.A. orchestra performances, maybe from Royce Hall. I still have it and I keep some of my most treasured Zappa sheet music in it. This was one of the many little coincidences that seemed to be leading me nearer to the Zappa universe.

Culture shock notwithstanding, the main thing I had to do in Los Angeles was find work. Phil had joined something called The Musician's Contact Service where a musician could actually find gigs, usually in top 40 cover bands. I had a lot of catching up to do in that department as I had not listened to much popular music during the previous four years in music school. The Musician's Contact Service had an office on Sunset where anyone could join for a small fee. They provided listings of people seeking musicians for various kinds of work. I signed up, went there daily and wrote down every listing I could find for people seeking guitar, bass, or Clavinet, then went home and started looking over my notes. I made a lot of calls and did some auditions, but most of the time nothing came of them.

One gig that did pan out was with an old time gal named Roberta Sherwood. She had a minor hit in 1956 with "Up A Lazy River" written by Hoagy Carmichael of "Stardust" fame.

She needed bass and drums for a two or three week stint in Jackpot, Nevada, just south of the Idaho state line. Phil and I auditioned, and we got the gig. It was a union gig, so I joined the union for the first time: Local 47 on Vine Street in Hollywood.

When the time came, I loaded up the Dodge and drove the 700 miles to the gig. Jackpot was pretty bleak, I have to say. It made Denton look like Paris. We were playing at a casino called Cactus Pete's. But it was a positive experience, all things considered. Roberta had a good piano player, Ernie, and he had charts for all the tunes. A lot of sight-reading on bass was exactly what I needed at the time, and it was a great learning experience to play all those old standards, like "You're Nobody Till Somebody Loves You," another of her hits.

Some months later, we did a week or so with Roberta in Palm Desert, the town next to Palm Springs. Roberta was friends with Hoagy Carmichael, who was in his late 70's by then and lived in the area. One night he came in and jammed with Phil and me before the set. We all just went free form, which is my favorite way to jam. He totally got it and seemed to have a ball. My dad, being a big fan of "Stardust," was quite impressed when I told him about meeting and jamming with Hoagy Carmichael.

One Musician's Contact Service call I made was to a guy named Bruce Powers. He had been a soap opera actor on General Hospital, but his real dream was to be a nightclub singer. He told me that he already had a keyboard player named Don Preston. I asked, "Do you mean the Don Preston that played with The Mothers?" He said yes and seemed pleasantly surprised that I knew who Don was. I knew that I absolutely, positively *had* to get this gig. I went up to Bruce's lovely home in Laurel Canyon, not far from Zappa's house, as it turned out, and auditioned. Bruce liked me and wanted to set up a time to play a little with Don, to see if he would approve of me. When I went up there the second time, Don was there. It was my first real face-to-face contact in L.A. with someone in the Zappa circle. Don liked my playing right away, and gave me the thumbs up. I think he was flattered that I was such a Mothers fan. I got the gig, but also found it a bit disconcerting that someone who had been in the Mothers could be still scrounging for work at the same level as me, a beginner. And I could tell that he knew it was a come down for him, and was not really into playing songs like "Ease on Down the Road" from *The Wiz* with Bruce struggling to get the rhythm of the melody right.

We soon found a drummer and a female singer, or "chick singer" as they were called then. Her name was Sylvia Saint James and again, here was another Zappa connection. She was a vocalist on George Duke's new record, *The Aura Will Prevail*, his first release after his time with Zappa. I couldn't believe that everywhere I turned there was another thread leading to Frank. Bruce Powers had a two week booking at the lounge of the Holiday Inn in Stockton, which was the alpha and the omega of that band.

The time in Stockton gave me a chance to get to know Don. Soon after we got back to L.A. he invited me up to his house in Echo Park that was situated on the side of a steep hill on Morton Ave. Inside, it was like walking into the album cover for *Uncle Meat*, full of weird sculptures and artwork; a very bohemian vibe to say the least. But the coolest thing to me was his Moog, a big mutli-panel modular system with clear plastic cases so you could see the electronics inside.

Don, of course, knew a lot of the other Zappa musicians. Through Don, I got to meet Tom Fowler, who had played bass for Frank on some of my favorite albums. Tom was a big influence on me, and a great inspiration. One of the reasons I took up playing bass was hearing him play the melody of "Echidna's Arf." I could not believe that playing such difficult passages was even possible on a bass! I took a few lessons from Tom which were very instructive and helpful. He taught me a lot of things about playing bass. One thing that stands out was his admonition about how easy it is to "lose time," or get a little behind the beat, when you are changing hand positions on the neck. The hand has to move much quicker than the eye, almost instantaneously, in order to not "lose time." Thank you, Tom Fowler.

I also got to meet his big brother, Bruce, who I like to describe as "the Jimi Hendrix of the trombone." He did some amazing work with Frank. One of my favorite Bruce contributions was his beautiful solo on "Don't You Ever Wash That Thing" on the *Roxy* album. I had seen both Bruce and Tom play with Zappa several times, so it was quite a privilege to get to know them personally. I am still good friends with them and their incredible trumpet playing brother, Walt.

I can't recall how it came about, but soon Phil and I were at Don's house playing some music. At one point, Don pulled out charts for a Zappa sounding instrumental tune he had written called "Moon Unit," named after Zappa's daughter. It had a few time signature changes, but nothing too complicated. Phil and I read through it almost perfectly the first time. Don was impressed. Soon after that Phil had the idea that he, Don, Bruce, and me should form a band to play some of my music and some of Don's. This bold long-shot of an idea would not have occurred to me, but it sounded like it was worth a try. So, I gave Don a call, he liked the idea and called Bruce who also agreed, and thus our fusion band Loose Connection was born.

It was around that time that Don trusted me enough to give me Frank Zappa's home phone number - I couldn't believe it! I don't recall why Don gave me the number, but I wrote it into my little phone book, knowing that I had to wait for just the right moment to use it.

By early 1976, I was in a cover band with Phil called Half Moon that did a lot of high school dances and such. I moved into a large house in Hollywood on Martel Avenue near the Ralph's on Sunset with a bandmate where I set up a music room. I made quite a few recordings of my music there. The guitar player in the band at the time was an eighteen-year-old lad named Brucie who had somehow become friendly with the Zappa inner circle and was in touch with Frank himself. This turned out to be yet another thread leading me to Zappa.

He asked me one day if I would like to go down to the Record Plant recording studio where Zappa was working. It was a chance to meet Frank and hang out for a while. Of course I said yes! On April 11th, 1976 we walked into the control room, and there was Frank Zappa in the flesh. When he spotted me, he looked me right in the eyes for a couple of seconds without smiling or anything, just an intense stare, as if he were sizing me up. It felt like he was peering into my soul, looking to see if there was anything good inside of me. He had these very penetrating dark eyes, and I found it a bit unnerving. But then he smiled and extended his hand for a firm shake. He was big on hand shaking. I believe it was because he loathed the whole hugging thing, even with people who knew him well. He could head off a hug by extending his hand for a solid shake. After that, he just ignored me and went about what he was doing. I did not have a chance to speak with him that day, but just watched him work.

He was recording Terry Bozzio on drums; no other musicians were involved. I think the song was "Disco Boy" which was later released on the album *Zoot Allures*. He was doing the drums as an overdub to already existing tracks. Though I now work that way fairly often myself, it was the first time I had seen this done. Normally, the drums for a song would be recorded together with the other rhythm instruments like bass, guitar and maybe piano, along with a reference or "scratch" vocal. The idea was to get a complete take called a "basic track" to which more tracks could be recorded as overdubs. Since most songs were not recorded to some kind of a mechanical metronome or click track, the drums would define where the beat was. Because of this, overdubbing the drums was almost never done in those days. But Frank was an innovator, and had recorded the other tracks to some kind of steady beat thereby making the drum overdub feasible.

The huge set of drums were set up in the middle of a big studio room with lots of mics stuck everywhere imaginable. They did some recording and Frank was happy with most of it, but wanted to redo a section in the middle of the song. In analog recording you can "punch in" on the recording, listening to the tracks and playing along and at the right point the engineer hits the record button and the new recording begins there. This can be done almost seamlessly if the engineer is capable and the equipment is good. "Punching out" and keeping what comes after the punched in part is a different matter, because the erase head wipes the tape before it gets to the record head, always leaving a little gap in the sound. Frank, of course was aware of all this, but he still wanted to keep some of the drum tracks he had and redo a section in the middle.

His solution was simple, but drastic, at least to me at that time. Frank was a master of tape splicing, so he simply cut the big two-inch tape at the exact point he wanted to keep the drums, and inserted blank "leader" (non-recordable tape) as protection against erasing something he wanted to keep. The tape was then rewound, Terry replayed the drums up to the cut point, and Frank got the result he desired without damaging the parts he wanted to keep. He then took out the leader tape, spliced the cut point back together, and it played back perfectly. Voila! I was impressed. That was a fun day. I got to hang with Zappa – wow! And of course this put me another step closer to my goal of playing in his band. My orbit around the center of the Zappa universe was tightening.

Maybe it was because the city of Los Angeles was just crawling with Zappa related people, but I seemed to keep crossing paths with them. Here's another example. I occasionally did some work as an accompanist, playing piano for aspiring singers. One day I was waiting to accompany a singer for some kind of audition at the old ABC Records building on Vine street. I was waiting for our turn in a hallway when I saw someone else waiting with sheet music in hand who looked familiar. When I thought I knew who it was, I walked over and asked him, "Are you Ian Underwood?" It was, and he was there doing the same thing I was doing, trying to make a living in the music biz. He was polite and soft spoken, living up to his reputation as the "straight member of the group." It was yet another thread leading back to FZ.

Another good thing happened to me in the spring of 1976. I met my future wife, Randi, who was a singer at the time. We hit it off right away, were married in January 1979, and have been together ever since. I am a very lucky man to have such a good woman in my life. I was about to move again when we met, and she soon joined me in my new apartment in Echo Park on top of a hill overlooking Glendale and the San Gabriel mountains.

Don Preston, who lived just a few minutes away, had an eight-track studio in his basement called Zoo Studio. We started recording some of his tunes and some of mine there. It was a lot of fun and served to further improve my engineering and producing skills. One high point occurred when Don persuaded Ruth Underwood to bring her vibes over and record the melody for his tune "Moon Unit." According to my old date book it was on August 16th, 1976. I couldn't believe it - RUTH! For real! She was one of my idols. I was in awe of her, and here was yet another Zappa connection.

By then I had become acquainted with a very talented keyboard and mallet player named Marty Jabara, who was a perfect fit for the Loose Connection band. He is a great sight-reader, which was important since I had a lot of written out parts, and reading was not Don's forte. Though only in his forties, Don was a bit physically weak then. He was on some kind of macrobiotic diet and had a lot of stomach problems that seemed to slow him down.

The band did a few gigs, but Phil often had scheduling problems which led to us going through a few different drummers, including Frank Wilson, Mike Englander, and David Iglefeld (now David Eagle). Future Knack drummer Bruce Gary played on the last live gig we did on March 6th, 1978 at the Odyssey Theater in Santa Monica. If I recall correctly, that show was attended by ex-Mother Ian Underwood and Doors guitarist, Robby Krieger.

Robby had a band at the time with Walt Fowler on trumpet, Carlos Vega on drums, and Don Preston on keys. I first met Robby at Don's where they rehearsed. I was a big Doors fan, so I was stoked to meet Robby, a hero of mine. He saw me doing some engineering in the studio there, and at that time did not realize that I was mainly a musician, not an engineer. He was looking for someone to mix sound for his band at a show they had coming up at the Whisky a Go Go in Hollywood, and asked me to do it. I did, and to this day, it is the only live show I have ever mixed.

Of course there was still the issue of trying to make a living. Don had a connection with a husband and wife team consisting of Frank, who played drums and Mary, who sang. They were forming a top 40 cover band, and invited Don and I to join them. The band auditioned at a couple of clubs, including one that was in one of the beach towns, maybe Hermosa. Don was having stomach problems and seemed pretty ill that night. It was also clear that his heart was not in the music at all. In the middle of the audition, I noticed that he had stopped playing, so I turned around to see what was happening. He was nowhere to be found! He had become sick to his stomach and had to run to the bathroom. It was rather disturbing.

We finally landed a regular gig in a lounge at the Golden State Motor Hotel, right off the I-5 freeway in Burbank. We worked five nights a week, doing four sets a night. I played both guitar and bass on the gig. The tunes we played were not very memorable, but I do recall we played a disco song called "The Hustle" a lot. It was a pretty cheesy act. Don was still kind of weak and clearly unhappy on the gig, but needed the money too badly to turn down the work. After a while, Frank and Mary replaced Don with a really pushy and obnoxious Vegas style B-3 player. He was pretty good, but I didn't care for him personally, and I felt badly about Don being fired. At any rate, it was good to have a steady in town gig, but it wouldn't last forever.

Los Angeles in the 1970's was a place where a decent musician could make a living performing and recording music. Things were very different back then in a lot of ways. One was the use of the telephone. This is before the time that even *answering machines* were in common use, much less email, texting, and smartphones. Instead, there were entities called answering services for which a small monthly fee was charged. There were two that were used specifically by musicians: "Your Girl" and "Arlyn's." If someone dialed a number connected to a service and got no answer after a number of rings, the service would pick up the line and take a message about the gig or whatever. The musician could check in with the service to see if any calls had come in. As I recall, they even acted as a go-between for musicians, keeping track of their calendars to some extent. It was almost like having a secretary.

I played quite a few "casuals," which means weddings, office parties, holiday parties, and that sort of thing. (Ooo, I Hear Laughter in the Rain as I Tie a Yellow Ribbon Round that Old Satin Doll with the Girl from Ipanema, Proud Mary!) Pretty cheesy, but I was still making money through making music, and to me that's always better than having a "real" job.

The mid to late 1970's was actually a good time for popular music, by which I mean the kind that got radio airplay and generated money. Stevie Wonder was in his prime, and it was fun to learn some of his more challenging licks, like the one in "Sir Duke" that had to be mastered to play top 40. Linda Ronstadt was riding high, and Joni Mitchell was doing some of her best work, too. My beloved Weather Report was doing really great stuff, like *Heavy Weather* and *Mr. Gone*. I remember hearing their tune "Birdland" on AM top 40 radio one time driving down Santa Monica Blvd. into Silver Lake. And amazingly, I even heard Zappa's "Lemme Take You To the Beach" on an early incarnation of KROQ. This all tied in nicely with my continuing musical development. Having to learn some pop songs to earn a living gave me a new appreciation of what it takes to write a song that will touch people enough to make them open their wallets.

Of course, I was listening to a lot of other music, too. For the first time in my life I had enough money to buy records when I felt like it. In addition to every Zappa release, I was buying everything Weather Report put out, too. It was really cool to get *Black Market* and see that former Zappa drummer Chester Thompson was now playing with them. So *that's* why Zappa had to find a new drummer, I realized. I heard Jaco Pastorius for the first time on that album and he transported me to new realms of what was possible on the fretless bass. He was the greatest electric bass player ever, in my opinion, the Jimi Hendrix of the bass, and a great composer, too. I was also buying more classical and modern classical records, especially Stravinsky, Bartok, Carter, Stockhausen, Bach, Brahms, and Beethoven. I was exploring whole new universes of music and loving it.

I had one fairly serious album disappointment, though, in October of 1976. That was when I bought Zappa's *Zoot Allures*. Although I liked "Wind up Working in a Gas Station" and the title track, I was very turned off by "The Torture Never Stops." I thought it was dreadful, musically and lyrically. For the first time, I couldn't finish listening to a Zappa song. Though I later played it live many times, I have to admit that I have never listened to the album version all the way through. I had not been too thrilled with *Bongo Fury* either, the previous year's Zappa release, but this was worse. I began to think that I might be changing into an ex-Zappa fan, but I did not give up hope entirely.

In addition to playing in bands, I did numerous demo sessions. For the first time I got to record in real studios, with big mixing consoles, 24-track tape recorders, good mics and real engineers. I loved the environment and yearned to have my own studio some day. Of course, I continued to record my own tunes, both at Zoo studio and on my own home equipment. By this time I had upgraded a bit to a Sony reel-to-reel 1/4" tape recorder that sounded fairly decent.

I also fulfilled a dream of mine, something that had seemed unattainable just a few years back: I bought my first synthesizer, a somewhat obscure one, the EML Electrocomp 101. I was in oscillator heaven!

At one point Half Moon, the top 40 band I was playing with, got a new guitar player, a young guy still in his teens named Steve Lukather. He was very good, and I remember what a great job he did playing and singing the George Benson version of "On Broadway." He went on to have a stellar career as a session player and was in the band Toto. This later became a Zappa connection when a Toto song was quoted on Frank's *Joe's Garage* album in the track called "Toad-O Line."

A funny thing happened on the way to a Half Moon gig with Steve at Antelope Valley College in Lancaster, Zappa's old stomping ground. It was the first time I had been to that area, so I thought it was kind of cool to be there. I looked for the Village of the Sun, but to no avail. On the way up there, I got to thinking about the way the P.A. speaker columns were attached to the roof of the station wagon we were in. Just as I opened my mouth to ask about it, I heard a thump, and turned around to see them bouncing down the freeway behind us! Luckily, they did not hit any other vehicles or cause an accident, and after all of that they still worked. Incredible.

In the late spring of 1977, I got a call about a possible gig for the summer in Sweden. A pop star there named Bjorn Skifs was looking for some American musicians. Bjorn had been in a band called Blue Swede who had a hit in 1974 with a cover version of "Hooked on a Feeling," with an intro that went "ooga chucka, ooga, ooga, ooga chucka." Bjorn wanted some musicians from the U.S. to join him in Sweden for his annual summer "folketspark" tour. A folketspark is a public park for the folks, and most have an outdoor covered stage of some kind. Since Sweden is frozen most of the year, the people make up for it like crazy in the summer with non-stop heavy partying. Bjorn and another person, his manager, I think, came to LA to audition musicians, and came to a Half Moon gig. We had yet another good guitar player then, Michael Stevens, and though the Swedes were looking for two guitar players, they heard me play only bass on the gig. I told them that I played guitar as well as bass, and I guess they believed me, because Michael and I got the guitar gigs. They also hired a keyboard player named Max Gronenthal, who later went on to sing with 38 Special and Grand Funk Railroad.

I scurried to get my first passport, and off we went to Stockholm. We arrived on June 25, 1977, just after the summer solstice, the longest day of the year. In Sweden in the summertime the days are *really* long – there was roughly an hour of darkness at around midnight. The thing to do at night there was to go out to the discos, something I had never done before, avant-garde rocker that I was. It was kind of fun, but I found it very disconcerting to have a few drinks in the darkness of the club, then emerge at two a.m. and head back to the hotel in the broad daylight of the morning sun. Too weird for me!

It felt good to be part of a professional tour, with roadies and good equipment. I didn't have to schlep my own gear around and set it up, and I loved that. I was required to wear a costume on stage, which was pretty silly; they had me dressed up as a pirate. I don't know who came up with that brilliant idea, but what the heck, I had to wear something. I was having fun and I was really "on the road" for the first time.

It turned out that Bjorn Skifs was not the only band playing in folketsparks that summer. My all time favorite jazz group, Weather Report, was also in Sweden with none other than the great Jaco Pastorius on fretless bass. In a lucky turn of events, they were playing at a folketspark nearby us on a day we had off. One of the Swedish guys asked me if I wanted to go to their concert, and of course I said yes!

We found decent seats in the middle of the audience. I was enjoying the show except for one thing. I couldn't hear enough of Jaco's bass in the mix. The Swedish audience was very polite, and after each round of applause was over, the place was almost silent. I decided that I could take advantage of this, so after a few tunes, I waited for it to be quiet and then shouted as loudly as I could, "Turn up the bass!" I could tell by Jaco's reaction that he heard me. When the next tune began, he meandered out to the edge of the stage and cocked his ear toward the house speakers. Evidently, he agreed with me and motioned to the mixer to turn him up. The balance was much better after that, making the rest of the concert even more enjoyable than it already was.

Wanting to meet Jaco, I hung around after the show until he appeared. I introduced myself and told him that I was the guy who yelled out for the bass to be turned up. I think he found that pretty amusing. I also had the honor of shaking his hand. I have hands that are quite a bit larger than average, but his hands were so huge they practically swallowed mine up! He was very friendly and started talking to me like I was an old friend. I think that was partly because I was an American. When you are in a foreign country, it's always refreshing to talk to a person from your own culture. I am so glad I got to meet him then, when he was playing at the top of his game in the greatest electric jazz group that ever was. It is tragic that his life ended the way it did. What a great loss.

The punk rock craze had reached the shores of Sweden by that time, and Bjorn wanted to do a punk parody. At one point in the show, he would shout "Punk!" and we would move around awkwardly, make ugly faces and play a bunch of noise. I had never been exposed to punk at the time, but when I finally heard some, I thought it was pathetic. How could anyone like it when there was so much good music to listen to? (Later, in the 1980's, I worked briefly for Malcolm McClaren, inventor of punk via the Sex Pistols, the fake band I call the Monkees of punk. More on him later.) We also went into the EMI studio in Stockholm with Bjorn and recorded a few tracks for a new album. All in all, the Bjorn Skifs tour was a great experience and a fine intercultural time was had by all.

After returning from Sweden, I continued writing music and playing in bands. I was playing a lot of gigs with cover bands, casual bands, and original bands, including the Johnny Baltimore Band. John had been the guitar player in Half Moon when I first joined them and he went on to dedicate himself to writing songs and leading an original band. It was through John that I met my long time friend, Tom Brown, a fanatic Zappa aficionado. The rest of my time was spent mostly on continuing to write music and practice my instruments, especially bass.

I attended the Zappa December 31, 1977 New Year's Eve show in the Pauley Pavilion at UCLA with Tom and my future wife, Randi. I was really glad to see that there was a percussionist back in the band, Ed Mann, who is a great mallet player. I enjoyed Adrian Belew in his WAC uniform, and really liked the new keyboard player, Tommy Mars. Maybe I was not an ex-Zappa fan after all. The thing I did not expect or care for was when Frank put down the guitar and strode around the stage with a hand-held vocal mic. I was even more put off when he held the mic in front of his pants zipper as if it was his penis. I thought that was beneath him. I had always liked the fact that though it was obviously his band and he wrote all the music, he stayed off to the side of the stage and played guitar, letting the singers, like Flo and Eddie or Napoleon Murphy Brock, be the front men. But being the front man himself was the way Frank did it from then on, and after a while I got used to it. Fortunately, I don't remember him doing the penis imitation much when I was in the band. All in all, it was a good show, and through Don, I got to go backstage, which was exciting. I had never been backstage at a big rock show, whether it was Zappa or anyone else, so that was pretty thrilling. I don't think I saw Frank, but I did get to meet Ed.

The *Zappa in New York* album came out in March of 1978, and I liked a few cuts on it. It was a relief to see Frank writing interesting music again, like "The Black Page," and I loved the fact that Ruth Underwood was playing in the band. It was the first time I heard Ray White, and I was impressed with the sound and strength of his voice. Though I did not care much for the "Titties and Beer" types of songs, it still seemed that Zappa wanted to do some more challenging musical exploration again, the kind of stuff that would appeal to a guy like me.

In April of 1978, Robby Krieger contacted me about doing some synth work on a new Doors project they were working on. He and Ray Manzarek came over to our little apartment in Echo Park to see what I could do. What a thrill to have those two men over to my place! They liked what they heard, and told me to come to Cherokee studio on Fairfax at noon on Thursday, April 27th for the session.

It was my first "real" recording session, something that would be released by a major label and be widely distributed. I would be a synth "programmer," not a musician, but it was a real session nonetheless. I thought what they were doing was very cool. They had recordings of Jim Morrison reading some of his poetry, and the remaining Doors were writing new music to go with the poetry. They needed some special eerie synth sounds for a certain track. I came to the classy recording studio with my EML 101 synth and a few Serge Modular panels that I had by then. The Serge stuff was pretty funky looking at that time. I didn't have the panels in a proper case, they were just sort of laid out on a little table I brought with patch cords sticking out everywhere. I got some skeptical looks and comments at first about all the funky looking wires, but the producer, John Haeny, came to my defense, explaining that if you looked inside the studio's mixing console, you would see the same thing – wires and electronics.

It was pretty spooky hearing Jim's voice when they played me the track I was to work on. At one point he says, "Did you have a good world when you died? Enough to base a movie on?" I started dialing up some sounds and soon came up with something that worked and they all loved it. A few sound effects were added, but mostly what you hear is Jim and me. The track is titled "The Movie" and is on the album *American Prayer*. They were kind enough to give me a nice big credit on the album, too.

Years later, when Oliver Stone made his movie *The Doors*, he had the clever idea of starting the film with Morrison in the studio recording poetry and used "The Movie," which worked brilliantly. Maybe I am a bit biased, though, because that means that the first sound you hear in the film is me at the controls of my funky synth system. I was involved in the film in another way, too, but I will tell that part of the story in a later chapter.

In the spring of 1978, I was playing with a band called The Taylor Sisters. It was a very commercial top 40 cover band which was soon hired to play at Disneyland. That's way down in Orange County, but it was a steady gig, and it paid a decent $300 per week. I had to cut my hair, which I didn't like, but it was a good gig so I did it anyway. Disneyland is very clean and very conservative. They had their own sort of secret police, or spies, that went around checking on employees for things like making sure the guys' hair wasn't getting "good in the back." We worked at the Coke Pavilion in Tomorrowland. The stage was on a hydraulic lift system that would elevate the bandstand from the Disney underworld to the ground level for performances, then sink back down when we were through with the set. The best part about it was that the band got to see the underground world beneath Disneyland: there are tunnels with all the elaborate, massive hydraulics and electrical gear that made the rides and everything else work. It was quite interesting. I also have a strong memory of sitting underground by the hydraulic stage on the day I received the sad news that my father had lung cancer. He was not expected to live for very long, so I knew I had to make a trip back to Texas to see him soon.

Chapter Five

On Thursday, June 1, 1978, three years to the day from when I left Texas for California, I got a call from my friend Phil. He said that he been talking to a girl from our old high school in San Antonio who (surprisingly to me) was in L.A. working as an exotic dancer. Phil asked her if she had a boyfriend. She said yes, that he was a bass player and he had just done an audition for Frank Zappa who was auditioning drummers, too! Phil hung up the phone and called me with the news. I was thrilled and stunned. I knew that, at last, the time had come for me to get out my phone book and call the number Don had given me: Frank's home phone.

I nervously dialed the number, and soon Frank Himself was on the line. I introduced myself and explained that I had gotten his number from Don, and that I had gone to North Texas like Bruce Fowler and Sal Marquez. I also mentioned that I had learned the melody to "Inca Roads" on the bass as an exercise. I had the distinct feeling he did not believe me about that. He asked me if I was familiar with the instrumental melody in the middle of "Saint Alfonso's Pancake Breakfast." When I said yes, he told me to learn it off the record and be ready to play it for him when I came to my audition. He said to call him back the following Tuesday so he could give me the details about when and where the auditions would be held. As soon as I got off the phone, I made a reel to reel tape recording of "Saint Alfonso" from the album *Apostrophe*, slowed it down to half speed so that I could pick out all those fast, funny little notes, wrote it out, and started learning it. On the original recording, the bass does not play the melody in that section, however, it sticks with the bass notes in that part of the song. As I quickly found out, that melody is not at all easy to play on the bass guitar!

My audition was on Wednesday, June 15, 1978, at 4:00 p.m. at soundstage 16 on the old MGM lot in Culver City at 9339 Washington Blvd. A soundstage is a very large room with a high ceiling that is used for indoor filming. It was perfect for rehearsing a band like Zappa's because he could set up the full P.A. and light rigs just as they would be in a real live show. I arrived early and got to know a couple of the guys in the road crew a little. They helped me plug into the bass amp that was already there, and I started warming up. When Frank came in, I introduced myself and said, "Here's that melody from 'Saint Alfonso' that you asked me to learn." And then I "whipped it out." Zappa said, "Well, you've got a few wrong notes in there, but you have potential."

He wanted to test me on a few different aspects of my abilities, like how quickly I could pick up on strange melodic and rhythmic patterns by ear. This was called the Big Ear Contest. Tommy Mars had Frank's big new EMU polyphonic synth system as part of his keyboard set up. He had programmed the note sequencer on the thing to play one of Frank's odd time melodic patterns. This one, which ended up in part of "Keep it Greasy," was in 21/16(!) and it wasn't "quantized" (perfectly even rhythmically) which made it even harder to comprehend. Mars hit the play button on the EMU and Frank watched while I tried to figure it out and play along with it. I was so nervous that my brain completely locked up for just a little while, although it seemed like an eternity. I began to think I was not going to "get" the pattern and thus blow my audition. But then, seemingly at the last second, I grasped what it was, and was able to play along with it and stay in sync. Whew.

Frank asked me to stick around for the rest of the day and play with a few different drummers. There were around 25 or 30 other bass players there, and about as many drummers, including Vinnie Colaiuta. I found out later that the day before I auditioned, Frank had already auditioned some 30 other bass players. Ike Willis was auditioning at this same time, and Denny Walley was there also, re-auditioning for the band. As I waited through the other bass players' auditions, I sat with Denny for a while. He was very encouraging to me, saying that he could tell Frank liked me and I would likely get the gig. Sure enough, Frank asked me to come back the next day, and after some more playing, hired me on a trial basis. I was to rehearse till the end of the following week, and then he would decide if I made the grade.

We began the next day, Friday, with Vinnie on drums. At one point he brought out some sheet music for a little sight-reading test. Reading was not my forte, so I was nervous. But I really focused my mind and did my best. Unlike many players that he had auditioned, I was not thrown by the odd meters or the weird rhythmic groupings. Being Zappa music, I knew that when I saw a grouping of five, whether as a time signature or a quintuplet, it was almost always going to be grouped 1-2-1-2-3, for example. I knew how his musical mind worked to some extent, and was comfortable with the way he notated music. I was not as quick as some players at reading through a fast run of sixteenth notes, but I could handle the weird stuff. I must have done pretty well, because after a couple of hours he took me aside, smiled broadly, shook my hand, and said, "You don't have to wait until the end of next week. You're hired. You are one of the best bass players I've ever played with." I was so thrilled I remember feeling like I could have jumped 30 feet into the air!

He had a few questions for me. "Do you have a passport?" he asked. I was delighted to able to say "yes" because of my gig in Sweden. He asked me, "Do you like to fly?" I said yes. Back then, before the heavy airport security, it was still fun. He said, "I hope you're not a drug addict." Luckily, I was not. The pay was $500 a week, year round, whether I was rehearsing, on the road or off duty. That was a considerable improvement over the $300 a week I was making at Disneyland, and of course it was a better gig, to say the least!

I had a question for him, too, and asked, "I just recently found out my father has lung cancer and doesn't have long to live. I need to take a trip to Texas soon to see him, would that be ok?" I was thinking about being gone for a week or so. He replied, "Sure, can you go on a weekend?" I was a bit taken aback, but, not seeming to have much of a choice, I agreed. I was finally able to fly to Texas to see my father on the weekend of July 29th. He had already begun aggressive radiation treatment, and it was a shock to see him. His hair was all gone, and he was very thin and pale. At one point he felt so sick that I had to lift him into the back seat of his car so we could take him to a hospital. I remember sitting by his bed there telling him about my new job with Zappa. When I told him I was making $500 a week, he said, "I've never made that much in my whole life. You be sure to work hard for that money, because when a lot is given, a lot is expected."

On Monday, June 19th, the rehearsals began in earnest, with Vinnie, Ike and me as the brand new hires. Denny was hired too, but he was already a vet from the *Bongo Fury* days. Rehearsals were grueling and wonderful. We rehearsed at least 8 hours a day, 5 days a week, for about 6 weeks before the tour. Rehearsals usually got started at 4 pm, although Tommy Mars was almost always there early working with his keyboard set up that he loved so much. One of the band members, Ed Mann, served as "Clonemeister," leading the rehearsal for the first half of the day until Frank arrived and took over. He would often come in and change a lot of things that he had us learn the day before, which could get very confusing. Frank asked me at one point if I had a cassette recorder. I did not. Frank instructed me to purchase one and a lot of blank tape to record the rehearsals, which I did. I reviewed those tapes each night after rehearsal to ensure that I would retain as much in my head as possible. It helped a lot, and as a result of Frank telling me to buy that tape machine, I now own many hours of interesting Zappa rehearsal recordings.

There were many things that had to get done besides learning the music. I had to buy a second bass to have on stage as a back-up in case I broke a string or something during a show. I bought a used blonde Gibson Ripper for that purpose, but when Frank saw it, he liked the way it looked and encouraged me to play that instead of my Fender Precision. I think he liked the way it matched Vinnie's yellow drums. I had to buy road cases, and a big suitcase to carry the new clothes I needed to buy. I had no road cases at all, and they weren't cheap. I had to pay for all of this out of my own pocket, of course. Getting the bass cases made was no big deal, but Frank wanted me to bring my Electrocomp and my Serge modular, too. That was more involved. I ended up with a large fold out case for the Serge, which fit into an even larger road case that also held the Electrocomp. That heavy case got schlepped around to every gig, but I never once used the Serge on stage.

One of the first things Frank taught me was to get on good terms with the road crew and treat them with respect. He understood how valuable they were and how crucial it was to have a reliable group of pros on your side. He said they would come to the rescue when the inevitable crisis arose and save my ass. Frank was absolutely correct. Hardly a show went by without some problem on stage, like a broken string or a problem with an amp. The crew guys huddled off to the side of the stage during the shows. All I had to do was give a look and a nod to one of the guys and he was there in a flash to help.

However, treating them with respect was not the same as lending a hand, I soon found out. One day at rehearsal I went to help one of the crew guys move a heavy speaker cabinet. When Frank saw me, he made me stop immediately and told me that the heavy lifting was the job of the crew. He said, "I can't afford to have you break your arm or something and screw up the tour. I have too much invested in you." It made perfect sense.

Playing sports was also frowned upon if not forbidden outright for the same reason. Poor Ed Mann went out jogging on the beach barefoot once and stepped on some glass that injured him pretty badly. He hobbled around with his foot bandaged up for quite some time. Thereafter, jogging barefoot was verboten. An experience with one of my predecessors, Tom Fowler, probably had an influence on Frank, too. During a recording session for *One Size Fits All*, Tom injured his hand so badly playing football that he couldn't play bass. As I understand it, that's why there is a synth bass on "Sofa" instead of a bass guitar. But then, it is a great synth bass sound on that tune which is one of the things I love about that recording.

Frank taught me another lesson which has stuck with me over the years. It was about voicing self criticism. One day I was going on about how bad I was at sight reading or some such thing when Frank said, "Don't flaunt incompetence." It's good advice, and I have passed it on to other young musicians many times.

But the music was the main thing by far, and, wow, what an experience! I was really surprised at how much more difficult the job was than I had imagined it would be. For one thing, even though I knew quite a few Zappa songs already, I still had to catch up with the new songs the band was currently playing. Frank soon gave me a cassette of the yet unreleased *Sheik Yerbouti* album. I had to learn almost every song on it, including vocal harmony parts on a lot of them. I had my hands full right there, but that was just the start. I was also handed a stack of sheet music to work up and memorize. Some of it I was familiar with, like one my favorites, "Strictly Genteel." What an absolute blast it was playing that masterpiece with that band! And there were many I had never heard before, like "Envelopes" or "Sinister Footwear," then called "Slowly B."

An interesting thing Frank was doing at the time was writing what he called "insertion units." He brought in charts for us with numbers for titles, like "Number Two" or "Number Six." These instrumentals were usually fairly short, only a minute or two in length. He had us work them up as a regular part of rehearsal, but they were not part of the planned show. He said he would find places to use them in future songs, and that is what he did. "Number Six," for example, became the instrumental middle section of "Jumbo Go Away." Another was the middle part of "Wet T-shirt Night." This was an approach to composing I did not expect, but I thought it was quite clever.

One of my duties was to sing, which was not one of my strong points. But the boss wanted it done, so I gave it my all. One of the first songs we worked on was "Stick it Out," a bizarre little ditty about human/animal sex. I had a high part to sing at the very top of my range. There was a line that, to paraphrase so as not to infringe on any "intellectual" property, made a request: have sex with me, you unattractive offspring of a dog. The only way I could hit the notes was to sing it at full volume. I can clearly remember practicing in my apartment in Echo Park, singing the line at the top of my lungs while I played the bass part that went with it. No one ever complained, but I often wondered what the neighbors thought.

People interested in Zappa's music are often under the impression that all the music we played was presented to us on charts that we simply played as written. Although this was the case for some tunes, particularly the intricate melodic pieces like "Black Page" or "Uncle Meat" or the insertion units I mentioned, most of the time there were no written parts at all. They were all what are called "head charts," that is, they exist only as a memory inside your brain. If every tune had an arrangement that was written out and never changed, the band could easily have been ready to tour in a few weeks. But it would not have been nearly as much fun, or as educational. Observing how Frank composed and being part of his creative process as a tool for him to use was at least as fabulous as playing live shows, if not more so.

Often when Frank had a new song idea he would start with just the words, bringing in typewritten copies for all the band members. He often wouldn't have the melody or the chords until he started inventing them in rehearsal. He might pick up a guitar to show the band a vamp or a lick or a bass line, then put the guitar down. To my knowledge, he never played guitar and sang at the same time. He claimed to be incapable of it, which I found hard to believe, but that's what he said. I sure never saw him do it. We would make notes in the margins and above the always double-spaced lyrics about the chord changes and other musical shorthand notations to jog the memory. Frank would create the music right before our eyes telling us each what he wanted us to do, just making it up as he went along.

I also brought blank notebooks with me, like the ones I had used in school. They filled up quickly with hasty, scribbled attempts to make notes of what I needed to remember. Luckily, I held on to those notebooks and I'm sure glad I did. Looking at them now, I am struck by the mad scramble in which they were dashed off. It would be largely indecipherable to anyone other than me, but it was what I could manage to jot down before hearing Frank say, "Again, from the top: One, two, three, four!" (He almost always made us take it "from the top," or start of the song.) But the scribblings were just enough for me, the bare minimum I needed to remind myself of what was most important. All of the notes are in my handwriting with one small exception. At the top of a page with notes on "Sofa," in Frank's handwriting, or printing, really, in all capital letters, is part of the German lyric I wasn't getting right. Frank walked over with a pen and wrote the line down for me in my notebook and seemed very proud of himself for knowing the German spellings.

New songs went through a lot of different experiments and versions before they were performed or recorded. In fact, even after they had been recorded, many would still keep getting changed and rearranged. The recorded version was really just a snapshot of how the song was arranged on the day of the recording, and it could easily change by the next tour. Sometimes he simply changed his mind, and sometimes a tune needed to be adapted to a new band. It was what I had observed about the live version of "Peaches" I had heard in San Antonio in 1970 writ large.

One style Frank experimented with was reggae. I didn't really know anything about reggae, but Ed Mann taught me how it worked. He explained that it was really a fun thing for the bass player, that all I had to do was to avoid the down beat and play melodically. I heard a few examples and got the drift, and it *was* fun. Have the drums play the bass drum on beats two and four with the right kind of swing, and you got it. Of course, Vinnie created absolute *killer* reggae grooves that were a blast to play with. Soon Frank was trying just about every song reggae style. That can be a real challenge to a bassist if the tune happens to be in an odd time signature.

Learning new songs or songs I had not heard before was a very different experience from playing songs that I was already familiar with. Even if I did not know every note of a tune that I had heard on a record, just being familiar with how it sounded made it much easier to play than to learn something brand new with Frank breathing down my neck. This was completely new to me, as I had never even seen a Zappa rehearsal before, nor had I talked about this aspect of the job with the other Zappa players I knew. It was one of the most exciting things about being in the band, to be part of something all new and witness the evolution of the latest FZ creation. I sometimes had to pinch myself to be mindful and aware that I was now involved in the making of Zappa music history. I was humbled by that.

I clearly remember one of the first new songs he wrote when I got in the band. We were scheduled to appear on Saturday Night Live in the fall of 1978, which was exciting. Back then, that was a very big deal. Everyone I knew stayed home on Saturday night to watch it if they could. It was really good then, with the original cast and writers. Frank decided to write a song for the occasion, and so "Conehead" was born in rehearsal. It might not have been one of his most brilliant compositions, but it was still cool to be involved in its inception and creation.

Following Frank's hand and body signals was yet another skill that had to be mastered. If he felt like it, he could give an indication to completely change the style of a tune at any time in a concert without warning, and we had to be ready for it. For example, the signal for reggae was for him to pull up some hair on top of his head, as if to indicate dreadlocks. If he suddenly wanted us to go country style, he would make himself look very bow-legged and rock back and forth from foot to foot. We had to be on our toes and ready to change on a dime at literally any moment in the show.

My experience in those rehearsals had a profound positive effect on my musicianship and my playing. Zappa would push his musicians to their absolute technical limits. For example, he might show me a tricky part to learn. Once I had that down, he might ask me to play it up an octave, or play it double time, or do it up an octave in double time while doing a little dance and a "stunt vocal!" (I was the "stunt" vocalist in the band, which meant I did the falling off the cliff scream or silly voices like the Indian accented crystal ball mystery man from "Cosmik Debris.") By applying this pressure, Frank was at once exploring what I could do and at the same time pushing me to do things I would not have thought myself capable of doing. If he asked me to play something I thought I couldn't do, I would say to myself, *"It seems impossible, but Frank thinks I might be able to do it, so maybe I can."* Much of the time it turned out that with some hard work and intense mental focus, I could do what he asked of me, much to my surprise and delight. I think Frank enjoyed seeing it happen, too.

It was incredible to watch how his mind worked. He had a bottomless well of musical ideas to start with, and a seemingly endless amount of energy to try a multitude of different ways of arranging things. He was constantly telling the band to play a song a certain way, then changing his mind and telling us do things a different way. It was a lot to keep up with, believe me. The brain can get pretty scrambled after 4 or 5 hours of that. Sometimes we would start to space out by the end of a long rehearsal and begin to make mental mistakes. This could make Mr. Zappa a tiny bit cranky. If he was very annoyed he would snap at us and say sarcastically, "What's the matter? Are you guys *tired*? Again, from the top! One, two, three, four!"

One day we were working on some tricky passage and we were close to getting it right, but not quite. Somehow a wager of a cheeseburger ensued with Frank taking the position that we still wouldn't be able to do it correctly the next time we attempted the mind warping section. We tried it again but we still messed it up just a bit. After a brief pause, Frank said, "It is my contention that each and every one of you owes me a cheeseburger." We all had a good laugh. He never asked us to pay up with the burgers.

But what great brain exercise it was! I remember driving home from rehearsals feeling like my brain was wriggling and convulsing in my skull. Tommy Mars told me that he experienced the same sensation inside his head. I have heard that when the brains of classically trained musicians are studied, brain tissue is found connecting the right and left sides of the brain. I think what I was feeling inside my head was that new brain tissue forming and growing. I hope that's what it was, and not something I wouldn't want growing in there.

Another huge honor and challenge for me was playing with Vinnie Colaiuta. I consider him to be not just the best drummer I have ever played with, but the best drummer I have ever heard, hands down. I consider him to be the Jimi Hendrix of the drums, which is the highest compliment I can pay. The guy is amazing. If something is possible in the realm of physics to play on the drum set, Vinnie can do it. He can play in 3 or 4 time signatures at once, play all manner of convoluted rhythmic figures, make it swing, play it straight, or dig into trench sized grooves. He had perfect time, a seemingly endless imagination for drum parts and fills, and he could sight-read his ass off. Frank said, "The guy's a mutation." In the improvisation sections, especially the long Zappa guitar solos, he was masterful. Frank loved him and encouraged him to totally "go for it," to not hold back, and he didn't. Sometimes the rhythms would get very complicated, often with "across the bar" figures that lasted many measures before coming back to the original "one." This could be very challenging to keep up with, especially for me as the bass player who had to equate all this in real time while at the same time inventing the right bass part for the jam. It was even more challenging if Frank happened to give the hand signal to go into reggae style, for example.

All of these wild rhythmic goings on were a departure from what some of the "vets" in the band were used to. It even upset one guy so much he made a sign he'd hold up that said "Where's one?" in reference to the downbeat of the measure not being played in an obvious manner. This did not go over well with Vinnie, and I can see why. I got confused by Vinnie a few times myself, but I can pretty much guarantee that he was always keeping track of the beat in his head and those polyrhythms always came out correctly in the end. If I lost track of where "one" was, I knew it was me and not Vinnie who was off.

Each night after rehearsals, which were five days a week, I would drive from Culver City back home to Echo Park in my ancient VW van listening to either that day's rehearsal tapes, or one of the tapes Frank gave me of songs I didn't know but needed to learn, like the *Sheik Yerbouti* songs. When I got home I would take notes from the tapes and go over the scribbled rehearsal notes to be ready for the next day, then practice whatever needed practicing, which was a lot. It was definitely a full time job.

It turned out that part of the job description included occasionally giving the boss a ride. Frank didn't drive. One night after rehearsal, he asked if I could give him a ride home to his house in Laurel Canyon, and of course I said yes. I think if he had realized what kind of car I was driving, he might have asked someone else for a ride. I had a mid-sixties VW bus – the type before the sliding side door, a weak six volt electrical system, a bench seat in the front with no seat belts, and a hard metal dashboard. When Frank got in and saw that there was no seat belt, he braced himself by putting his feet up on the metal dashboard and rode like that all the way home.

We had talked before about us both liking Bartok, so I mentioned I had a cassette of a Bartok Piano Concerto (number two, I think) and began fumbling around for it in the glove compartment, looking for it while I was driving. Frank got a little spooked and suggested that it would be better to forget about the tape and concentrate on driving. It was wise advice.

Early on I told Frank which of his compositions were my favorites. I mentioned the 1971 Fillmore version of "Little House I Used to Live In," and he said that if I wanted to transcribe it, he'd have the band attempt to play it. I spent quite a bit of time on it and brought in copies for the other band members. We tried it a couple of times, but it never became part of the show, to my disappointment. Unfortunately, I didn't keep a copy of the chart for myself. I recently transcribed it again, this time in greater detail, and I now have a lovely arrangement of it which was performed in my April 2015 concert at the University of North Texas.

I also mentioned to Frank how much I loved *One Size Fits All*. He sort of cocked his head and gave me an odd, slightly sad, puzzled look and said, "It didn't sell very well at all." I got that funny little puzzled look from him only a few times over the years, but I came to recognize it as a rare glimpse of sincerity in expressing a lack of understanding about something that was going on. Looking at the liner notes for "Sofa" on the *Zappa in New York* album recently I noticed that he described the *One Size Fits All* album as "not very popular." I find that it is now mentioned as the favorite Zappa album of most Zappa fans I talk to. It started to become clear to me why he had changed direction with *Zoot Allures* and *Sheik Yerbouti*. He must have felt that by dumbing down the music a little and being more of a rock star he would sell more albums. This also explained why he would put down the guitar and roam the stage with the hand-held mic while fronting the band.

I had a fretless bass by this time which I had been playing more than my fretted one, and it was becoming my main axe. I auditioned for Zappa on the fretted Precision bass, though, because I thought that sound suited Frank's music better. I was even playing it with a pick instead of my fingers to get more of a rock than a jazz sound. I asked Frank about playing the fretless in his band, and he said no, that he preferred the fretted one, saying that he didn't like all that "slippin' and slidin'" on the fretless. Imagine my surprise when I found out - only after the album came out - that he hired Pat O'Hearn to record fretless bass on two tracks for the first Zappa album I played on, *Joe's Garage*.

Contradictions like that were not uncommon with Frank. Another example: he told me that he fired Bozzio and O'Hearn because they were taking too many liberties with his arrangements instead of playing the parts he had given them. Then he hires Vinnie who was allowed, even encouraged, to pretty much play whatever he wanted to play. I doubt if Vinnie ever played a tune the same way twice, but whatever he did was always great, and Frank loved it.

As great as it was to be in the band, it was not all a bed of roses. I did not mind the long hours and hard work, but there were other issues. Early on, maybe it was even during my audition days, we were working on one of the guitar solo sections. Vinnie was doing great, able to keep up with Frank perfectly. Of course the drummer has to worry about the rhythms only and not be concerned with the musical pitches, unlike the bass player, who must keep track of all the musical elements. Frank praised Vinnie, then turned to me and said something like, "not too bad, but you're only getting about 80% of it." Of course, I was dismayed, and asked, "Jeez, am I supposed to have ESP or something?" He nonchalantly replied, "Yes." I was a bit taken aback, but did my best to improve my psychic powers. They are a lot better now.

People often ask me what it was like to be in the Zappa band, and I try to explain it like this: if you have ever been in a band, you may have had one member of the band who was much more musically advanced than the others, but more often than not, that person was a bit off his rocker, if not totally nuts. The Zappa band was mostly comprised of *those* guys.

On top of that, there was a small faction of Mean Girls in the band, too, who seemed to feel that I was not as good at accompanying their solos as well as their former bandmate and pal, my predecessor Pat O'Hearn. At one point, in between bites of his favorite snack, an entire stick of pure butter, the moldy-toothed leader of the anti-Barrow faction told me that he had advised Frank not to hire me. What a guy. This was hard for me to take. After all, I was fulfilling a long worked-for dream of playing in this band, and here were some of my bandmates pissing on it. I soon realized that this Mean Girl was also annoyed because I really enjoyed learning Frank's more challenging music, and the Mean Girl didn't want to be bothered with all the work that entailed.

Early in the first tour, I clearly remember feeling down over this one day and having a talk about it with Vinnie over a burger in Florida. I said, "I guess those guys don't think I'm good enough to play with them." Vinnie had the perfect answer. He said, "Frank thinks you're good enough, and that's all that matters." I will always be grateful for those words, Mr. Colaiuta. I even tried to talk to Frank about it, who said, "What do you want, for people to like you? There will always be people who don't like you. Get used to it."

On balance it was *way* more good than bad, especially as I look back on it now. My God, I was getting to play some of my favorite Zappa music in *Zappa's own band*, like "Sofa," "Strictly Genteel," "Village of the Sun," "Saint Alfonso's Pancake Breakfast," and great new tunes like "The Meek Shall Inherit Nothing" and "Packard Goose." It was a terrific high, to be sure.

The first tour was originally scheduled to be a U.S. tour, with the first date scheduled for Miami in mid-September. But one day in August, Frank announced that some dates had been added before the start of the regular tour at some big outdoor festivals in Europe. The first concert would be on August 26th. Consequently, there was a big push to get the show properly whipped into shape pronto! The moment of truth - my first big rock concert with the real Frank Zappa - was about to happen. Would I be able to perform on stage in front of an audience under "battle conditions" as Frank called them? I would soon find out.

Chapter Six

On Saturday, August 19th, 1978, at 12:30 pm, we boarded a TWA flight to London. We went there first to rehearse a few days before heading off to Germany for our first gig. I went for a walk around London one day with Guy, one of the roadies. I recall standing on a corner near our hotel studying a map of London, when a lovely, kindly old British woman saw us looking at it. She stopped and asked us if she could be of any help, and proceeded to point out a few sights that we might enjoy seeing. Since then I have stood on a lot of street corners in a lot of cities looking at maps, but that was the only time anyone offered to help.

After five days in London we jetted off to Germany. Our first show was a huge outdoor festival on August 26th in Ulm. The other acts included Joan Baez, Genesis with Chester Thompson on drums, which was cool, and John McLaughlin's group The One Truth Band which was an acoustic group with L. Shankar on Indian-style five-string violin. I was able to listen to some of the other sets before we played, and I was very impressed with Shankar. When I saw Frank backstage, I told him about Shankar. I think Ed knew L. already, and pretty soon Shankar was in Frank's tent. This meeting led to Frank inviting Shankar on stage with us in New York. Frank later produced a Shankar album called *Touch Me There*.

That first concert happened to be the biggest audience I ever performed for with Zappa or anyone else, with an estimated 70,000 people in attendance. Because it was a festival, there was no sound check, something that almost never happened at a Frank show. We usually had extensive sound checks. As luck would have it, I plugged into my amp and it didn't work! My amp was really just one of the Tycho Brahe side-fill monitor speakers wired up with a preamp for bass. I tried not to panic as I was looking out into a sea of faces as far as the eye could see, and there I was with no sound. Nothing! I got the attention of one of our great crew members, and they immediately wheeled another amp onto the stage, and within a minute or two, I was ready to go. It hadn't taken long to find out that Frank was right about those guys coming to my rescue.

Once we started the show I looked out into the audience and saw that there were a bunch of tough looking young guys with crew cuts near the front who were holding their middle fingers high above their heads. It was my first show and people were out there giving us the finger! What the hell was going on? Frank explained to me later that it was American army guys. He said they always did it as a sort of display of affection or something. I'm not sure if I ever really bought that explanation, but it helped anyway. Maybe it was just Frank's way of teaching me not to worry about such trivialities.

Of course I had been nervous as hell, but I managed to get through the set without any major screw-ups. Before I knew it, I had completed my rite of passage. I could play in front of 70,000 people without choking.

Most of that first leg of the tour in Europe is pretty much of a blur. I do recall one amusing incident, however. Vinnie and I were in a cab together in some German city and we struck up a conversation with the driver. When he asked about us, we said we were musicians, then asked him if he knew who Frank Zappa was. He turned around with a shocked look on his face and replied, "Of course I know who Zappa is! You might as well have asked me who Jesus Christ is!"

At some point we had a few days off in Munich. Frank rented the Circus Krone for more rehearsals on the days without any gigs booked. Right after we left the U.S. Frank had given me a piece of sheet music, the bass part of a composition I had not yet heard of called "Mo's Vacation." This version was a duet for bass and drums. It was two pages long and *very* challenging. I was thrilled. This was a first for me: a brand new Zappa chart and I had a chance to be the first bassist to play it. Very cool.

As soon as I got settled into my room in Munich, I dove into the chart full steam ahead, spending about 15 to 20 hours on it, memorizing as I went. I was totally into it even though there are parts of it that are all but unplayable.

There was a moment during the rehearsals, a food break, probably, when I had a chance to try to run through it with Vinnie. When I asked him about it, he said that he hadn't had a chance to look at it yet, but would be happy to sight read through it with me. He had a plate of sushi which he opened up and started eating while he located the drum part. He got the chart set up on his music stand, lit up a cigarette and he started reading through it. Incredibly, he was able to play it almost flawlessly the first time through! I was floored. Scarfing sushi and smoking a butt while sight reading "Mo's." I couldn't believe it.

We played "Mo's" for Frank when he got there, and he beamed with delight when he heard it. That night I was sitting next to him in a club. He was very curious about how I learned it, asking how long I had worked on it and so forth. I told him I had spent about fifteen hours on it. He was clearly pleased and impressed. I had met the challenge, and man, did that feel good.

It was during that time at the Circus Krone that the German video *We Don't Mess Around* was recorded. What appears to be a live concert was actually a rehearsal in which Frank put on a show for the camera. It contains our version of "St. Alfonso's Pancake Breakfast" in which I played the fast melody part ("Rollo Interior") on the bass, the same thing I had auditioned on. It's gratifying for me to see that a clip of that performance is now available on the Internet.

Frank wrote another new song at that time which later became a favorite track on *Joe's Garage*. It was inspired by the road manager, Phil Kaufman, who was quite a colorful character. On a bus ride one day he got up from his seat and announced that he was going to go "vote," by which he meant he going to use the tiny toilet in the rear of the cabin. We soon heard a horrible scream from the back of the bus. He emerged after a few moments and asked in a plaintive voice, "Why does it hurt when I pee?" That was the kind of humor that Frank loved, so naturally it inspired a new song. He came into rehearsal with the lyrics and started composing the music on the spot. My favorite part of the song "Why Does it Hurt When I Pee?" is the instrumental middle section. He wanted it to sound similar to one of those English "art rock" bands like King Crimson or Genesis. He described what he wanted as "pseudo English pomposity." I think the climax at the end of that section with the big D major vocal chord is absolutely glorious.

After the rehearsal time in Munich was over, the rest of the European leg of the tour seemed to go by very quickly. We started in Saarbrucken, Germany on September 3rd, and were back in England at Knebworth on the 9th. I thought the band was starting to sound pretty damned good.

Then on September 10th, it was a flight back across the ocean to the states straight to Florida, where we had a few days off at a hotel on the beach. It was during this time that a club in Miami provided another source of inspiration for Frank, a Wet T-shirt contest.

The first date of the U.S. tour was in Miami on the 15th, followed by St. Petersburg on the 16th, Atlanta on the 17th, and so on as we worked our way up the east coast on a tight, grueling schedule.

Atlanta had a little surprise in store for me. It was a double show at the Fox Theater, and Frank always liked to change things up for the late show. The difficult new piece, "Mo's Vacation," was not part of the regular show, but to my horror, in the second set, he unexpectedly turned around to face Vinnie and me with a big smile and said, "Mo's Vacation!" Now, I had assumed that since it wasn't part of the regular show, I didn't need to keep it polished up for performance. I didn't have time to practice it every day, anyway, so I wasn't ready for it at all. We did pretty well, all things considered, but as soon as there were a couple of mistakes, Frank's smile turned into a frown of disappointment and a flash of the evil eye.

Once we were back in the states, Frank let it be known that band members were welcome to join him in his room after the show to listen to mixing board cassette tapes from that night's performance. Vinnie and I often took him up on the offer. I have a clear picture in my mind of Frank in his robe sitting in a chair with his feet propped up on an ottoman. I was sitting on the floor next to him, watching him wiggle his toes in time to the music, doing a sort of "air toe tap." But I also remember one night when some things did not sound too great, especially in the vocal harmony department. He got agitated and said something like, "I can't believe I spent all that money rehearsing this band and it doesn't sound any better than this!" I was shocked. I thought things had been going along so well! But he was right, some of the vocal harmonies did not sound good. I could be a bit shaky at times, and although we had good singers like Ike, Denny, and Tommy, it was not always easy to get a good blend. He also mentioned that this was the first time he had allowed musicians who were also "fans" like Ike and me into the band, and wasn't sure yet that it had been a good idea. Ouch. But really, would he have preferred musicians who didn't like his music, or were unfamiliar with it? Maybe he was just trying to spook us into trying a little harder and improving our performance by a couple of percentage points. I found out later that Frank actually *had* hired fans before, like Bruce Fowler and Ruth Underwood, for example.

In another conversation I had with Frank in his room after a gig I mentioned how I hoped that we would play my home town of San Antonio some time, and how great it would be to return in triumph, impressing all my friends. He offered me some sage wisdom. He said that he didn't know if we would play there or not, but if we did, it wouldn't give me the satisfaction I expected it to. He said that most people wouldn't understand the significance of it, and the ones who did would probably be jealous. Since we never played in San Antonio, I never had the chance to find out if he was right, but human nature being what it is, he probably had a point.

The tour proceeded and we were sounding pretty good, in spite of, or maybe because of Frank's concerns. We hit all the major spots in the eastern part of the continent, going as far west as Milwaukee, and as far north as Montreal. It was a whirlwind – we were working 5 or 6 nights a week, every gig in a different city. That meant flying every day, often having to change planes in the "hub" airports.

Like Frank said, touring really can make you crazy. You wake up too early in the morning in a Holiday Inn (or equivalent) after too little sleep due to the performance adrenaline pulsing through your body, get your bags packed, wait in the lobby, go to the airport, wait, (at least there was not the airport security there is now) fly to a hub airport, dash to the right gate, wait, fly to the city where the gig is, go to the venue, do a long sound check, get a bite to eat, wait, get butterflies in your stomach, play an insane show for two hours, get off stage full of adrenaline and ready to stay up late and hang out because once again, you are too wound up to go to sleep. Then do the same thing all over again the next day. A life like that can *definitely* make you crazy.

Frank had a huge amount of experience in handling audiences, and one night I saw just how brilliant he was at doing that. It was October 6th, 1978 in Augusta, Maine, at the Augusta Civic Center. At that time, my stage position was next to Frank, to his left and a bit behind him. He was playing his heart out in a guitar solo, facing slightly upward with his eyes closed as they often were when he played. Suddenly, I saw him get violently knocked backwards and stop playing. At first I thought he had been shot. I was horrified. It turned out to be a pint sized glass liquor bottle thrown by some idiot in the audience. Frank stopped the band immediately, got on the mic and explained to the audience what had just happened. He instructed the people in charge of the lighting to turn on the lights and said, "We aren't going to play another note until whoever threw that bottle at me goes to jail." The lighting people started shining the spotlights on the audience, but Frank said, "No, I mean the house lights, those bright ugly big ones in the ceiling." The big fluorescent overhead lights came on, which is pretty jarring to the eye in the middle of a show after it's been dark for a while. Soon, the attention was going towards some seats up high and to our left. Audience members began to point to a certain area as security guys climbed up the aisles on either side and zeroed in on the suspect. The jerk that threw the bottle was removed without incident, and we resumed the show. To me, that is a textbook example of audience control mastery.

Shortly before we played in Passaic on October 13th, I got a surprise visit to my hotel room from Frank and his wife, Gail. I was informed that Patrick O'Hearn would be added to the group for the remaining two weeks of the tour. Frank said he would work out some two bass arrangement ideas for some things, and that Pat would be doing the jamming parts. I was devastated, to put it mildly. Gail could see this in my face, and sarcastically uttered something like, "Oh, don't take it so hard, Arthur, it's not the end of the world." And so it came to be that there were two bass players for a while. I assumed it meant the end for me in the band after the tour. It was like a bad acid trip.

My least favorite question to be asked about my time with Zappa is, "Why were there two bass players in 1978?" I don't know for sure, but I heard that the Mean Girls in the band had been complaining to Frank about my playing. They were in touch with Pat, and influenced Frank to add Pat to the line-up. So there you have it; please don't ask me again. Pat is a nice guy, and we got along fine. He is a great player, and I learned some things from listening to him which improved my approach to the Zappa band jams. I thank him for that.

But here I had been telling my friends and family all over the country that I was going to be on *Saturday Night Live* with Frank

Zappa and that they *had* to tune in *for sure*. Only now there were going to be two bass players. Great. To make matters worse, most of the time the camera work made it look like there was only one: Pat. I felt like a complete ass when I later talked to people and they asked, "Who was that other guy up there? You didn't say anything about him, and we barely caught a glimpse of you." And so it went for the final couple of weeks of the tour.

    There were still a couple of high points left, though. For one thing, I got to see what it was like to be on SNL, and experience the feeling of knowing that millions of people were watching our performance. In the week before the show, we had a rehearsal with the SNL band. I remember thinking how cool it was that Paul Schaefer was handing me my union contract. Frank had a special arrangement of "Rollo" that was scheduled to be performed by our regular band plus the SNL horns. This horn section was comprised of some of the best session musicians in New York including North Texas alumni Lou Marini and Tom Malone. They were the top of the heap, man. We ran through the tune a couple of times, but the horns weren't really getting it. Frank turned to us and told us to play it down once without the horns so they could hear how it was supposed to sound. We whipped it out flawlessly, and then Frank turned to them and said, "OK, let's try it again." They did, but they still weren't playing it right. Frank said, "I think we better forget about the horn arrangement on this one. I don't think you guys are going to cut it." That evoked an outcry from the horn guys who were saying, "No, man, we can do it – we'll take it home and shed it real good, we promise!" I couldn't help but be tickled that some unknowns like us had shown up the hot New York players. Apparently, they did practice their parts, because they nailed them on the show.

    By the way, Frank was a master of reverse psychology. I recall a time when we had been working hard on a very difficult piece and almost had it right. When we played it for Frank in rehearsal, we made a couple of mistakes. He said, "Well, you can take that one off the list. I don't want to have you guys embarrass me on stage." This was agonizing to us because we had worked on it so hard and were close to getting it down. So we replied with something that in effect said, "Oh, please, Frank, let us keep torturing ourselves some more trying to play your impossible music, oh please!" He would then grudgingly allow us to work on it a little more. See how that worked? Brilliant.

On the day of the live SNL broadcast, Saturday, October 21, 1978, there was a dress rehearsal of the show before a live studio audience in the afternoon. The show was supposed to run 90 minutes, but it lasted more than 2 hours! The writers had to scurry to do a lot of cutting before the live broadcast.

There was a meeting in Frank's room before the show in which he said that he thought the script for the show was weak, and he intended to do something radical to save the show. There was obvious friction between him and some of the SNL people, although he seemed friendly with Dan Akroyd and Laraine Newman. She even came to one of our shows later at the Palladium.

When it was time for the broadcast we were instructed by a stage manager to stay in our places on stage with our instruments ready to go during the entire 90 minute show. I thought that was a bit strict, but found out later why it had to be done that way. (While were waiting for the show to begin, she told me about having the Rolling Stones on two weeks earlier. They came in and asked, "When do we tape?" not realizing that *Saturday Night "Live"* really meant that it was a live broadcast. The Stones were apparently quite surprised and not terribly pleased about it.)

Before the broadcast, we were handed sheets of paper with the revised, final version of the order of the sketches and the musical numbers for the night. We got through the show smoothly, though Frank seemed pretty uncomfortable reading his lines in the sketches. Apparently, his big idea to "save the show" was spitting out some chips in the Coneheads scene, and letting the audience know he was reading from cue cards. I am not sure that did anything to save the show, but it did seem to piss off the SNL people.

It was interesting to see how the show worked. There were 4 or 5 different stages set up around the studio ready to go for whatever sketch was lined up next. I had always wondered why after commercial breaks there would often be periods when they would air still pictures on the screen while the house band played. It turned out it was because there was always a mad scramble during the commercial breaks to prepare for what was next, and sometimes they just weren't ready yet.

We got to a point in the show where my sheet indicated that there was going to be one more sketch and then we were to play our last number. Vinnie had just lit a cigarette and I was looking all around the studio trying to figure out where the next sketch would be, when suddenly the lights came on *us* and Frank was running up to the stage with baton in hand! Holy shit! They had ditched the scheduled sketch, and we were on! Frank gave us four beats of the baton, and we were off to the races playing Rollo. Now I knew why they had insisted that we stay on the stage the whole time, and that also explains why Vinnie had a cigarette in his mouth throughout the performance. John Belushi joined us in the middle section as "Samurai Rock and Roll Guitar Player." He had a guitar strapped on, but rather than play it, there was a mic attached to it that he sang into. We played a funky vamp as he sang riffs, and we would answer them with random notes as a kind of atonal call and response. I really enjoyed the experience of doing the show, but was disappointed later when I found out that I was hardly even visible on the TV screen. Oh, well.

Another high point for me on that tour was the night L. Shankar, the great Indian violinist, sat in with the band at the Palladium in New York. Before the show, there was a meeting in Frank's dressing room. He had an electric piano in there, and had written a little C Lydian vamp in 13/8. It was a bit tricky to feel at first, but it basically consisted of a bar of 5/8 plus a bar of 4/4. It was certainly nothing I had tried before. Frank said that we would use that as a vehicle for L. Shankar to improvise over. I thought to myself, "I'm sure glad I don't have to do this one since Pat is doing all the jams. Have fun, Pat!" Then Frank turned to me and said, "I want you to play bass on this one." Oh, great – thanks a lot, Frank, give me the one in 13/8, a time signature I had never played in before, a perfect set up for failure. I don't know why he chose me, to be honest. I guess in a way it might have been a vote of confidence. Maybe he didn't trust that Pat could pull it off. I'll never know. Terrified as I was, I went out in front of the New York audience and played in 13/8 for the first time in my life without having a total train wreck. Whew.

Looking back on the whole two bass thing and the idea of having Pat do the improv parts, I take some comfort in the fact that when all was said and done, Frank released a lot of recordings of jams with me on bass, especially on the first *Shut Up and Play Your Guitar* albums. I guess I was good enough after all.

The Halloween gig was the last of the tour. I was exhausted and glad to head for home, but I couldn't help wondering if it was the end of my days in the Zappa band. After all, Frank would constantly remind the band that we had absolutely *no* job security, and that he had a filing cabinet full of names of musicians who wanted our jobs. On the other hand, I had not been terminated and the paychecks kept coming.

Chapter Seven

When I got home, I rested up a bit and was soon into my old groove of doing a variety of gigs. It felt good to be back in town, and I was eager to get into a studio to do some recording. I had written three new Loose Connection tunes I wanted to get on tape, and it occurred to me that it would be great to use Vinnie on them. He agreed, and I began looking for a studio. I found a 16-track place on Hollywood Blvd. just across from the Chinese Theater that I could afford. Since I was making more money than I'd ever made in my life, I was feeling generous and paid the guys for the session. Vinnie was awesome, of course, and even had to replace his drum tracks on a tune because the original recording had some bad dropouts on the tape. I didn't think that he would be able to redo the drums because there was no reference "click track" or anything to play to. Amazing as always, Vinnie nailed it in one take! I was very happy with the recordings we got.

We ended up recording at odd hours, late nights and early mornings, because before we got into the studio, a call from Frank's office came in saying that rehearsals for an upcoming European tour would begin on December 11th at a rehearsal place in Hollywood called Mars. This meant that we had to find time to record my new tunes outside the always heavy Zappa schedule.

But this call was good news - it meant I was still in the band after all. I got to the first rehearsal, and, to my relief, I was the only bass player. There were, however, a couple of changes to the line-up. Frank had hired Warren Cucurullo on guitar, and Ike was back in the band. Ike had been sent home back in October when he was spotted by Gail at the Gramercy Park Hotel bar in New York after skipping the gig in Stony Brook, saying he was too sick to perform. That was a big No-No. You were expected to play in that band unless you were too sick to stand up or sit on a stool next to bucket, as I was soon to find out.

There was another change in store. Not only was I not fired, but because Ed did not want to continue to be the Clonemeister, Frank asked me if I would do it! Of course I said yes. How could I have said no to Frank Zappa? Even though it paid double during rehearsals, I actually didn't particularly want to do it, mainly because I would much rather have had Frank there himself doing it. I think everyone in the band would have preferred that, too. So there I was. One day I'm wondering if I'll be fired, and the next day I'm running the rehearsals. Some roller coaster, but that was just the beginning.

It was no surprise that when I assumed the role of rehearsal director it did not sit well with some of the other band members, especially the "vets" who had been in the band longer than I had. This I can understand. I probably would have felt a little of that, too. But to the main Mean Girl, it was a travesty, so he became dedicated to trying to make my job as miserable as possible. This Clonemeister gig was not going to be easy.

Nonetheless, it was a great set of rehearsals when Frank was around. There were now *four* guitar players in the band, and Frank was experimenting with textures that twenty-four amplified guitar strings made possible. He was also getting very creative with his method of writing "on the band," seeing how far he could push us in terms of piecing together more and more ideas for us to remember on the spot. It was as if he wanted to see how much he could cram into our heads before they exploded.

A tune he was working on that really stands out in my mind was something he called "Saddle Bags." I think he was calling it that because of a section utilizing three hand-muted guitars playing redundant, stacked up, neutral sounding chords that produced a gentle loping feel and then a livelier section he referred to as the "Heidi Ho" part. This had a bold synth French horn melody played over a bass part that was on the off beats with a lot of very inventive orchestrations involving keyboards and percussion. There were several other sections that he experimented with in various combinations. Nothing was written out, so Frank would sing or play parts to us instead. This could get tricky when we were playing in odd time signatures. We were usually just going on feel without worrying about what it actually worked out to in mathematical terms. Here's an example of how he would throw ideas at us to instantly remember. There was a certain odd time lick that existed in two slightly different versions, a shorter one and a longer one. He described how he wanted a certain section played by saying, "When it happens three times, do the longer version, ok? Got the breakdown on it? It's one bar of the vamp, then you play one, then it's two bars of the vamp, and you play two, then it's two bars of the vamp and you play three of the long ones. Got it? OK, one, two, three, four!" This kind of work went on for hours at a time, with him constantly trying new ideas and changing his mind. It was great fun and totally mind boggling.

"Saddle Bags" was becoming a brilliant new Zappa composition before my very eyes, but alas, he never finished it. One little part survived and ended up in "Fembot in a Wet T-Shirt" on *Joe's Garage*. It's the lick after the line about serving them right.

I was also very pleased that Frank began adding some of my favorite songs to the set that were a treat to play, like "Inca Roads," "Andy," "Florentine Pogen," and "Brown Shoes Don't Make It." Fortunately, "Brown Shoes" was in the very accurate Zappa songbook, thanks to Ian Underwood's meticulous work. Striving for accuracy, I even recall working closely with Warren to get the tremolo setting on the amp just right for the end section. He was a big fan, too, and we were both in Zappa heaven.

This set of rehearsals ended on January 5th, 1979. I flew to Texas the next day for a visit with friends and family, then came back to LA before our scheduled departure date of January 27th. Frank was already in London producing an album for his new friend, L. Shankar.

Frank often had favorites in the band that he liked to hang with because he found them entertaining. At this point, they seemed to be Warren and Vinnie. Frank got bored in London (that's when he wrote "Dead Girls of London") and decided he wanted them to join him over there to keep him laughing for the remaining week or so before the rest of the band was due to arrive. I was also asked to drop everything and come early, not to amuse the boss, but to go to work. Frank said that Shankar was going to be joining the band, and that I was to start tutoring him on the vast amount of music he was going to have to learn very quickly.

It was a wonderful experience for me working with L. What a fantastic musician and deep, lovely person. I was surprised to hear that he had agreed to join the band for the tour, but I was very happy about it. Doing the Clonemeister tutoring with him was quite an undertaking though, especially in such a short period of time. He was trained in the Indian style of music notation but did not read western notation at all. I had to teach him all the parts, note by note, while he made his own notations on paper. This was very time consuming, and I could see that he was getting overwhelmed by it. As it turned out, he did not do the tour after all, but it was a pleasure to work one on one with a musician of his caliber.

One evening, Frank invited Vinnie, Warren, and me out to dinner. We took a cab from our cut-rate hotel in St. John's Wood to his swanky one by Hyde Park. Gail was in town by then, and we were all going to go out to dinner together. As we waited in the living room of his suite, a visitor came to the door for a quick hello. It was none other than a hugely successful brocade coat wearing British folk/pop star who I shall not name, along with his wife and two beautiful daughters who looked like they were about 7 to 9 years old. Frank was still getting ready in another room, so Gail greeted them and then left to get ready herself. The visitors sat down on the couch, where the folk/pop star proceeded to pull some hash and a pipe and out of his pocket and load it up! He lit it, took a hit, handed it to his wife, who had a toke, then she handed it to the little girls, each of whom had a smoke! Not cool. Warren, Vinnie, and I looked at each other in horror not knowing what to do. We knew about Frank's staunch anti-drug views, so it was clear that this was not going to end well. Naturally, we all declined the pipe when it was passed our way. It was pretty obvious that smoking hash in Frank's hotel room was not a good idea.

We didn't have long to ponder the situation, however, because in a few minutes Gail returned while the smoking was still in progress. She freaked, and ran to Frank's room to tell him what was going on. He appeared in a matter of seconds and started shouting, "No drugs! Get out, get out!" as he pushed them out the door into the hallway, without so much as a hello! It was one of those times when I wanted to pinch myself and ask, "Did that just happen?" Then we went to the restaurant where Frank treated us to a wonderfully lovely dinner.

Speaking of Warren, it was around this time that he did a little clothes shopping in the London fashion district. He came back with earrings, furry boots, and other somewhat flamboyant attire. This lead to Frank inventing the perfect nickname for him, "Sophia War-rén." I still chuckle when I think about it.

I spent a fair amount of time in the studio with Frank where they were recording Shankar's album. One day I saw a man leaving the studio just as I was arriving. I thought he looked familiar, but couldn't place him. It turned out to be the great Van Morrison, who had just recorded a version of "Dead Girls of London." Frank was impressed with him, saying that he came in, took off his hat, sang the shit out of the song, put his hat back on, and left. Unfortunately, his version didn't make it to the album because of record company legal issues or some such thing.

As I said, Frank was bored in London. He said he found producing very tedious, because all the producer did was listen for mistakes and fix them. I didn't know any better at the time, but I was to learn later that there was *a lot* more that a producer did than just find mistakes. A good producer usually picks out the songs, works out the arrangements, oversees the engineer and the sound quality, coaches the players and singers, oversees the mix and more. Looking back on it now, it is hard to imagine that Frank really thought that way, but it could be based on his own experience. I recall Frank saying that the producer for the early Mothers' records, Tom Wilson (who had produced some of the early Bob Dylan recordings, including "Like a Rolling Stone") was the guy sent to the studio by the record company to watch the clock and make sure the recording session didn't run up too much of a studio bill going overtime, and that was about it. I don't know if that's how Tom Wilson produced his other artists, but that's how Frank described what he did in his case.

The rest of the Zappa band members arrived in London on January 28th, and rehearsals began at the Rainbow Theater on the 29th. This was the very same place where Frank had been seriously injured in December of 1971, when an audience member pushed him off the stage and he fell ten feet into the orchestra pit. Frank rented the theater for us to use as a rehearsal space. Since a lot of his time was still being spent in the studio with Shankar, Frank's attendance at the rehearsals was minimal. That meant I was the one in charge of running them most of the time. This of course gave the Mean Girls more opportunities to harass me, and it got pretty ugly. I don't want to dwell on it, but I can remember times when I would spend the breaks in the toilet stall with tears of hurt and frustration filling my eyes. My life long dream had turned into this? What was with these guys, anyway? I gradually came to understand who they really were, and of what kind of character. For an example of what kind of person the Main Mean Girl was, one night in France he and Mars got jumped by some local skinheads. Mean Girl spotted a cab, hailed it, jumped in and took off, leaving poor Tommy to have the crap beaten out of him. But I survived the harassment, and got the band whipped into shape in spite of the friction.

My time not spent in actual band rehearsal was spent doing other Clonemeister work, like continuing to tutor Shankar and transcribing songs Frank wanted to add to the set. I remember one time I was struggling with the dense vocal harmonies in "Florentine Pogen" when Ike Willis stopped by my room. I was amazed when he easily found each of the parts and could sing them back to me for transcription. Ike has a huge musical talent, and it was really obvious to me that day. Thanks, Ike.

The last rehearsal was on February 8th, and the first gig was in Birmingham, England, on the 10th. We went on to play in Manchester, Newcastle, and Brighton. Frank didn't really seem to like England much. I guess he had his reasons, like nearly being killed at the Rainbow in 1971. But a lot of it was the British pop music press who are very fickle and self-important. In 1979, they were peddling punk rock, so anything that began in the 60's was old news and not of interest to them. I think that's how most of them viewed Zappa and thus they were dismissive of him. The day after one of those shows, Frank showed me a "review" of our previous night's performance in a newspaper. It listed the band line-up from the year before, with Terry and Pat! The writer had obviously not even attended the show and just made stuff up. Talk about *dismissive* - I couldn't believe it.

In London we played at the Hammersmith Odeon on February 17th, 18th, and 19th. As Frank had expressed in song, the food in England could be pretty awful. So bad, in fact, that some of the band members got food poisoning from the rancid swill we were fed backstage at the Hammersmith. I was so sick by the last of the three days that I skipped the sound check. When I got there and told Frank I would do my best to make it through the show, he said, "Well, I've got bad news for you. We're recording tonight and I want to play everything we know, which means it will go on for three hours or so. You'd better get yourself a stool and a bucket." That is exactly what I did. I was too weak to stand, and I was still vomiting. I literally puked into the bucket on stage during the show, but I made it through. This show was memorialized by Frank in "Diseases of the Band." He ended up releasing quite a bit of material from those shows. I am especially proud of our version from that disease-ridden night of "Don't Eat The Yellow Snow," replete with me somehow pulling off the high speed, blazing bass line in the "Rollo" section of "Saint Alfonso's Pancake Breakfast." Frank included that and "Diseases of the Band" on the *You Can't Do That On Stage Anymore Vol. 1* album. For Frank, poisoning his band was one more reason to dislike the U.K.

After England, we were off to the continent. The first stop was Brussels where another backstage food incident occurred. I was sitting next to Frank when we were served beautiful looking big steaks. I eagerly began to devour mine, but when Frank took his first bite, he spit it out, shoved the plate away and said, "That's horse meat!" I don't know if he was right or not, but it tasted good to me, and I was hungry, so I finished mine off. I think it was beef, myself. Maybe Frank was a bit jumpy after his band had just been poisoned in London.

Somewhere in the south of France, I think it was Montpelier, we had a little excitement one night at a gig. It was a relatively small venue which was sold out, leaving a throng of disappointed would-be attendees unable to get into the show. We had barely started the concert when things got out of hand. Someone ran to the stage and said something to Frank who immediately stopped the show and got us off the stage. He herded the band into a dressing room and said, "Don't anyone leave this room. I'm gonna go find out what's going on." He came back in a few minutes and explained that somebody had ripped a signpost out of the ground, concrete base and all, and threw it through a big plate glass window in the lobby area. The people who could not get tickets were pouring in across the broken glass and into the hall. Frank said, "We have to go back out there and finish the show. If we don't, there will probably be a riot." I think we were all a bit shaken, but we went back and finished the show without any more trouble. It felt like it was right on the edge though, and scary, because being a smaller place, the crowd was pressed up against the edge of the stage. Once again, I was extremely impressed with Zappa's masterful handling of a bad situation.

A similar incident occurred in Madrid. Things were already a little tense because Spain had only recently gotten rid of the fascist dictator Franco. We were one of the first rock bands to play there as the country began its transition to democracy. I recall that Frank even had to submit the lyrics of the songs in the show to the Spanish government for their approval before allowing us to perform.

We were playing some kind of big outdoor sports venue that was used for bullfights. Shortly after the show began, some doors at the opposite end of the place came crashing open and a horde of people poured in. The flood of humanity came rushing down the center aisle towards us, filling every available space. We were a safe distance from them, though, and this time we just kept on playing. It often seemed as if being on the road was a bit like going off to war, with each gig being a battle. It was the few of us on the stage with our instruments versus thousands of people in the audience. We had to play all the right notes at the right times to make them happy so they wouldn't turn on us and lay waste to us and our equipment, which they could easily have done.

Madrid was also the scene of some colorful air travel memories. When you fly almost every day you have the privilege of experiencing the occasional anomalies. Our landing in Madrid was the bumpiest I have ever been on – it seemed like the plane bounced 5 to 10 feet in the air 3 or 4 times before finally staying down on the runway. The airport did not have modern jetways, so we deplaned the old fashioned way via a stairway onto the tarmac. I was walking with Frank over to the terminal and I commented, "I sure didn't like that landing!" He replied, "You're here, aren't you? You liked it." He was great with the quick comebacks. When I mentioned that the big new army-surplus down jacket I got for the trip was supposed to be "good to 40 below," he said, "Good for what? Preserving the corpse?"

Getting out of Madrid turned out to be not so easy. For some reason our scheduled flight had been cancelled, and there was a mad scramble to book a private jet to get us to France. This meant we had a lot of time to kill at the airport. Some of the band members were approached by sexy young girls who were trying to find converts to some weird cult called The Family of Love, an offshoot of The Children of God, with Father David as their leader. They were doing something called "flirty fishing," which meant that they would offer sex in exchange for joining the cult. They even had porno comic books with images of Jesus Copulating and having Oral Sex! I think a couple of the guys almost went for it. We later saw the girls get into a fancy private jet with their cult name painted on the side. It seemed Father David was making a nice living while having a grand time. Praise Jesus.

This was all very entertaining to watch while hanging out at the bar with a couple of Spanish pilots who were knocking back quite a few drinks. We finally got word that we had a plane to use and hurried to board it. What a surprise when we climbed in and were greeted by our pilot drinking pals from the bar at the controls of the little jet! Oh, great! On top of that, our luggage would not all fit in the luggage compartment, so after we were in our seats, they filled up the aisles with the rest of the suitcases. When it came time to take off, it felt like that little jet was so overloaded it just barely got in the air, but it got us where we needed to go.

We went on to play more shows in France, Germany, and Austria, all on a full throttle tight schedule, doing 3 to 5 shows in a row on a regular basis. A lot of it is a blur to me, but a conversation after a show in Munich near the end of the tour stands out in my mind. Several of the band members were hanging around with Frank talking about our garage band experiences as kids. It was a lot of fun comparing stories and laughing about the funky gear we used to use. I mentioned that I had a secondhand Stratocaster, and that we played next to the old green Dodge in the family garage. We all had some good laughs, and normally, that would have been the end of it. But Zappa, of course, was nowhere near normal. This conversation gave him the idea to write the song "Joe's Garage" which then gave rise to the entire three act album *Joe's Garage*. This was a great insight for me into another aspect of the man's genius. It didn't occur to any of the rest of us to write a song about garage bands, but to Frank it was yet another creative opportunity. Pretty amazing, I think.

The last gig of the tour was Zurich. It was the end of four cities in a row, and after the show, it was time to celebrate a successful tour. Unfortunately, we had an early flight out the next morning, so I ended up staying up almost all night. Frank was not going to be on the same flight that we were on, as he usually was. Looking rather bleary, we got to the airport and onto the plane, one of those jets with three engines in the rear of the plane – one on either side of the body and one mounted in the rudder. We taxied into position for takeoff and the pilot hit the gas, but after a few seconds, throttled down and put on the brakes. We taxied off the runway onto a side taxiway and sat there for a few minutes, wondering what the heck was going on.

Soon the pilot came on the intercom and explained that the third engine, the one in the rudder, did not seem to be working. He said it wasn't a problem, though, because it was only used for a boost during take off. He assured us that we could get into the air safely without that third engine, and that was what we were going to do. He did *not* say that if anyone did not agree with this plan they could deplane and take another flight, so there was no choice but to hope he was right. It was a bit eerie to know that Frank was not on the plane. I feared that after all that work and being away we would die on the trip home! The pilot, of course, was right, but it seemed like we were going down that runway for an eternity, *very* gradually gaining speed before we were airborne. But we made it.

Chapter Eight

I got home on April 2nd, had a bit of rest, and by the 21st, we were at Village Recorders for the first studio recording sessions with the current band line-up. There we recorded one of Frank's most loved albums, *Joe's Garage*. This was very exciting for me, because it was the first time I would be recording master tracks for an album as a musician. That was way cool enough on its own, but it was even better because it happened to be an album by my hero and mentor, Frank Zappa.

We recorded the basic tracks of bass, drums, keys, guitar, and temporary guide or "scratch" vocals for about 10 days, often working for 10 or 11 hours a day. After most of the basic tracks were done, Frank did the overdub recordings of vocals and more instruments. I was not around for most of that, although Frank did bring me back in the studio for a couple of things. One overdub I did that got overlooked somehow in the album credits was playing electric guitar on the title song, "Joe's Garage." I played the cheesy surf guitar parts on my secondhand Stratocaster with a whammy bar. On the main two note guitar motif, Warren and I both played the same part at the same time through two amps picked up by one mic.

Most of my contribution to the album, of course, was playing bass. *"Joe's"* turned out to be a very popular album among musicians, largely because of the unusual rhythmical adventures. I am often asked about the odd meters and time changes, some of which can be quite puzzling to listen to until you grasp what is going on. I probably get the most questions about "Keep it Greasy." Up until the time we got into the studio, we had always played that song in a normal 4/4 time signature, but Frank decided he wanted to do a new version for the recording. The choruses were to stay in 4/4, but the verses were to be changed to odd times: 19/16 and 21/16. Frank was doing the guide vocal as we recorded it. As we played the odd time tracks for the verses, he sang more or less in 4/4 over what we were doing in 19 or 21. We were to play the vamp until he reached the end of a verse, then transition back to 4/4 on the choruses. We never knew how many times we would play the vamp before going into the transition. I can't remember if we did many takes of it, but the one that is on the album was the one that just happened to come out the way it did. We never stopped to count how many bars of what we were going to play, we just did it by the seats of our pants on the fly.

I know a lot of people are afraid of math, but for the hardcore rhythmic encyclopedia fans, here's the basic breakdown of the rhythm track with CD times given:

00:36 - 19/16: count 16th's as 4+4+4+4+3, or 4/4 + 3/16. Last bar has an extra quarter note added making it 23/16 (4+4+4+4+3+4), then a bar of 7/4 at "chances are..."

00:59 - 21/16: 3+2+2+2+3+2+3+2+2

02:26 - 19/16 again

03:18 - 19/16 again

Hope your head does not explode – use with caution.

One of my favorites from that album is "Packard Goose," with its masterful lyrics about Frank's music business troubles. Having seen first hand what he meant about the sleaze of the music critics and their selling the disease of punk rock, I really understood what he was saying, and felt it personally. It really bothered me to see such talentless impostors get so much attention and praise while a genius like Frank couldn't even get a label to sign him by the time I was in the band. He paid for the sessions out of his own pocket.

It might come as a surprise, but all of the odd time rhythms going on in "Goose" in the vocal sections of the song are based almost entirely on the lyrics. We worked off the lyric sheet, following the words on the page only; there were no music charts. We didn't stop to figure out what we were doing, as we were mostly just playing the rhythms of the words with the type of musical feel or groove that Frank wanted.

The length of the drum solo part in the middle of the song was not defined, and I had no idea as to what direction Vinnie might choose to go. My job was to play the tight, choppy, repeating bass riff without getting off the beat. Warren was standing next to me, doubling the bass line on the guitar. At one point, Vinnie does some incredible "across the bar" stuff that I did not see coming. It was very difficult to keep my concentration focused on the beat when it got as far afield as it did. Somehow, by stomping my foot really hard, praying, and squeezing every brain cell as tightly as I could, I managed to do it, but man, that was a hairy one. Years later I talked to Warren about it, and asked him what he was thinking in that section and how he managed to stay on the beat. He replied, "I was watching you!"

"Catholic Girls" was a brand new song that we had not yet performed live. Frank wanted an odd time version of the verse chord changes to serve as an instrumental middle section. He asked Vinnie and me to invent some kind of an arrangement for it, which we did. Frank liked what we came up with and that is what is on the album. After we got a take that Frank was happy with, Vinnie took me aside and whispered, "Artie, I missed the first back beat coming out of the middle section. Do you think I should tell Frank?" Frank had not noticed this little missing beat, nor had anyone else. I thought about it for a second, and I said, "Nah, let it go. He seems happy with it." And so it stands forever. It was one of very few mistakes I ever heard Vinnie make, and I have heard him play a lot of drum notes, believe me.

Frank decided that he wanted some of the songs segued together the way we did when we played live, and so that was how we recorded the songs on side two of Act I. Although the listener might understandably assume that the segues were edits, that was not the case. We played the basic tracks to "Fembot in a Wet T-Shirt," "Toad-O Line," and "Why Does it Hurt When I Pee?" straight from start to finish without stopping, about twelve minutes worth. The latin part that begins in the middle of "Wet T-Shirt" was to be of indeterminate length: we were instructed to play the vamp until Frank gave a cue to go into the next section. There was no guitar solo yet – that would be added later. I wasn't exactly sure what I would play, just something latin. I found a nice but active part similar to a Jaco line I liked and locked into a groove. I thought Frank would have us play it for about 32 or 64 bars, but he let it go much longer, so long that my hands began to get very tired. I was glad when he finally gave the cue for us to transition into the next section, the repeating "Saddlebags" lick in 18/16, but that was also very taxing. I was greatly relieved when he finally gave the cue to go into "Why Does it Hurt When I Pee?"

When we started recording, there was no concept yet of the storyline that runs through the album; it seemed at first that Frank just wanted to get some of his new songs on tape. Except for the few times I was called back to the studio for overdubs, I was not present for the rest of the recording after the basic tracks were done. I talked to Frank shortly before the album was released, and he told me I was going to be in for a big surprise. When I heard Act I for the first time, I found that he was right. I had no idea that he had turned it into a "rock opera," if you will pardon the term. Once again, Zappa blew my mind. What a great honor to have *this* be the very first real album I ever played on.

After I was done with my parts in the recording studio, I had some free time while still on salary, an agreeable situation for a musician. I had received decent additional pay for the *Joe's Garage* sessions at union scale, and I was doing a few gigs with some of the bands I had worked with before I was hired by Frank. I was in the best shape financially I had ever been in, and my wife and I decided we wanted to move out of our tiny Echo Park apartment and rent a house. We looked around until we found a guest house for rent in Hollywood. We decided to take it even though it was a much higher rent than we had been paying before. Unfortunately, it was too close to the Hollywood freeway, and we had failed realize how bad and relentless the noise would be.

To make matters worse, after we had committed to renting the place, I got a call to go to a band meeting at the Zappa management office on June 26th, 1979, a year and ten days after I was hired. Frank told us he was dissolving the band and that we now qualified for unemployment which we should begin to collect ASAP. The band was fired. Uh-oh.

The timing could not have been worse. We moved into the more expensive new place a week after I lost my job. We had thought we could block out the freeway noise by putting some thick foam rubber in the windows, but it hardly made a dent because the whole building shook from the vibrations. I had a few gigs here and there, but it wasn't enough to pay the rent and the bills. Things were bad enough that I took part-time work at the Serge Modular

Synthesizer company which happened to be close to our new residence.

We had to get out of that place. It was messy because we had signed a lease, but we did it, then stayed with friends for a short time until we found an apartment in Santa Monica.

Things began to pick up a bit in late August. Robby Krieger called to find out if I would be interested in putting together a band with him and a British singer and bass player named Andrew McKensie, or Mack, that he had been working with. Of course I said yes, although I was a bit dubious at first since it was clear when I met him that Mack was very much punk or new wave oriented. But when I heard the songs they had been writing together, I was pleasantly surprised. It would be a new challenge, because I'd be playing keyboards and some keyboard bass, not bass guitar. They were also looking for a drummer, so I gave Vinnie a call who was willing to give it a go, too. We called the band Red Shift.

We rehearsed in a house in the Hollywood hills that Robby and the other Doors rented to have a space to use for music. For each rehearsal I lugged my Rhodes, my Clavinet, all my synth gear and an amp. We worked up a set and played some of the popular clubs at that time: Blackie's, Madame Wong's, Club 88, and so on. In early November, Vinnie got too busy to stay in the band, so we had to find a replacement. We did a few more gigs with the new drummer, as well as some recording. Though we had high hopes, the band never really got off the ground. I did, however, become good friends with Mack. A couple of years later, he was a big help to me with some recordings we made together that helped lead me into another important phase of my musical life. More on that later.

In mid-September, I got a call from Denny Walley who wanted to know if I would be interested in joining a band he was forming to play his original songs, with Vinnie on drums. This call was gratifying for me. It was the first time that a fellow Zappa band member had asked me to do something musical together outside of Frank's band. Of course I said yes, and we soon recorded some music and did a few gigs. I am very grateful to Denny for asking me to participate.

Along with the Johnny Baltimore Band and my friend Phil's new wave band Hit and Run, I was in four different original bands there for a while. That kept me pretty busy, but there was not much income involved.

Once again, however, things were about to change.

Chapter Nine

In mid-January of 1980 I got a call from Frank's wife, Gail. She told me that Frank was putting a band together and he wanted me to come down for an audition. I thought this was ludicrous. I said, "Frank has heard me play and knows what I can do, so I don't think I need to audition. Tell him if he wants to hire me, I will do it, but I am not interested in auditioning." He hired me.

Things were different as far as the pay on this tour, however. Instead of being on a year round retainer of $500 a week, we would be paid $500 a week for rehearsals (I got extra as Clonemeister) and then $1,000 a week on the road. This time, when we were not working, there was no pay.

Rehearsals began at Frank's warehouse in the San Fernando Valley on January 28th, 1980. It was a smaller six piece band. The front row was Ike, Frank, and now Ray White on vocals and guitar. The back row was Mars, Vinnie, and me on a big riser. I doubled on bass and keyboards, and covered the Clonemeister duties again.

During the time I was in the band, this proved to be Frank's most creative and productive period. With a smaller group, it took less time to invent and convey new ideas to the players. Everyone in the band was extremely quick at learning new musical parts almost as fast as Frank could come up with them. With Mars, Vinnie, and me in the back handling the heavy artillery, and Ike and Ray flanking Frank in the front to complete the vocal sandwich and guitar parts, we could do whatever Frank threw at us. I remember one time Frank was looking for a particular kind of piano part for Mars to play in a new arrangement of a song called "Broken Hearts Are For Assholes." He asked Mars to come up with something that sounded like "Devo cocktail piano." Tommy thought about it for a couple of seconds, and came up with the perfect part with just the right aroma. (Let me know when there is a computer that can do that.) With Ike and Ray singing harmonies above Frank, all Frank would have to do is turn to them and ask them to sing harmonies to his melody, and bingo, there they were. They usually did not even have to figure out who would sing what notes, they just found them instinctively. Quite impressive. I can tell you without a doubt that

Frank was thoroughly enjoying himself, and so was the band. He wrote most of the *You Are What You Is* album during that time. I loved every minute of it. Being part of his creative process was more amazing than it had ever been.

Around this time a new band called The Knack had a huge hit with a song called "My Sharona." The drummer in that band, Bruce Gary, happened to be a former drummer for my band Loose Connection, so I had been aware of them for a while and was amazed by their success. I told Frank about knowing the drummer for The Knack, figuring he might be amused, and suggested we do a "Sharona" take off somewhere. I was surprised when he liked the idea and soon was inserting the famous "Sharona" guitar riff hook all over the place. For some reason, I found this particularly entertaining.

A composition Frank spent a lot of time working on in these rehearsals was based on the "Thirteen" vamp that we had jammed on with Shankar in New York. Frank made up a whole new piece around it, incorporating some other melodic fragments he had been fiddling with on guitar for a while. It was shaping up to be something very cool. It involved some more of those complex rhythms that we played but never stopped to figure out what the math was, including "metric modulations." (A metric modulation is more complicated than a simple time signature change. It has to do with a note value on one side of a bar line equaling a different note value on the other side. Composer Elliot Carter used them extensively.) It was up to me to put it all down on paper at some point, which meant a lot of head scratching on my part. It's a good thing I did, because this nifty tune might have been lost forever. Part of it was used in "Tink Walks Amok" on *The Man From Utopia* album, but it's missing a lot of the cool parts that we had done in rehearsal. Shortly after Frank died, I resurrected the original version of it for a Zappa tribute performance with The Band From Utopia. A few years ago I did an arrangement of it with Tommy Mars, and have played it several times since then, including performances at the University of North Texas and the University of South Dakota.

Another song that could have been lost was one called "Solitude." It was written shortly after Frank found out that his wife had some serious health issues. I gave Frank a ride home from rehearsal one night and he told me that he was really pretty worried about her. Soon after that, he came in with the lyrics to "Solitude." He went to the Wurlitzer electric piano he had set up for rehearsal and played the basic chords and melody for us to learn. We went over it a few times, but it was never played live, and seems unfinished to me. Nonetheless, it is beautiful and sentimental, which is almost unheard of in the songs of Frank Zappa. It's clear to me that it was written for and about Gail Zappa. After Frank passed, I made a recording of it with the Band From Utopia guys as a gift for her. I hoped it would serve as an olive branch after our falling out over *Beat the Boots,* which I will discuss later. I don't recall if she had ever heard it before then, but she seemed to appreciate the gesture. I hope it made her feel good to know that Frank had written a song for her.

I recently got an email from Joe Travers, who works for the Zappa Family Trust. He was doing some research on "Solitude" and wanted to know if I had the definitive lyric sheet. He seemed to want it for posterity. I dug around and was able to find it and make a copy of it for him. He was very happy to get it. Shortly after that I learned of Gail's death. I'm glad I took the time to make that recording for her. Rest in peace, Gail.

Joe told me something interesting that I had not known before. According to him, Ruth Underwood said that the music to "Solitude" had been floating around since the time she was in the band in the early 1970's. I guess it should come as no surprise. That seemed to be the case for a number of songs we played while I was in the band that had not yet been released. "Stick it Out," "Easy Meat," and "Keep it Greasy" had all come from previous eras, though they were new to me.

Current events played a part in some of the new songs, too. At that time there was speculation that the government might reinstate the military draft. This inspired Frank to write "I Don't Wanna Get Drafted." He wrote it quickly, and came up with a spiffy arrangement with me playing keyboards instead of bass. He liked it so much that he decided we should go into a studio and record it right away. He thought with the timeliness of the subject matter he could have a hit single on his hands. So off we went on February 16th to Ocean Way studios in Hollywood to record the single version of the new song. Frank got it released almost immediately, but disappointingly, no hit single.

Just after the recording session, about five weeks before the tour was scheduled to begin, I got word that Vinnie had decided to quit the band. He had been asked to record an album with some other group. It was his dream to do session work, and apparently he thought doing the record was more important to his career than doing another Zappa tour. I can't really blame him since it was the dream of most musicians to be able to stay in town and do studio work. But for the rest of us, this was terrible news. This band line-up was sounding so great! How could we ever find anyone who could do anything near what Vinnie could do? We had all these new songs, but nothing much was written down. There weren't many drum charts anyway, and nothing at all for the new songs. This was really going to throw a wrench in the works, and bring the beautiful creative momentum we had to a standstill. When we did find a new drummer it was going to be my task as Clonemeister to get him up to speed.

The call went out to the L.A. musician world, and immediately there were 30 or 40 top players who wanted to try out for the gig. Frank figured a good way to audition drummers was to start by seeing if they could handle the basic "Thirteen" rhythm, which, as I mentioned before, consists of a bar of 5/8 and a bar of 4/4 glued together. It was a good way of separating the boys from the men. Most of the drummers couldn't do it, so it proved to be a good tactic for speeding things up. But still, the auditions went on for days. Frank finally settled on David Logeman, who was quite good, but no drummer we heard could really fill Vinnie's shoes. I recall giving Frank a ride home during that time and he said about David, "He really stomps the piss out of the vamp on 'Society Pages.'" The next day Logeman was hired. At first I was a bit puzzled by Frank's choice, because I thought we had heard some players that were a little better, but I also understood what he liked about David. He was more of a rocker than some of the other drummers. I set about bringing him up to date on the ton of music he needed to learn, and to his credit, he busted his ass and got it all down. I think he is an excellent drummer and did a damn good job on the tour.

Of course, the drummer issue slowed down Frank's creative process, but it didn't stop it. Remember Chris Geppert from San Antonio that I've mentioned a few times? I heard from my old friend

Phil (the drummer in Chris' high school band, Flash) that Chris had signed a record deal with Warner Brothers. One day on my way to rehearsal I was thinking about how great my life was playing with Zappa, and that I guessed I was just about the coolest, most successful musician to have emerged from my high school, triumphant after they had walked out on me in that auditorium, when a familiar sounding voice came on the radio. It was Geppert, now calling himself Christopher Cross, singing his soon to be hit single, "Ride Like the Wind." I couldn't believe it. My feelings of coolness and high school revenge took a severe nosedive.

When I got to rehearsal, I told Frank about the song, and I think that because Chris was signed to Warner Brothers, Frank's current archenemy, he took notice. I went to an electric piano and played and sang what I could remember of "Ride Like the Wind" after that one partial hearing of it in my car. Frank said "Get me a pencil and a piece of paper. I can write a song like that in 5 minutes." Sure enough, he proceeded to whip out the "Teenage Wind" lyrics in just about 5 minutes. I thought it was hilarious, and it raised my spirits back up considerably. When I got home that night, I called Phil and told him all about it. Phil then called Chris and told him that Zappa had written a song mocking "Ride Like the Wind." Phil quoted Chris to me as saying, "Oh, I hope he doesn't release it while I'm peaking!" When I told Frank that the next day, Frank said in a silly voice meant to be Chris, "Ooooo, I've been in the business 15 minutes and I'm peaking!" I almost died laughing. Chris would eventually get his revenge on me, but that story comes later.

On March 24th, 1980, we hit the road, first going north to Seattle and Vancouver and then working our way south for about two weeks back to southern California. When we got to San Bernardino, Frank had a lovely surprise for me. He was so impressed with the Yamaha CS-80 polyphonic synthesizer he had bought for Tommy to play that he bought a second one for me to use. I was playing keyboards on about 25% of the show by then, but had a very humble set up. I was stoked – it was the coolest keyboard around at the time. I used it on the show that very night, and when we got to the middle section of "Easy Meat," Frank, as usual, turned to face the band to conduct us in the mock-classical instrumental part. I was banging away on the brand new instrument with Frank looking right at me, when a can of soda I had foolishly put on a stand above the new keyboard slipped and spilled right into the face of the CS-80! I got the dagger eyed look from Hell, to be sure! Luckily, the great crew guys were able to clean it up, and no damage was done. Not a great way to start off with my new toy, however.

After playing the Sports Arena in L.A., we headed east. We had a day off between Kansas City and New Orleans, so I used the time for a side trip to San Antonio to see my father who was very ill with lung cancer by then. It was a brief visit, but I am glad I was able to squeeze that trip into the tight touring schedule. He told me that he felt at peace with his maker and was ready to go. I was pretty sure I would never see him again. I was right.

The first half of the tour continued around the states, ending up in Baltimore on May 11th, then we came home for a week before leaving for Europe. We played Brussels and Rotterdam, then headed to Berlin for a day off and then did a show there. That is when I got word that my father had finally succumbed to his illness and died. Of course I would have gone to the funeral under normal circumstances, but being in Europe in the middle of a tour, I knew that I would really screw things up for Frank if I left for a few days to go back to Texas. Out of loyalty to Frank and the band, I decided not to go to the funeral. It was not an easy decision to make, to say the least. Before the Berlin show, I went to Frank's dressing room and told him, "If I seem a bit sad or gloomy today, it's because I just found out that my father died. But don't worry, I am not going to leave the tour to go to his funeral." He rewarded my loyalty by saying, "Well, I hope you don't use that as an excuse to mess up the show." I was stunned by his icy response. He added that he was on the road when his father died and didn't go to his father's funeral, either. Was that supposed to make me feel better? Zappa was not Mr. Warmth, that's for sure.

We went on to play the Scandinavian countries and eight gigs in Germany before arriving in France, but were soon heading back to Germany. We had a day off in Cologne before our June 7th gig at the Sporthalle there. Bob Marley happened to be playing at the same place on the 6th, our night off. I wanted to go to the show and went to the hall, but before I bought a ticket, I had an idea about how to get in for free. I went around to the back door, showed my Zappa backstage pass to the guard at the door, and he let me right in. I don't know if he was being nice or just didn't notice that the pass said

Zappa, not Marley, or he just didn't care. Anyway, I was in. I found myself in a dressing room that was filled with women cooking up some great smelling food, and a lot of ganja smoke. I smiled and said, "Excuse me," and found my way into the hall. As usual, I located the sound mixing desk and found a place to sit right behind the console. I figure the best sound in the house is probably going to be where the mixer is. The guy behind the console was a crack-up, dancing around as he did his cool Reggae dub effects with the delays. Marley put on a stellar performance, and I am glad I got to hear him live at least once.

The next night was our gig at the same place with Santana for our opening act. (This was a rarity. Zappa almost never had an opening act.) Carlos seemed like a nice fellow. I recall playing darts with him before the shows. I listened to their very enjoyable performance for a while before going into Frank's dressing room. He was warming up on guitar as he almost always did before a show. I mentioned hearing Carlos play and how good his trademark fluid soloing still sounded. When the thought crossed my mind I laughed and said, "Hey, maybe we should do a Santana take off." Then something shocking happened: he thought I had a good idea again!

I suggested the G minor to C vamp from "Evil Ways" and told him how Bob McCready, an old college friend of mine, used to jokingly refer to it as the *Carlos Santana Secret Chord Progression*. Frank liked the vamp from "Evil Ways" idea too, and said we could do it in "Tiny Lights." I thought this was a good call because it would replace a ponderous half time dirge with something more lively, and it also happened to be at the right tempo and even in the same key. We did it that night, and from then on, that was what we used for the solo section of "Tiny Lights." To my surprise and delight, Frank released a version of it on the first *Shut Up and Play your Guitar* album with the title "Variations On The Carlos Santana Secret Chord Progression." That particular solo was from a show in Dallas on the fall 1980 tour, which is an interesting coincidence. Bob McCready is from Dallas, which is only about 35 miles from Denton where the phrase Frank used was invented.

We were in for a treat when we got to Paris, because Frank had invited his new friend, conductor and composer Pierre Boulez, to come down to one of our shows. It was quite a thrill for me to meet him. Some months earlier, Frank had written to him to see if he would be interested in conducting some Zappa music. During a rehearsal before the tour, Frank excitedly came over to me to show me his reply letter from Boulez. I rarely saw Frank as happy and proud as he looked when he got that letter. In it, Boulez expressed an interest in recording some of Frank's music with his chamber group. This eventually led to *The Perfect Stranger* album.

Boulez even told a little joke backstage before the show. Here it is: There was a violinist stranded in the jungle who had soothed and tamed vicious tigers and gorillas with the sound of his music. They were all calmly sitting around listening to the music when a big lion comes over and attacks and kills the poor musician. The other beasts all cried out, "What did you do that for?" The lion held his paw up to his ear and said, "Eh?"

In the middle of the show, Frank mentioned that there was a special guest in the audience. He then stopped the concert just so that Tommy could give Boulez demonstrations of the various keyboards. Frank didn't seem to care what the audience thought. It was as if we were at a rehearsal or something, but no one seemed to mind. After the show Mr. Boulez was generous enough to invite us to see the electronic music facilities at the Centre Pompidou. Unfortunately, when we got there the next day, there was some kind of strike going on and the power was off, so we didn't see much. An electronic music center is not much use without electricity.

France brought about more inspiration to Frank, this time providing a morale boost to the band as well. After Paris, the tour had gotten pretty bleak. It rained a lot and we were playing outdoor shows in tents, often set up on grounds that were all mud. Because of the drummer change, we had a limited amount of material, so we were doing pretty much the same show every night. There was a synthy pop song that was getting a lot of attention at the time called "In Cars" by Gary Numan. Frank came up with a parody of it called "In France," which was a hilarious dig at the French. There is a little instrumental middle section of "In Cars" with a robotic sounding synth melody. I was playing second keyboard on "In France," and when we got to that section, I would play the robotic melody while Mars would simultaneously play the French national anthem, Charles Ives style. It was all good fun and definitely revived the morale of the band. Worried about copyright infringement, Frank re-arranged the song for recorded release without any trace of the Gary

Numan song, producing an inferior version, in my opinion. It turns out that he could have kept the original parody version. Soon after that time, the Supreme Court ruled that parodies were legal, as long as the original writer got a fair share of the royalties.

France also had the coolest outdoor venue I have ever seen or performed in. We played an amphitheater called Theatre Antique in Orange that had been built in the *first* century. This place had the best outdoor acoustics I have ever heard. It was designed so that anyone in any seat would be able to hear sound coming from the stage without amplification, and I have no doubt it would have done that. It worked great for our amplified music, too. This amphitheater seemed to have an almost magical quality to it. Even Frank seemed to feel it. Whereas he usually remained unseen by the audience before the shows, that night he stood at the edge of the stage in his purple spandex pants and greeted the fans as they filed past on their way to their seats. There was something about being in that place that made us all happy and a bit giddy.

Frank did not use recreational drugs, but he did enjoy a glass of good wine now and then. One night in France, someone gave Frank a bottle of Chateau Latour from the 1920's that must have been worth thousands of dollars. He opened it and wanted to share it with the band. All he could find were some Styrofoam cups, so that's what he used. It was fabulous – thick, rich and kind of chocolate tasting to me. I drank the best wine I ever tasted from a Styrofoam cup!

Though Frank was anti-drugs, he had a lot of dental problems that often resulted in bad toothaches for which he would sometimes take pain killers. I recall once or twice when the pain must have been pretty severe, because he was full of enough pain medicine to be noticeably high on stage, and considerably looser than normal. It was a side of Frank I had never seen before, but he certainly seemed to be enjoying himself.

Speaking of Frank's bad teeth, my dentist told me recently that Nicolas Slonimsky, the famed conductor, author, and lexicographer, had been a patient of hers. Slonimsky and Zappa became friends in the 80's and Frank was still having dental problems then. Slonimsky told my dentist that he begged Frank to go see her, telling him that she could fix his teeth, but he wouldn't go. Dental floss, anyone?

We went on to play in Switzerland, Austria, and more venues in France and Germany, doing our final show in Munich. That show was notable because it was recorded on an early Soundstream two-channel digital system, a brand new contraption way back in 1980. Frank released the digitally recorded version of "You Didn't Try to Call Me" from this concert on the album *You Can't Do That on Stage Anymore, Vol. 1* in 1988. Within a few years, digital recording took over the world of audio. Once again, Zappa was ahead of his time.

We got home on the Fourth of July, and after that long tour, I was ready for a break.

Chapter Ten

It turned out that there was not much of a break to be had. After barely enough time to drink a couple of beers at the beach and recover from jet lag, the phone rang. It was Frank, who was eager to get into his new home recording studio for the first time to record the new songs we had been playing. We began on July 8th, 1980. I was very impressed with what he had done. The studio was beautiful, and even had a lovely, fresh woody smell to it. I commented on how great it looked, and Frank told me it had cost a million dollars. He said, "You gotta play 'Dinah Mo Hum' a lot of times to get something like this." He was clearly very proud, and we were there to record the first album of many that would be done there, *You Are What You Is*. He called the studio the Utility Muffin Research Kitchen, or UMRK.

Frank approached recording albums differently from what was the norm in the music business at that time. Most bands or artists would go into the studio and record new songs first, then go on tour when the record was released to help promote sales of the record. A lot of bands would make little or no money on their tours, but it was worthwhile for promotion if it helped to sell a lot of records. I think that because Frank rightly believed he would get better recorded performances of his music when the band had already been playing the songs for a while and had the arrangements down cold, he did it the other way around. We usually played new songs on the road many times before going into the studio to record them. He didn't sell a lot of records by music business standards, but he did manage to make good money on the road. Things were kind of upside down for him compared to most artists, but he made it work anyway.

As we did for the *Joe's Garage* album, we sometimes recorded the basic tracks to several songs in a row without stopping, just as we had been doing in the live shows. From the notes I took at the time to keep track of my hours, it appears that we did the entire side two sequence of "Society Pages," "I'm A Beautiful Guy," "Beauty Knows No Pain," "Charlie's Enormous Mouth," "Any Downers?" and "Conehead" in real time without stopping. However, it appears that we did those same songs on three different days, July 20th, 22nd, and 26th, so it could be that Frank did some editing between the various takes. We recorded the tracks for "Fine Girl" on July 26th. I got a good laugh when we were recording "Teenage Wind." Frank came up to me and said with a broad grin, "Hey Arthur, I finally heard that Christopher Cross song 'Ride Like the Wind.' I thought it was good!" I don't know if he was serious or just teasing me, but it was a funny moment.

"Dumb All Over" was a brand new song that we had never played before. The first time I saw the lyrics was when they were just a few minutes old. We were on our way home from Europe when I got up in mid-flight to stretch my legs. I strolled over to Frank's seat to say hello, and right away he handed me a piece of paper and said proudly with a big smile, "Look what I just wrote." It was the complete lyrics to "Dumb All Over," and I was dumbfounded all over. To this day, I think that those words are absolutely brilliant and reflect my feelings about religion exactly. I feel the same way about two other songs from the album: "The Meek Shall Inherit Nothing," and "Heavenly Bank Account." By the way, Frank said he had heard some TV preacher talk about having money in his "heavenly bank account" which is what gave Frank the idea. What a fertile mind Mr. Zappa had.

There was a credit mistake on the album which has never been corrected as far as I know. It was probably just an oversight, but the cheesy Doors-like organ solo on "If Only She Woulda" is performed by me, not Tommy Mars, so don't blame him.

We worked on basic tracks on and off through August 3rd. According to my notes, I made a total of $1,756.27, which comes to about $88 per song. By the way, Zappa sidemen at that time got no share of any kind of royalties from record sales. I'm not complaining, as this was understood out front, but I think a lot of people have the mistaken impression that it was otherwise.

After I was done recording my parts for the new album, I did some gigs with various bands to keep busy and keep some money coming in. I got word in early September that rehearsals for another Zappa tour would begin in a couple of weeks, so I made a trip to Texas to see how my mother was doing after losing my father. She was a trooper, and was holding up pretty well.

When I got to the rehearsal studio on September 15th, 1980, I was surprised to see that David Logeman's drums were not set up. A completely different set was in place. That was the first time I heard that Vinnie was back in the band. There were other changes, too, with the addition of Bob Harris on vocals, keys, and trumpet, and a 19-year-old Steve Vai on guitar. This would be the Tinsel Town Rebellion band. I was the Clonemeister again, but this time, the biggest problem I had was getting the band back on their instruments to resume rehearsal after breaks.

This turned out to be a pretty good band, especially in the vocal department. Ike, Ray, and Bob are all very strong singers. Getting vocals to sound consistently good in a live rock band is no easy task. The proof is in the pudding when you listen to *Tinsel Town Rebellion*. No weak vocals on that live album, and thus no need to overdub vocals in a studio later as Frank had done in the past. On the other hand, here we were with *four* guitar players again! Vai is a nice guy and a good melody player, but I could not see the value of adding another guitar player to the band. On the recordings of that tour, about all that can be heard of his guitar playing are a few stunt whammy bar effects noises. I got along with him just fine, and he was always very respectful, so it's nothing personal. But I just think sometimes about what a truly great band it could have been with a percussionist like Ed or Ruth instead of a fourth guitar player.

At that time, Frank was going through a cool and very loosely constructed style phase that I call "neo-beatnik." A good example of this is the song "The Blue Light." He brought in copies of the words for all the band members, and started describing in general terms the sounds he wanted. He had us do a lot of what he called "meltdowns," in which we would improvise mostly atonal weirdness as he recited the words. Some parts were a bit more organized where we might play a repeating pattern an indefinite number of times until he reached a certain phrase that was a cue for a change. It was great fun to do, and we were the perfect band for it. A jolly good time was had by all. I even enjoyed playing "The Torture" once it devolved into full neo-beatnik meltdown mode. The earliest versions of "Drowning Witch" and "Truck Driver Divorce" were also done as neo-beatnik free-form meltdowns.

As I mentioned, the music biz at that time was obsessed with new wave and punk rock. All the record companies were clamoring to sign the next Clash or Sex Pistols. Bands in Hollywood were cutting their hair and changing their images as fast as they could to jump on the bandwagon, however fake they might be. Of course, being fake was what punk was really all about anyway. Malcolm McLaren formed the Sex Pistols as a way to sell punk-style clothes to fashion lovers in London. It is obvious when you hear the recordings of these bands that it was always more about the look and the shock value than about the music.

    For the record companies, it was a dream come true. They had just been through a period that featured a lot of talented artists like Steely Dan, Stevie Wonder, Joni Mitchel, and Weather Report, to name a few. These were the kinds of artists that did not come along very often, and once they became popular, they could ask for better terms in their recording contracts. The record companies would have to go along, because they knew there weren't a dozen Stevies or Jonis out there who could do what these very talented people could do. But anybody with the right look who knew three chords could be in a punk band. Since it didn't matter what the music sounded like anyway, they could sign a punk band to a typical "fuck you" contract, spend $10,000 to record a crappy sounding album, and quickly shove it out there with a shocking cover and a lot of hype. That way the record companies could quickly recoup their minimal investment and start to make money right away. That was a lot cheaper and easier than making an expensive album with a true artist. If one of those punk bands became popular and asked for a better contract, the record companies could laugh and say "We have a dozen bands more shocking than you waiting to be signed, and you're old news now. Goodbye!"

    This situation gave rise to another of my favorite Zappa songs written while I was in the band, "Tinsel Town Rebellion." Frank totally understood what was going on in the music biz and put the phoniness of the whole thing out there for all to see. I think it is a masterpiece, from the cheesy opening lick all the way through to the "I Love Lucy" ending. It is perfection in expression of words and music. Sometimes a visitor to my studio who doesn't know much about Zappa will want to hear an example of something I played on. I will usually play them "Tinsel Town" and "Pick Me I'm Clean." "Pick Me" has what I consider one of the best, if not the best, guitar, bass, and drum jams of any that I played on with Frank.

Our first show of the tour was on October 10th, 1980 in Tucson at the University of Arizona. Then it was on to Albuquerque, New Mexico on the 11th and Phoenix on the 13th. The place in Phoenix we played, the Celebrity Theater, was a hoot. Not only did they serve alcohol there, it's a theater in the round with a rotating stage. We were going around in circles as we played, as if the meltdown stuff didn't make me dizzy enough!

By October 15th, we were in Austin Texas, the closest we would ever get to my home town of San Antonio. We were off that day, and my sister Mary hosted a "Welcome to Austin" party for the band. For some reason, Frank liked Austin, and to my surprise, he accepted the invitation. I told my sister to please make sure nobody lit up a joint around Frank. He came, but seemed pretty uncomfortable, to be honest. He was most at home being the center of attention, so it was hard for him to be a normal person at a party, I guess. I think it was also a bit disconcerting for the Austin crowd that Frank had his body guard, John Smothers, at his side the whole time. John was a big, bald headed black man who looked pretty intimidating, though he was generally a nice fellow.

The next night was our show at the famed Armadillo World Headquarters, where I had seen Zappa play twice in the early 70's. It was exciting for me to be back there, but this time on stage rather than in the audience. I had friends coming up from San Antonio, and my mother even made the trip with her friend Mrs. Wyatt. They got there early in the afternoon as we were getting ready for the soundcheck. I introduced my mother to Frank who seemed to take a liking to her, and asked if she would like a taco. My mom, of course, said yes, so Frank trotted off and soon returned with the tasty little snack.

We played two shows that night, and even in October, it was very hot and muggy at the Armadillo. Perhaps the air conditioning was on the fritz or just overwhelmed, but it was brutal on stage once the lights came on. Because San Antonio is a 90 minute drive from Austin, my hometown friends chose to come to the early show, as did my sister. I was really looking forward to playing for them, and even hoped that Frank would be kind enough to give me a solo, something I rarely got. I sweated buckets of sweat all through that first set, but no solo. After the show, I said goodnight and thanks for coming to my friends and family, and then went on to sweat through the second set. I finally got a solo in the second show, when nobody I knew was still there. Oh, well.

We performed next in Dallas at the same Convention Center where I had seen Zappa play when I was studying music at North Texas. I had a couple of old friends from Denton show up for that, and it was good to see them again back stage. That was the night we performed the "Variations on the Carlos Santana Secret Chord Progression" jam just down the road from where the very idea of a *Carlos Santana Secret Chord Progression* was conceived. We also played in Houston in a place that smelled like it had recently been used for a rodeo. That was it for my triumphant return to Texas with Frank Zappa.

As the tour went on, I became more and more weary of the constant partying after every show. By that time, I was trying to cool it and get away from all that, so I began to isolate myself from the other guys. When we checked into a hotel, the first thing I would do was change my room to one as far away from the others as I could, so I could try to get some sleep.

I was also getting pretty sick of the decadence of it all. This was the tour where Frank, having heard that women voluntarily threw their panties on stage at Tom Jones concerts, decided it would be entertaining to solicit girls in the audience to take off their panties and throw them on stage. Some did, and he had the roadies collect them and save them in a big box which they toted around to each gig, eventually stringing them up like laundry on the stage. Somewhat amusing, I guess, but... Then there was the time when some crazy girl stood up during the show and flashed her bare chest at the band. Of course, she ended up back stage after the show. I walked into the food room, and there she was with her top off while Frank smeared mustard, ketchup, and mayo all over her breasts. And I can't forget the disgusting fat girl who did something gross with Vai involving a hairbrush. Steve made the mistake of telling Frank, who thought it was a worthy subject for a song he called "Stevie's Spanking." That song rates right down there at the bottom of the barrel along with songs like "Ms. Pinky," in my opinion. At one point, Frank made a tape recording of himself having sex with some girl, then had the sound mixer play that tape over the P.A. during some of Frank's solos. I'm no prude, but I was beginning to find this kind of stuff a bit repellent.

On top of all that, I wasn't all that wild about many of the songs we were doing on that particular tour. Without a mallet player, we couldn't do a lot of the early 70's material that I enjoyed so much. "Andy" was about the only one from that era we did. I was getting very tired of "The Torture," and all of those *Sheik Yerbouti* rock songs.

As much as I loved a lot of Frank's music and playing in his band, I began to think that perhaps my time in the band should come to an end. It was hard being on the road, but at least most of the time the music had still been fun and had made the rest of it worthwhile. The pleasure of playing took a nosedive when he came over to me as we were walking through an airport shortly before we were to play in New York. He said my playing was too busy during his solo in "The Torture." I couldn't believe it – I was too busy? He and Vinnie were going completely over the top during every solo on every song, and *I* was too busy? He said, "I want you to play the note 'A' in my solo. That's it, no other notes, just 'A,' got it?" Now I was pissed.

So, the next time we got to the solo section of that dreadful song at the Palladium in New York, I was a bit of a stinker, I'm afraid, and not very professional. I played "A," all right, the stiffest, most expressionless, robotic quarter notes on my open A string that I could do, at least for a while. Then I purposefully started playing them off the beat, a little ahead or behind in a deliberate attempt to do what I could to disrupt the rhythmic flow. Of course, nothing can throw Vinnie, who didn't seem to care what I did, and Frank didn't react so I assumed that he didn't notice anything. My attempt at revenge had been a dud, except for one thing. I was up at Frank's house shortly before the release of *Shut Up and Play Your Guitar* to hear some of the cuts from the new album. He prefaced one of the jams by saying, "I don't know if you were pissed at me or what, but you really played your ass off on this one!" Of course it was that "Torture" jam, now titled "Beat it with Your Fist." I didn't see that one coming.

One of the worst nights of the tour was a horrible night for anyone in the world who loved The Beatles. On December 8th, 1980 we played in Santa Barbara at the Arlington Theater. I had just stepped up onto the stage and we were about to start the opening vamp when one of the roadies ran up to me and said, "John Lennon has just been shot to death in New York City!" I was in shock, then seconds later I heard Vinnie count off "One, two, three, four" and the show began. I played that whole show with tears in my eyes and my heart in my throat. Frank knew, also, I think, but wisely did not announce it to the audience. Because this was before the age of cell phones, they didn't find out till after the show. For the last few shows of the tour, we actually had some security checks at the doors of the venues.

After Santa Barbara we played in San Diego, then ended the tour back home in Los Angeles. The last shows I played with Zappa were the two sets we played on December 11th, 1980 at the Santa Monica Civic Auditorium, which is about 10 minutes from where I lived in Santa Monica. Of course a lot of friends came to the shows, but it was bittersweet for me since I had decided by then I didn't want to do any more long tours with the Zappa band. I recall taking a slow walk around the auditorium between the two shows, and thinking very hard about whether I was making the right decision. Then I went back in and played a show with Frank Zappa for one final time. There was, however, no reason to say anything to Frank then, since the tour was over and we were not on any kind of salary or retainer. The next day I filed for unemployment again.

Chapter Eleven

No sooner had I gotten settled in back at home when the phone rang. It was Robby Krieger on the line, who wanted to start doing some recording. By this time, a friend of mine from the Johnny Baltimore Band named Mark Avnet had a 24-track recording studio in Venice on Lincoln Blvd., close to where I lived. I had told Krieger about the studio, and he soon became a very good client at Mark's Mad Dog Studio. Robby and I did a lot of recording together there. Mark was kind enough to let me have free run of the place sometimes when it wasn't booked. This was a great opportunity for me to get better sounding recordings of my songs. When I saw Mark recently after a Krieger gig in New York, I mentioned how generous he had been about letting me use the studio. Mark said, "Of course I was – you brought me my main client, Robby Krieger!" It was great to be able to stay in town doing studio work. Soon I was back in my old groove again, playing with some of my old L.A. bands and doing some sessions.

The phone rang again on Monday, January 5th, 1981. It was from the office of Bennett Glotzer, Frank's manager, announcing that rehearsals were to begin again at 6 p.m. on the 7th at the Zappa warehouse in the valley. It was time for me to bite the bullet and make my move. I called Frank and told him I wanted to come up to his house and talk. He said he was busy, and asked if it could be handled on the phone. I said I wanted to talk face to face and he reluctantly agreed. I went up to his house that Tuesday evening and told him that as much as I loved his music, I knew it was time for me to leave the band. I cited personal reasons, and said I wanted to pursue a solo career and spend time writing and recording songs at my home studio. He mentioned that Vinnie was not going to be in the band. Maybe he somehow thought I wanted to quit because of Vinnie, but that was not the case. Frank was understanding, said he was sorry to see me go, and we parted on good terms. At the time, it seemed like the best choice for me to make. I can't say that I haven't had moments of regret, for several reasons, but especially because he got sick and died so young. There is now, of course, no possibility of playing with him ever again, at least in this world.

But I had made my decision, and it was time to move on. I didn't look back, at least for a while. I was eager to get to work on my own music. By then I had a pretty decent Otari 8-track recorder and a Tascam mixer in our Santa Monica apartment, enough to do some good demos. I wasted no time in putting my money where my mouth was, and wrote quite a few songs. I spent a lot of time honing the arrangements and recording them, and I thought some of them were sounding pretty good. I also began co-writing songs with a few people, including Mack, the singer from Red Shift, the band with Robby from a couple of years back, as well as continuing to record with Robby. All this and doing gigs with various bands was my life for the next few months.

Then, from out of the blue, the phone rang again in late May with Frank on the line. Apparently, the January rehearsals had never materialized and Frank had to cancel whatever touring plans he had once he realized he had no band. He wanted to hire me to prepare some click tracks for some tunes he wanted to record that required more than a simple steady beat. As I explained earlier, a "click" is a mechanically or electronically produced clicking sound like a metronome that musicians can listen to while recording to keep a steady beat or stay in sync with a film. I was only too happy to oblige; it would be an interesting challenge, and I would earn some much needed dough. I had been using my synths to create some fairly complex click tracks for some of my own music, so I was getting pretty good at figuring out how to make a simple analog synth do such a thing. I went up to the house nine times between May 27th and June 13th to record the click tracks, as well as some bass, guitar, and piano parts that would end up on the *Drowning Witch* and *Man From Utopia* albums. The credits on MFU are vague, so for the record, I am playing piano and guitar on "The Radio is Broken," and I came up with the idea to use the chord progression from the Doors' "Love Street" in that song, too. I recorded multiple bass tracks on "Tink Walks Amok," of course, and I'm pretty sure that's me playing bass on "We Are Not Alone," too.

I was still working on my own songs during this time, and even got Frank to listen to a couple of my demos. After hearing them, Frank was kind enough to offer to let me come up to his house while he was out of town to record vocals and mix two of my songs with engineer Bob Stone, free of charge. That was generous of Frank and I was very grateful. However, between that and doing all those sweet recording sessions, I had the feeling Frank was buttering me up, and sure enough at one point he asked if I would consider changing my mind about being in the band, but I declined. Soon after that he hired Chad Wackerman on drums and Scott Thunes on bass. To my surprise, Frank asked me if I would stay on through the first set of rehearsals to be the clonemeister and get the new guys up to speed, and of course I said yes.

I began clonemeistering the new band in early August, 1981. I put in an average of about thirty hours a week and was being paid $15 an hour. It was a lot easier running the rehearsals with this band than it had been in the past. First of all, it was better to not be in the band where I would have to worry about my own parts as well as everyone else's parts. Also, I was the clear authority, and got no crap from anybody. Frank had added Bobby Martin to the band, and he and Chad in particular were consummate professionals in every way. The biggest problem I had was getting Steve Vai to keep his volume down. Like most guitar players, he could not resist the urge to inch up the volume as the rehearsal wore on. At one point I threatened to make a repeating tape loop that every five minutes would say, "Steve, turn down!" Now that he is a big guitar hero I get a kick out telling people the it used to be my job to tell Steve Vai to turn down.

Although he is a good player and always treated me with respect during the rehearsals I ran, I have to admit that I was surprised at Frank's choice of Thunes. He was competent playing the difficult parts, but to me he had a tone that didn't fit with the band, and he didn't seem to groove with Chad. I think one reason he was hired was because he looked real "punk," and maybe Frank wanted to update the image of the band, like he had done with the glam rock cover of *Zoot Allures*. There was, however, no doubt that Scott had the chops to do the gig.

Ed Mann was back in the band on percussion, which was a great addition, and re-expanded the universe of sounds at Frank's fingertips. Frank was bringing in very cool new instrumental material, the kind I really enjoy, like "Moggio." Now, I doubt if it was for my benefit, but if he was trying to work his mojo on me in a "see what you're missing?" kind of a way, it was working.

The rehearsals continued for almost two months, until September 25th. As usual, I would leave shortly after Frank arrived to take over the rehearsal. It would be the last time I saw them all before they started the tour, so I said my goodbyes to everyone. Just as I was leaving the huge sound stage, the band struck up "Montana," one of my all time favorites, and it felt like a knife through my heart. All at once, I was filled with the realization that they were all going and I was staying behind. I had to fight back the tears, and hope I had made the right decision about leaving the band.

For the rest of the year, my life was back to writing songs, alone and with others, and doing gigs and a few sessions. I spent a lot of hours at Mad Dog Studio working on my original songs. I also made a good investment at about that time. I had been very impressed with a Roland synthesizer that Bobby Martin was using in the Zappa band, a Jupiter-8. It was one of the early polyphonic synths, and I liked the way it sounded and the way it was set up. It was a very expensive purchase for me, at around $5,000.00, but I bought one. This was the beginning of the 80's synth pop era, and I quickly started getting more sessions as a keyboard player than as a bass player. I was on the cutting edge with my JP-8, and it soon proved to be worth its weight in gold.

1982 brought more of the same kinds of activities, including playing again in Denny Walley's band with Vinnie on drums at the Blue Lagoon in Venice, just down the road from Mad Dog Studio. I was doing gigs with Johnny Baltimore, and even tried to put together my own band to do the songs I had been writing. We had only a few rehearsals and made a few recordings before I got another call from Zappa that was going to result in most of my time being consumed by him again for a while.

The call was to do another recording session up at Frank's house on March 10th. It was a nice fat double session, going from 9 pm to 3 am. I'm not sure, but I think that was when we recorded "Tink Walks Amok," the tune that features me on multiple bass tracks. It did not have that title at the time we recorded it. The first section was part of something he called "Atomic Paganini" and most of the rest of the bass part was from the version of "Thirteen" that we were working on in early 1980, just before Vinnie quit the band. That's the tune I mentioned earlier that was almost forgotten.

Sitting in the control room, I was recording the bass to a click track with Frank sitting right next to me. The "Paganini" part is mainly just a repeating riff in 11/8 time. Frank started inventing the arrangement on the fly, as we were recording. We started off with me playing the riff in one position, then he would say, "Move up two frets – OK, now!" or "Move the whole thing over to the A string position – OK, now!" After we had done that for a while, he remembered the "Thirteen" arrangement we used to do, so he had me do the bass part to that. I fully expected that he would overdub all the great keyboard and guitar parts that were part of it, but he never did. He seemed to like it as a track featuring me on bass, and I sure can't complain about that, but I always miss those other parts when I hear it. It's also pretty flattering to have a Zappa composition named after me. I did not find out about Frank naming the tune after me until I had the album in my hands for the first time. That was a surprise and quite an honor.

By the way, this is where Christopher Cross enters the story again. When I arrived at the house for one of the sessions during this time, Frank greeted me with a big smile and said, "Hi, Tink!" My immediate thought was to wonder who had told him about my old childhood nickname, which I had always hated. I didn't have to wait for long; he was eager to tell me the story. One evening at some fancy restaurant in New York there was a meeting, a chance meeting of Frank and Christopher Cross. Frank said he noticed Chris was there, and had the waiter send over an opened, half finished bottle of wine that Frank was done with. They ended up hanging out for a while, whereupon Chris took the opportunity to inform Frank that my childhood nickname was the despised "Tink." I think it was Chris's way of getting his revenge on me for inciting Zappa to write "Teenage Wind."

During this recording session, it seemed like Frank was buttering me up again. Sure enough, after a while he told me he was gearing up for another tour, and asked again if I would change my mind and rejoin the band. I declined, but said yes to helping out with the clonemeister duties one more time. That set of rehearsals ran from March 15th through April 28th.

I can't be certain, but I think it was around this time that Frank was in talks with Bob Dylan about the possibility of Frank producing a Dylan album. Bob had already been up to the house, and Frank was interested, but he said he was too busy to do it himself. He told me he would subcontract out songs to various other producers. He even named Giorgio Moroder as a possibility. He told me that he wanted me to be the musical director for the project. I found the idea thrilling, but unfortunately, the whole thing never happened. I suspect that when Bob's record company got wind of it, they lowered the boom and killed the idea. Zappa was not very popular among the music business people known as "record company executives."

A notable recording session happened soon after those rehearsals were over. I went to engineer Earle Mankey's house to record with The God of Hellfire, Arthur Brown, who had emerged from the crazy world of himself to do a new record. He was actually a very nice man who was living in Austin by then. Earle Mankey is a fine engineer and producer who had engineered some Beach Boys records. He pointed to a black box under a desk and said it was the reverb unit that had been used on the song "Good Vibrations" for that long sustain of the vocals when they cut off after holding that gorgeous chord near the end of the song. Cool.

Another series of memorable sessions occurred in August. I got a call from my Knack friend, drummer Bruce Gary, who asked me if I wanted to work on a new Bette Midler record with him and Berton Averre, also a Knacker. Of course I said yes. She was trying to make a musical comeback after a big flop in the movie business with *Jinxed*. She had been very upset by the failure, it seems, and though she was pleasant, she was a bit standoffish. To be honest, this group of musicians was not right for what she needed at the time. I was happy to do the sessions, but I could tell it wasn't really going to work. The producer was Chuck Plotkin of Springsteen and Dylan fame, but he seemed pretty clueless in this situation. He was constantly drinking cognac and liked to play along with us on congas to supposedly help with the vibe or something. He provided me with one of my all time favorite music biz quotes, though, when he told us at one point to play in such a way as to make it sound more "horizontal." Right. I am pretty sure none of the tracks we recorded were ever released, and it's just as well.

Soon after the Midler sessions were finished, I got a call from Krieger again, who wanted to put together a live band to do a short tour of just a few weeks. This was a lot easier to swallow than the prospect of the months long tours with Zappa, so I agreed. We put together a good band with Bruce Gary on drums, Berton Averre on guitar, and Marty Jabara on keys. We toured the east coast for about three weeks starting in mid-October. It was an enjoyable tour, and just about the right amount of time to be away from home.

One day during rehearsals for that tour I had an unexpected treat. Mitch Mitchell, the drummer in The Jimi Hendrix Experience, dropped by to say hello to Robby, and I got to meet him! What a thrill it was to be face to face with the man I consider to be the best drummer that ever played with Jimi. Hendrix was like a god to me, and Mitch had played in Jimi's best band and on his best recordings. I was totally in awe, so much so that I was too tongue-tied to say anything more than "Wow, I can't believe I'm shaking your hand!" It is sad to think that all three members of that band are no longer with us.

Unfortunately, my career as a solo artist was going nowhere. I had recorded decent demos of about twenty songs by then, and had been shopping them to record companies to the best of my abilities, but none were interested in what I had to offer. Unperturbed, I was not yet ready to give up, and recorded another song which was crucial to my future, though not as a boost to my solo career. Andrew McKensie, aka "Mack," the singer from Red Shift, was still around and living in Santa Monica. We collaborated on a new song called "A Crush." We wrote the music together and he wrote the lyrics. We used my synths in a kind of euro/techno style, with the fast repeating synth bass part called "trigger bass" and a drum machine. It was the most modern sounding thing I had done, and the direction of it was mostly guided by Andrew's good taste and knowledge of pop music. We borrowed a new drum machine called a Linndrum for the recording at Mad Dog, and it sounded great. With Andrew's guidance, even my vocals were not too bad. Although I never got a record deal as a solo artist, this tape opened up the door to the next important phase in my musical life.

Chapter Twelve

By 1983, my old friend from San Antonio, Will Alexander, was working for Fairlight in an office space above the Village Recorders where *Joe's Garage* had been recorded. The Fairlight CMI (computer music instrument) was an Australian built digital synthesizer, and one of the first digital sampling devices. Like its American counterpart, the Synclavier, it was expensive, and only the very rich or, as it sometimes turned out, foolish people invested in one. It was a cool machine for its day, though, to be sure. I occasionally visited Will at the Fairlight office to play with the machine. I even programmed it to play a bit of Zappa's "Uncle Meat" for laughs. One day, Will told me that famed disco producer Giorgio Moroder had just been up to the office for a Fairlight demonstration, and had mentioned that he was looking for a good synth oriented keyboard player for recording work. There was also another fellow I knew named Larry Lee who knew Giorgio and had told me the same thing.

Moroder was a well known producer and songwriter who had made Donna Summer a star in the mid 70's. He basically invented the European electronic dance music (EDM) sound that continues to be popular to this day. He was widely respected. Even Zappa knew about him and thought highly of his work. But the music biz is very fickle, and when the bottom fell out of the disco market, Giorgio's career appeared to be over.

I soon learned that the reason he needed a new keyboard player was that he was making an unexpected comeback with a hit song he had written and produced for the film *Flashdance* called "What a Feeling" sung by Irene Cara of *Fame* fame. Giorgio had done the song for the movie, but thought the film was so bad that it would be a flop. He was surprised and delighted when it was a hit and all at once he was a hot commodity again. Giorgio immediately realized that with a hit single on his hands, he needed to make an album to go with the single as fast as he could. Otherwise, there was no album to go with the hit single other than the movie soundtrack.

I got Giorgio's number, and after a few tries, got past his rude secretary and spoke with the man himself. Larry Lee knew

Giorgio pretty well and his recommendation seemed to carry some weight. I think that's what finally opened the door for me to meet with the famous producer. Giorgio invited me up to his mansion in Beverly Hills, and when I got there, I was encouraged when I saw that he had not one, but two Jupiter-8 synthesizers just like mine, and a Linndrum. This was a great sign, since I knew the JP-8 inside and out and already had a little experience with the Linndrum. He had asked me to bring a tape to play that would give him an idea what I could do. I chose "A Crush," the song I had done with Mack, since it was the best thing I had and seemed to be right up Mr. Moroder's alley. He liked it, and asked me if I would like to audition to do some work for him as a musician and possibly as an artist. Of course I said yes!

My audition was on May 16th, 1983. Auditioning for Giorgio was a lot different from auditioning for Zappa. Giorgio put me in his deluxe home studio with engineer Dave Concors where he gave me a demo tape of a song he had just written and told me to create an arrangement and record master tracks for it, right then and there, with no preparation. I can't remember the song now, but I think it was something for Irene Cara. I whipped out a track with help from Dave, who is one of the coolest, most unflappable guys I know. He kept my nerves calm enough to get something done. We ended up doing a lot of work together and are still good friends today. I guess the track was good enough because Moroder had me back the next day, and the day after that, and by May 23rd, I was in New York along with guitarist Richie Zito recording a new album for Irene Cara at Electric Ladyland Studios.

Unlike Zappa, Moroder encouraged those working for him to write songs for the artists he was producing. Of course, he would keep the publishing, which is 50% of the song's total royalties, but 50% of something is better than 100% of nothing. Richie and I put our heads together and wrote a song called "Keep On" that made it onto the Cara album. It was my first pop song that would actually be released on a real label and had a chance of going somewhere.

It was exciting for me to be at Electric Ladyland, a studio designed by Jimi Hendrix himself, though he worked there only briefly before his untimely death. I could really feel the vibe there, for sure, and I found it just a little eerie. But I didn't have much time for feeling spooked, because there was a whole album of songs to be recorded as quickly as possible. I remember one day when Giorgio came into the studio very excited to announce that "What a Feeling" had reached #1 in the charts, knocking David Bowie's "Let's Dance" out of the top spot. It stayed at #1 for several weeks. Of course, I was not playing on "What a Feeling," but some other songs on the album that I did play on charted decently, with "Why Me?" making it to #13 and "Breakdance" reaching #8. I was playing on a top ten song for the first time in my career. Yahoo! And, I was making the best money I had ever pulled in. Life was looking up.

By June 1st we were back in L.A., and I went right to work again in Giorgio's home studio. Keith Forsey, Billy Idol's producer, was producing an album for East German singer Nina Hagen. I was conscripted for keyboard and bass duties. Nina was an unusual character, sometimes bringing in a baby carriage holding her two year-old daughter, Cosma Shiva, who would be wearing full make-up! Nina often talked about the UFOs she had been seeing lately. You get the picture. I thought the music was pretty cool, though, and I enjoyed the experience. It was exciting to work with Keith, too. He was very intense and intent upon making great records. It was during these sessions that I heard "gated reverb" for the first time, in this case on a cowbell. It adds a very explosive, short burst of reverb that would soon be heard on just about every pop record ad nauseum for the next few years. But the first time I heard it I thought it was cool and a clever idea. The single "New York/N.Y." from Nina's album, *Fearless,* made it to #9 on the U.S. Dance chart. It was also on the Hagen album that I met my future collaborator, guitar player Steve (Schifty) Schiff.

My non-Giorgio work continued to expand, too. I was doing lots of synth sessions with my JP-8. Sometimes I would do double duty, like doing a session with Robby at Mad Dog at 11 a.m. then up to Giorgio's for a session with Nina and Keith at 5 p.m. I was making good money doing sessions in town, and I was loving it. It was 180 degrees away from Zappa musically, but that was a good thing. With Frank, I had proved to myself and the world that I was capable of playing complex music with the most advanced rock band that ever existed. Now I was learning what it took to create music that could get played on the radio and sell records. This was a completely new, and equally difficult challenge to face. I recall driving home one night after working at Giorgio's thinking to myself that I had really "made it" now, and that things would be great for me and my career forever more. Foolish me!

But things were really hot there for a while. I am amazed when I examine my date book from that time in 1983. In addition to Nina, there were still a lot of dates with Robby Krieger and others at Mad Dog and elsewhere. By mid-June, we had already started working on Giorgio's music for the film *Scarface* starring Al Pacino. There is even a note in my datebook that indicates I did a session at Zappa's house with Dweezil Zappa, but I have absolutely no recollection of it at all.

Giorgio had bought a studio on Lankershim Blvd. in Studio City he named Oasis. He made some alterations, turning one big room into three smaller rooms to suit his way of recording, which was mostly done electronically in the control room. All he really needed were small isolation booths to record things like vocals and percussion. We did our first day of recording there on the summer solstice, June 21st. By then, Richie Zito and I were basically Giorgio's band. Giorgio had not known at first that I was also a bass player, and was pleased when he found out, because he loved the slap style funky bass playing along with the synth bass. So Richie handled the drum machine and guitar parts while I handled the keys and the bass. Voila! That was all we needed to make a Moroder track, ready for vocals and mixing.

As I mentioned, Giorgio was suddenly very hot again with the success of "What a Feeling." Several offers for him to do film scores came in all at once. It seemed every film producer in Hollywood decided they needed a hit single in their movie, and Moroder was king of that realm. It didn't hurt that in addition to his many hits with Donna Summer, he had received an Oscar for best original score from the movie *Midnight Express*. Giorgio needed to write a lot of music in very little time, so he got right to work - on his own kind of schedule, that is. He liked to get up in the morning and go to his favorite breakfast spot, the exclusive Beverly Hills Hotel Polo Lounge. When he later got into the studio he would regale us with stories about the stars he would see there. Of the gorgeous Nastassja Kinski he said, "Her nose is too big" or of Brooke Shields, "Wow, now she is really beautiful!" This was before the days of cell phones, but you could reach him at the Polo Lounge if need be. The Polo Lounge staff would bring a phone to his table, just like in the old movies.

After breakfast at the Polo Lounge, a typical day working for Giorgio when he was composing went something like this: Giorgio, an engineer, (usually Dave Concors or Brian Reeves) Richie, and I would arrive at Oasis at about 2 p.m. Giorgio would tell us what style he wanted – dance, latin or whatever - and we would program the appropriate beat in the Linndrum. The engineer would set him up behind a Rhodes electric piano or a synthesizer with a microphone, headphones, access to the drum machine and to the remote control for the 24-track tape recorder. Once he was all set, the rest of us would leave Giorgio alone while he tried to come up with something. After about 20 minutes he would come out of the control room. Sometimes he would say, "Nothing today, boys," and we would either go home, or move on to something else. But if he had an idea, he would excitedly invite us back into the control room to hear what he had come up with. He would usually have a basic melody, chord structure, arrangement, and lyric "hook" line, with the rest of the melody sung in nonsense syllables or lyrics. We would all listen to it while he described what he wanted us to do. "OK, boys, I need a trigger bass, a funky slap bass guitar, a big synth chord sound in the chorus, some beautiful strings, a clean funky guitar in the verse and a heavy one in the chorus, some synthesizer "bubbles" in the bridge, and some electronic drum fills," he might say. He would then leave us to work on it, and often as he was leaving, he would say in his thick Italian accent, "I'll listen to what you do tomorrow. I have to go now. Tonight I have centerfold!" That meant a hot date with some gorgeous babe.

About once every six months he would get in a Latin mood and "write" a song that sounded almost exactly like the 1967 Classics IV song "Spooky." One time I said, "That's really good, but it sounds an awful lot like that old song "Spooky." He said, "Oh really? Was it a hit?" I replied that yes, it was a big hit. "That's good!" he said, seeing that as encouragement to keep working on it.

There always seemed to be beautiful women around Giorgio. In fact, one of the perks for a while at Oasis was the presence of a former Miss World, an exquisite six foot tall blond from Europe. Her job was to make and bring us coffee on demand. It seems we needed a lot of coffee when she was around. Then there was Shawn, another tall, curvaceous woman who Giorgio was dating. Ostensibly, he was fostering her career as a singer. I was assigned the task of trying to write some songs with her, but nothing much came of that. She ended up married to a famous television personality who was much older than her.

I had free run of Oasis whenever it wasn't booked. Giorgio encouraged all of us who worked for him to use the studio to try to write hit songs. The catch was that, as I mentioned, he kept the publishing (50% of the whole) for anything we wrote there. I had a blast in that place with all that cool gear, but alas, I never came up with a hit song. Hits were the only thing that mattered to Moroder, by the way. He thought any song that did not have hit potential was a waste of time. He also believed that one should release as many songs as possible, because the more songs that were out there, the more chances there were of having a hit. The man knew what he was talking about. He has at least eleven number one hits to his name.

Giorgio sure knew how to live the rich man lifestyle. When I first met him, he drove a sleek Ferrari. He soon grew tired of that and got an even more expensive Maserati, that had the kind of doors that open up instead of out. One day he was sitting in that car parked in his garage with the driver's side door open. He decided to back out of the garage, but failed to close the open door. It hit the garage door on the way out and ripped the Maserati's door right off! When he worked in New York, he would sometimes take the Supersonic Transport to Paris for lunch, then return to New York the same day. Speaking of New York, he kept a full length mink coat in a locker at the airport, the kind where you could put a quarter in, take out the key and leave stuff in there as long as you wanted. That way, in the winter, rather than bring a coat from L.A., he would simply go to his locker when he got to New York, get the coat, wear it while in the city, then return it to the locker on the way home. Quite practical, really.

Though I did not witness it myself, and can't swear that it's true, I heard a funny story about a Giorgio party at his mansion. He was not a drug guy at all. I never saw him smoke or snort anything even though there was plenty of that going on all around him. I never even saw him have a drink, although I think he did enjoy fine cognac now and then. But he wanted to be a good host at his party, so in addition to food and drinks, he bought a large amount of cocaine and put it in a bowl on the coffee table so that anyone who wanted some could help themselves. This kind of hosting was something I had never heard of before.

Giorgio also had a pretty good sense of humor. Guitar player Richie Zito is a very ambitious and hard working Italian-American from Brooklyn. Giorgio hailed from northern Italy, which made him almost as much German as Italian. (When Giorgio left home to pursue his musical career, he naturally went to Munich, not Rome.) One day over lunch he asked Richie what part of Italy his family was from. Richie said they were Sicilian, to which Giorgio replied, "Sicily – isn't that part of Africa?" Although it was before my time with Giorgio, I heard a story told about the day the disco label Casablanca Records went under, and Giorgio's meeting with them about it. He reportedly came back to his studio, gathered his crew together and said, "Bad news, boys. We have a budget."

But for me, being on the Giorgio team was about our work, writing and recording music, and a lot of it. Work continued on Nina Hagen's record simultaneously with work on *Scarface*. This was the first big movie I had been involved with, and it was very exciting. Giorgio divided most of the work into 2 parts: Sylvester Levay handled most of the underscore, (background music) while Richie and I did most of the songs. For some of the dance songs, lyrics were needed. Giorgio gave me a shot at coming up with some, so I whipped off the first ideas that popped into my head for submission. They were good enough that they made it into the movie. I even got screen credit for them.

Our team did do at least one of the underscore cues, the scene in the beginning in which the marielitos are coming onto the Florida shore from Cuba. I am proud of this work and feel that it still holds up well when I hear it today. I think Moroder wrote some impressive and inspired music for that film, especially "Tony's Theme" and "Gina's and Elvira's Theme." It was also a thrill for me to work on a song sung by Debby Harry, "Rush, Rush," though I did not get a chance to meet her, I'm sorry to say. The song was not a big hit, but did reach #28 on the U.S. dance charts, and has since been sampled and covered a few times. I dig it. I used my Serge synth a lot on that, and my slap bass playing is prominent, too. Throughout the songs for the movie and most of my recordings with Moroder, I used the same Fender Jazz bass I played with Zappa on *Joe's Garage*, and a careful listen to the *Scarface* songs will reveal that it's the same sound in two different settings.

We did a 12" remix of "Rush, Rush," too, the first such remix I was involved with. Giorgio was there and really got into it, coming up with all kinds of cool ideas, and I think it turned out great. As with Zappa, it was another chance for me to see first hand how a successful creative mind works. It turns out there were a lot of things I was going to be learning from Giorgio, and fast.

One thing I was not expecting, just because I had never thought about it before, was what a typical movie soundtrack album consisted of. Most of the music on a movie soundtrack album is usually re-recorded or edited, with arrangements and structures more like pop songs, as opposed to being geared toward fitting into the actual scene in the film. Writing music for film demands particular attention regarding timing and visuals. Very little of a soundtrack album is exactly the same as what is heard in the movie.

Scarface work continued, but by early August Irene Cara was in town to finish working on the album that we had begun at Electric Ladyland. Since I had not met her when we were in New York, it was the first time I got to know her. Though talented, she could be a handful, and very moody at times. I can remember calling her at her hotel one time and she answered the phone by picking it up and screaming, *"What??!!"* But she was a good soul, I think, just trying to find her way in life like everyone else. I imagine that she was fairly surprised herself about the hit with "What A Feeling." Irene and *Scarface* were my main jobs through July and August. I guess Irene didn't realize that I had not worked on "What a Feeling," although Zito had. Months later, when she was on stage to receive the Oscar for Best Song on behalf of Giorgio, she graciously thanked Richie Zito and Arthur Barrow. Thanks Irene, but... Well, the karma of that would kind of balance out for me later. Read on.

Also in August, Richie had landed the gig of producing an album for Toni Basil, who had just come off of a #1 hit with her novelty song "Mickey." She had already had a pretty impressive career as an actress and dancer. She was in *Easy Rider* (one of the girls in the cemetery scene) and was a dancer on *Shindig!* and *The T.A.M.I. Show,* to mention just a few of her accomplishments. I was heavily involved in the recordings which became her next album, *Toni Basil*. It yielded a #4 hit on the dance charts with the song

"Over My Head." I liked her. She seemed pretty level headed, and was always trying to keep up with the latest trends in pop culture. At one point she called Richie from New York to tell us about the "scratching" craze that the DJ's there were into, manipulating the record while the needle was in the groove. She excitedly related how everything sounded like "waka-waka-waka," so of course we had to throw some of that onto her record.

By mid-August, I was working on three major projects, often on the same day. On Friday, August 12th, for example, I worked from noon to 3 p.m. on Scarface, 3 p.m. to 7 p.m. on Irene Cara, and 8 p.m. to 12:30 a.m. on Toni Basil! Man, was I busy, and I was loving it. I felt I had reached the top of the heap. I was an in-demand session guy, and it felt like it would go on forever.

As if that weren't enough, I got a call from Zappa again to do more recording at his home studio. I recorded with him the whole week of August 15th. The first thing we did was put a forward (normal) bass track to a backwards version of his song "No, Not Now," that would be called "Won Ton On." It was a pretty hairy enterprise attempting to stay in synch with all the backwards sounds, and at first I didn't see how it would be possible. But Frank seemed to believe I could do it, so I closed my eyes, concentrated as hard as I could and managed to pull it off by the skin of my teeth. Frank was so pleased with it that he loved to play it for visitors. I saw Terry Bozzio up at the house shortly after that session who looked at me wide eyed and told me how blown away he was by it. "How did you do that?!" he asked incredulously.

The rest of the week was spent doing bass overdubs on *We're Only In It for the Money* and *Lumpy Gravy*, replacing the bass parts on the original 1960's recordings. Frank had won a legal settlement in which he gained control of the original master recordings to use as he saw fit. He said that he had never been happy with the original drum and bass parts, and wanted Chad and me to record new tracks to the original versions. I couldn't believe he wanted to do it. Those two albums were among my favorites, and, as a fan, the thought of altering them so many years later seemed like a terrible idea. I actually told him that, and that I didn't think the fans would like it at all. He basically said it was his music, and he wanted to do it, so that's what he did. He was a hard man to say "no" to, and besides, it *was* his music, after all. Besides, if I had refused, he would have called someone else to do it, so of course I said yes.

Though as a fan I philosophically disapproved of replacing the bass and drum tracks, it was actually a lot of fun for me. *We're Only in It for the Money* was the first Zappa album I really got into, so it was very interesting to see what was on those original tracks. In spite of the fact that I had never played most of the songs before, I had heard them so many times that I pretty much knew them anyway. I found some oddities, like the way the tempo varied so much in "Mom and Dad." When Frank left the room one time to make peanut butter and jelly sandwiches for us, I played the tape and listened to the individual tracks to hear what was there. There were a few "Aha" moments when I would think, "So *that's* how he did that!" It was also amusing to enjoy a peanut butter and jelly sandwich made by Frank Zappa. I chuckle every time I think about that.

In the psychedelic part of "Flower Punk" as the LSD is supposed to be coming on to the Flower Punk, Frank told me to insert the "My Sharona" lick that he loved to stick in anywhere and everywhere. He seemed to find it particularly entertaining to hear the new wave lick in the context of the old recording. This was seized upon by the pathetically misinformed Barry Miles in his Zappa biography, in which he accuses *me* of inserting the Knack lick into the song. He said that I must not have been aware that *We're Only In It for the Money* had been recorded a decade before "My Sharona." How ridiculous. Of course I knew that was the case. It was my favorite album at the time! And if it wasn't for me, Frank probably would never have parodied the Knack at all. It also shows a complete lack of understanding by Miles about how Zappa created and scrutinized every detail of his music. Frank would never allow a musician to insert something into his music without his permission or knowledge.

Sure enough, as I predicted, when the re-recorded versions came out with the new bass and drum tracks, the fans were not happy. I tried, folks, I really did. On the other hand, I have met younger fans whose first exposure to the album was the one with the new bass and drums and they love it. Maybe Frank was right after all.

Then it was back to work at Oasis, mostly on *Scarface* and Toni Basil. By early September, another movie arrived for Giorgio: *Electric Dreams*. It was an early take on home computers in which Edgar, the computer, becomes sentient and begins to imitate the sounds of a cellist practicing nearby. It's a sweet little science fiction romantic comedy which I enjoyed working on.

Taking another look at my datebook, I see another example of a busy day for a musician. September 6th, 1983: noon to 2 p.m. - *Electric Dreams*, 2 p.m. to 8 p.m. - *Scarface*, 8 p.m. to midnight - Toni Basil. A long day, but still, I loved it. And so it went until late September when another movie called *D.C. Cab* was in need of the magic Giorgio touch. I was done with Basil sessions by mid-October, but work on the films went on through the end of the year.

Before I met him, Giorgio had acquired the rights to do a soundtrack to the classic Fritz Lang silent film *Metropolis*. By early December, I was working on that project as well. I had heard some of the music he was composing for it when I auditioned at his house. I thought it sounded really interesting, and would fit the film very well. Unfortunately, after the success of "What a Feeling," he decided to write several pop songs for the film and get "name" singers to sing them. For me, this diminished the integrity of the project. I think it would have been much more effective done instrumentally, letting the picture tell the story without the forced sounding lyrics vying for the viewer's attention. And in spite of the name artists like Freddie Mercury, Pat Benatar, Jon Anderson, and Adam Ant, who were meant to make it a commercial success, it was mostly hated by the critics. A lot of credit has to go to Giorgio, however, if only for how he tracked down whatever bits and pieces from the original film he could find to make a restoration and bring this classic to a wider audience. The instrumental parts are still pretty good, I think, and I even have a fretless bass solo in one of the songs.

In between all the Giorgio work, I was shoehorning in other sessions as much as possible, and it all kept me quite busy for the rest of the year.

Chapter Thirteen

In 1984, things continued full steam ahead. One day in early January, I found myself with Giorgio in his office at Oasis along with guitarist Richie Zito. Giorgio had just had a meeting with David Geffen about an album by the band Berlin that Geffen was about to release. Berlin had already had some minor success with their independently produced songs "Sex (I'm A...)" and "The Metro" but never had a top 40 song. David Geffen signed them to do a studio album with a real budget which they had just completed.

Geffen was concerned that there wasn't a song that sounded like a hit, and had asked Giorgio if he thought he could do something to improve a couple of the songs the band had recorded. Giorgio, Richie, and I listened to the songs from the album, and we all agreed that "No More Words" and "Dancing in Berlin" were the best candidates for us to work on. Giorgio talked about his ideas of how we should approach the arrangements, then Zito and I went into the studio and recorded all new tracks with very little oversight from Giorgio. He knew he could trust us to come up with something strong, which we did. Our versions of those two songs are the ones that ended up on the *Love Life* album. What you hear on those recordings are Terri Nunn, Richie Zito and me. No other Berlin band members are playing on those two songs. Released on February 27th, "No More Words" was a minor hit at #23 on Billboard. It was the first top 40 hit for Berlin, and the video for it was played a lot on MTV, still something new and fresh in 1984.

There was a little unpleasant surprise in store for me, however, a little catch. When I saw a copy of the album for the first time, the credits said that the two songs Richie and I had created were produced by Giorgio Moroder and Richie Zito! I couldn't believe it! We had done those songs as a team in the same way that we had been recording tracks the entire time I had been working for Giorgio. There was no hint that Richie was producing as we arranged and recorded the tracks. I asked Moroder what the deal was, and he said something about Riche supervising the recording of the vocal tracks and the mixing. OK, that, and the fact that Zito had been working for Moroder longer than I had would give him the edge, I suppose, but I still felt betrayed. They could at least have mentioned it to me before I found out by seeing the credit on the album cover. My credit is on the inside paper album jacket in small print, "additional synthesizer programming: Arthur Barrow." In reality, I had done arranging, programming, and I played all the keyboards on the two songs, as well as playing fretless bass on "Dancing in Berlin." I was not at all happy about this. Richie seemed to understand how I felt, and assured me that he realized that I had gotten the short end of the stick, promising to make it up to me somehow. I'm still waiting for that.

In late January and into February, I worked on Janet Jackson's second studio album, *Dream Street*. I came into Oasis one day to find lyricist Pete Bellotte and keyboardist Phil Shenale working in studio C on a track they were writing for Janet. I happened to mention that I'd had a dream the previous night about some kind of big parade going down Hollywood Boulevard. Pete said "That's it! "Dream Street" – the title I've been looking for!" So I got credit as co-writer of the song which also became the title of the album. I went on to arrange and play keyboards on five of the songs on the album. One song, "Two to the Power of Love" was a duet with Cliff Richard. The album credits say I am playing bass, but I think that's a mistake. It all sounds like synth bass to me.

The first time I met Janet, she was just seventeen, and kind of shy. I was alone with her in a control room at Oasis with some keyboards trying to find the right keys for some songs she was going to sing on the album. When she sang, it came out very soft and timid. I asked her to go ahead and sing out a little more strongly so that we could find out which key was going to be the best for her. She replied, "I'm not really much of a singer." Great, I thought. *I'm trying to work with a singer who says she isn't much of a singer.* After we were done we said goodbye and she left the studio. I assumed she had a ride waiting for her. But when I went out about a half hour later to get a bite, she was sitting on the curb in front of the studio on busy Lankershim Boulevard as if she were a vagrant. She said a ride was on the way, but given that her brother Michael was such a huge star by that time, I couldn't believe the security for his little sister could be so lax. When I got back she was gone, and obviously unharmed as we all know, because she went on to be a huge star. Unfortunately for me, *Dream Street* hardly got noticed and did not sell well.

In 1984 Los Angeles hosted the Olympics, and Moroder, being hot stuff at that moment, submitted a song called "Reach Out" that became some kind of official theme song for the Olympics. The tracks were played by Zito and me, and it was sung by Paul Engeman, the brother of one of Giorgio's girlfriends. I thought the song was one of the corniest things Giorgio had done, but it was chosen by some committee to be the theme song, and even became a #1 hit on the German singles chart. Go figure.

As we got to March and April of 1984 work continued on *Metropolis* and Janet Jackson, as well as some preliminary work on the movie *Breakfast Club*. Keith Forsey was doing music for the John Hughes film, a very 80's movie about high school kids in a detention class. Keith hired me to do some keyboard and bass work for that project, which I greatly enjoyed. I even have a lovely fretless bass part on the instrumental "Love Theme." Keith wrote some of the songs with Steve Schiff, including the #1 hit "Don't You Forget About Me" that was performed by the band Simple Minds. Amazingly, I did get credit for playing bass and keyboards on the soundtrack album which, as I previously explained, was quite a rarity. Upon release, *Breakfast Club* received wide critical acclaim and is considered one of the best "high school" movies ever.

I also worked with Keith on some songs he was producing for the Psychedelic Furs. I enjoyed working with Keith. He was a British guy who had moved to Munich and hooked up with Moroder in the 1970's. He was a drummer, and played those "four on the floor" (relentless, pounding quarter notes on the bass drum) disco drum parts on a lot of the Donna Summer stuff from the seventies, and had also co-written some of the hits. Although he was very much from the Moroder camp, he had a quite different producing style from Giorgio. While Giorgio would usually tell us what he wanted then leave us to do the work on our own, Forsey was totally hands on, scrutinizing every detail of the recording. He said he felt like he wasn't doing his job if he did otherwise. He was very intense and liked to get right up in my face when I was recording to help infuse me with his enthusiasm. He was also much more creative than certain other of Moroder's associates, who always went by the book. By that I mean they stuck to whatever was the most conservative, by the pop song handbook way to go. Not so with Keith – he was always looking for new sounds and creative approaches to the music. I found it refreshing and inspiring. Forsey was hot stuff in the biz at that time because of his success with Billy Idol and "What a Feeling," which he co-wrote. I found his enthusiasm contagious.

Among the many record production tips I got from Keith, one stands out in my mind. Never give the record company rep a copy of a song that is unfinished. It is better to invite them over to the studio and play the track through the big studio monitors with the artist in the room. That way, they get the full effect of the music under the best possible conditions. If you give the record company person a copy of it, it is likely that they will listen to it over and over until they find something about it they don't like. It's much better to let them have the memory of how great it sounded in the studio and recall the vibe in the room of those who are working on the music.

There was a band called Sparks who were signed to some kind of contract with Giorgio. I worked with them on their album *Pulling Rabbits Out of a Hat*. The band was really just two brothers by then, and they did not seem happy with their contract. They made it pretty clear they were doing the record mainly to comply with the terms of the deal and then be done with Moroder. It was not a fun experience. Though I worked doing synth work with them for about three weeks, the only credit I got was one in a long list of "special thanks," not even a grudging "additional synth programming." The album was not very good, and it stiffed.

Another film project came Giorgio's way in mid-April, *The Never Ending Story*. The movie already had an orchestral score by German composer Klaus Doldinger of the band Passport, but the director, Wolfgang Petersen, wanted a pop song for the American release of the film. Mr. Moroder was up to the task, of course, and wrote "Never Ending Story," the title song for the movie which was sung my Limahl and Beth Anderson. It's pretty schmaltzy, but still, I kind of liked it. Amazingly, it made it to #1 in Japan, Norway, Spain, and Sweden, the top ten in Austria, France, Germany, Ireland, Italy, Switzerland, and the U.K., and #17 in the U.S. Billboard hot 100.

We also did four other tracks for the film that were instrumentals. It was a huge rush job, so there were a lot of 11, 12, 13, and even a couple of 16 hour days to get it done. On May 6th, 1984, for example I worked straight through from 1 p.m. till 5:30 the next morning. I remember driving home on the 405 freeway in *morning* rush hour after one of those work days and thinking that things were getting a little weird. But I was still liking it, and I was "making real good bread" as the Beach Boys had put it. Of course, like most movie soundtrack albums, the musicians were not credited. Not even an "additional programming" crumb! But that was the deal, take it or leave it.

In May we were back to work again on *Electric Dreams*. Giorgio wrote a song for the movie called "Together in Electric Dreams" which was sung by Phil Oakey, the singer from Human League. The song became a worldwide hit, reaching #3 on the UK singles chart. In addition to that song, Moroder wrote some good music for the film. I especially liked "Madeline's Theme," a classical sounding number which has some lovely harmonies. Again, being a movie soundtrack, no credits for Arthur or Richie.

In the summer of 1984, I had the privilege of working with Joe Cocker for the first time. Keith Forsey was asked to produce a song for the Nick Nolte film *Teachers* called "Edge of a Dream." Keith asked me to help out in the keyboard and arranging department. As with Janet Jackson, it was first necessary for Joe to come to the studio so we could find the best key for him to sing the song. Before then, I had never thought much about Joe Cocker one way or another. I knew a couple of his hits, but that was about it. Based on what I had heard of his recordings, I did not expect him to have a lot of vocal power, but, man, was I wrong. When he opened up his mouth to sing, a great big sound came out! What a very pleasant surprise, and I took a personal liking to him right away as well. He seemed to be a good-natured Englishman, and he sure loved his beer. He said he enjoyed having musicians come visit him where he lived near Santa Barbara, and invited me to come up to hang out any time. At one point as I was exchanging phone numbers with his bass player, Vito San Filippo, Joe was looking over my shoulder as I wrote down my name and commented in his thick accent, "Arthur Barrow, now that's a solid name!" I got a kick out of that. It is always refreshing how British people know how my name is pronounced. I guess it figures with a name like Arthur William Barrow. You can't get much more Englishy than that.

Keith wanted to use real drums so we recorded at Westlake Studio instead of Oasis, which did not have a good room for recording drums. At my suggestion, Keith hired my former Zappa bandmate Vinnie Colaiuta to do the drumming. I had brought a bunch of synth gear and was playing keyboards. Joe was in a separate soundproofed room with windows called an isolation booth to record a scratch vocal. We rehearsed the song a few times and were ready to do a take, when we realized that Joe had disappeared. It turns out he was in the restroom - somewhere between the Heinekens and the nerves, I guess, he had to vomit. He seemed OK when he got back, and we carried on. I thought it was odd and sadly touching that a singing star like him would get that nervous after all those years of experience. It wasn't even the "real" vocal, it was just a guide vocal for reference. The final vocal for the recording was done later as an overdub. Again, as usual, no credits for musicians were listed on the soundtrack album.

Speaking of Westlake, I'm not sure of the date, but at some point during that time, Michael Jackson was there working at the same time I was. I can't recall if he was in the men's room first or I was, but I found myself peeing in the urinal next to him. He seemed kind of shy as he looked over at me in his full Sgt. Pepper outfit and smiled slightly as if to say, "I know you know who I am. Please don't hurt me." So that's my brush with super-duper star fame.

Looking through my old business records, I found some invoices regarding a Moroder project called SP2 which was a code name for "Secret Project #2." It was so secret that when I looked at the invoices, I did not realize at first that it had to be demos for Diana Ross. It seems there were hush–hush negotiations between Giorgio and Ms. Ross about him possibly producing her next album. Moroder was very much a *writer*/producer, and of course wanted to write the songs as well as produce them. "Giorgio's Vision" is written on one of the invoices, which refers to his vision for the album, I think. I racked up a lot of hours that June, July, and August working on about a dozen Giorgio pop songs for SP2. Soon the secret was revealed, and Giorgio, as usual, encouraged us, the Moroder team, to write songs to submit for the Ross project. I quickly came up with a nice little island sounding hook and verse pattern using a synthetic digital kalimba. I brought it to Zito and we came up with a chorus idea, then Joe Esposito, a long time Moroder associate, helped with the lyrics and came up with the title, "Touch by Touch." As usual, the deal with Giorgio was that he would keep the publishing rights and income. So with a song like "Touch by Touch," for example, having three writers, for every dollar I might get, Moroder gets three. Still, 16.67% of a song on a Diana Ross album is better than 100% of a song that isn't.

Not too long after that I found myself flying off to New York again to meet with Ms. Ross in a studio to find the right keys for some of the songs. It was pretty exciting for me, as I have always loved her voice and her extraordinary poise and beauty. I even wore a coat and tie for the occasion, something I almost never do. I sat down at a piano in the studio with her and Giorgio next to me, and played one of the songs to find a key. I was a little nervous, and had to struggle with key transpositions a couple of times, and she had a little trouble with her voice and finding some notes. At one point she laughed graciously and said, "If only people out there in the world could see us fumbling around like this, what would they think!" We all laughed, and it helped release any nervous tension. She seemed to be a very classy lady in the best sense. When we were done, we gave her a cassette of the songs and flew back to L.A.

However, things were about to go downhill on the project, for Giorgio, anyway. After listening to the songs on the cassette, Ms. Ross called Giorgio and told him she didn't like any of them! She had a point; most of them were awful. I remember a particularly bad one called "The Captain of Love." He was sailing away, of course. Her rejection did not sit well with Moroder, who decided to forget the whole thing. She called back after a while and said that she did like one song, "Touch by Touch," the one I had written with the other guys. This was great news, a song on a Diana Ross album, how cool! Richie and I were hired by her record company to record master quality tapes. We laid down some killer tracks and sent them off to New York where she would record vocals and mix the song. So that Ms. Ross would have a guide vocal on tape for reference, we hired Beth Anderson to record a guide vocal track, too. Beth had an uncanny ability to imitate other singers, and she did a *perfect* Diana Ross imitation for us.

I did not hear the final version of the song until I got a copy of the album, *Swept Away,* upon its release. Ms. Ross had recorded a nice vocal which was note for note *exactly* the same as Beth's guide vocal down to the last detail. That was fine, but the mix left a lot to be desired. A look at the liner notes revealed that not only had Ms.

Ross failed to give us credit for playing the instruments and doing the arrangements, she took credit for *producing* the track! I actually complained to the record company about our missing credits. They said they were very, very sorry, and would absolutely fix that in the next issue of the album. Take a guess if that ever happened. Still, I got a song on a Diana Ross album and a gold record of it hanging on the wall. Over the years I have earned easily tens of dollars in royalties from it.

    Apparently she continued to like the song, because I found out years later from Walt Fowler (who played trumpet and keyboards in her band for a while) that it was part of their live show. I loved the idea of Walt playing my synth horn parts. I wish I could have heard that. I recently found out that in 1987 she hosted the American Music Awards on TV, and she opened the show with "Touch by Touch." How in the heck did I miss that? She seems to be singing to prerecorded tracks, which I can tell were the tracks we recorded for the album, edited and remixed. I also recently discovered that "Touch by Touch" was released as a single in Europe and elsewhere, and made it to #18 in Holland, which makes it the closest I ever came to writing a hit song. There are even some remixes of it, one by mixer Chris Lord Algee, who was a hot property at the time.

    Unfortunately, multi-millionaire producer Giorgio Moroder decided that since he was not going to produce Diana Ross, he didn't want to pay me for all the time I had put in recording the demos of his songs. Typically, with bad news, he had it delivered by his secretary, the same one I had to get past to even meet Giorgio. When I complained about not being paid for work I had done, she told me I was *nothing* before I worked with Giorgio. Funny, all these years later, it's the work I did with Zappa that has held its interest among fans. I hear from them all the time. I occasionally hear from fans interested in my work during the Moroder years, but much less so than the Zappa fans.

    This secretary told us that Giorgio would make it up to us by getting us more work, which was ridiculous. We were already working for him all the time. If something came along that Moroder needed us for, he'd call us. I think eventually, Giorgio's conscience must have caught up with him because a couple of months later he finally did pay me for at least some of the invoices I submitted for the Ross songs.

It turned out that the big reward for Richie and me was a gig doing some music for the worst movie you've never seen, a Canadian film that was a cheap imitation of *Flashdance* called *Heavenly Bodies*. It was about a "dancercise" studio with lots of sexy dancing done to throbbing 80's music. We did some underscore, and wrote a few songs that were sung by The Tubes, Bonnie Pointer, Joe Lamont and Dwight Twilley. We even flew up to San Francisco to produce the Tubes song at Fantasy studio, which, given their egos and "lifestyle," turned out to be a fairly unpleasant experience.

The whole business side of the deal was being run through the Moroder organization, so his secretary was handling all the billing for our time and for studio time. I never learned the details, but she must have engaged in some "creative" bookkeeping. We worked with a pair of Hollywood music supervisors on the project who came around to Oasis once in a while. When we were done, we were hit with a written complaint from these guys citing a bunch of overcharges for our time and the studio time! I can assure you that I certainly never submitted any billing for work I did not do – that's not my style. So, was this how I was going to be compensated for underpaying me on the Ross project? I would have rather taken the loss of money than the tarnishing of my reputation. I doubt if Giorgio knew about the actions of his staff in this incident. I can't believe he would have approved.

Various sessions continued in the fall, and by October, it was back to work on *Breakfast Club* with Keith and Steve Schiff in Studio B at Oasis. My records show that I worked on several other projects that I don't even recall doing, like "American Dream Come True," "The Touch," and Darwin Hastings. Who was that? I don't know, but they are all in my invoice book. I was so busy these projects got wiped from my memory, I guess.

Around this time I found myself in the middle of arranging a great "meeting of the minds" event. Zappa was one of the first people in L.A. to buy one of the brand new $90,000 Sony 24-track DASH digital audio recorders. It was a reel to reel machine that allowed physical editing of the tape with a razor blade, just like an analog machine. Some time in mid-1984 or so, Frank bought one and began recording with it. He loved it because he could edit to his heart's delight, something he really seemed to enjoy. Moroder was always trying to stay on the cutting edge of technology, so he asked me if I could arrange for him to go up to Frank's house to see his new machine. Frank said it would be fine to bring Giorgio over, so one day Giorgio and I went to the Zappa home in Laurel Canyon. We were greeted at the door by engineer Bob Stone, I think, and went into the studio control room. Bob, or whoever it was, promptly disappeared, and we sat there and waited, and waited, for about a half hour. While we were waiting Giorgio noticed the drums set up in the studio drum booth, and the king of the drum machine made a little joke. He pointed to the drums and said, "What are those things?" Finally Frank showed up and said, "Oh, I didn't realize you were down here waiting. I thought the engineer was here with you." Frank showed us the machine, said he loved it, and that was about it. We thanked him and left. There was no great rapport or anything like that. Frank had warned me about those great star meetings. He told me he had gone out to dinner with David Bowie one time. He said it was totally boring, that they had little in common, and really had nothing much to say to each other.

In October 1984, Giorgio was attending the Audio Engineering Society's convention in New York, where Sony was showing off these new machines. He called me from New York to ask me if Zappa still liked his Sony. I said that he did, as far as I knew. Giorgio came home with two of the $90,000 machines! We recorded everything digitally at Oasis after that. He soon bought a third one, so all three studios at Oasis were fully digital.

Earlier in the year, Martha Davis, the singer, songwriter, and leader of The Motels had approached Moroder about producing her next album. He was not interested, but suggested she use Zito instead. Based on Moroder's recommendation (and the fact that Zito had gotten co-production credit on the Berlin songs, no doubt), Richie got the gig and hired me to do some keyboards and bass for the project. However, because the Motels were a real band, my participation proved to be a bit awkward. Apparently they made a deal with Richie that the Motels would hire him to produce, but the guys in the band would actually get to play on their own album this time. It seemed that a previous producer had used studio musicians instead of the band, and the guys in her band were not too happy about that. Richie didn't really want to use her band, either. He wanted to do it with me the way we had done the Giorgio stuff, but a compromise was found. It turned out to be a combo of the band and me doing the work. I got credit for - you guessed it – "additional synthesizer programming" and fretless bass on "Icy Red." I also did a few sessions produced by Zito for America of "Horse With No Name" fame, including a song I liked called "Special Girl" for their album *Perspective*. And so ended my 1984, except for one little thing: I found and rented a space in Mar Vista which I turned into a recording studio I called Lotek. Incredibly, I still have the studio going as of this writing, which is taking place right here in the Lotek control room.

Chapter Fourteen

Things did not let up as 1985 came in with a roar. I was back at Oasis on January 2nd to record a remake of Giorgio's classic chase theme from *Midnight Express*. This was a 1978 film about a young American hash smuggler who got busted in Turkey. It was one of the earliest synthesizer music soundtracks for a movie. Giorgio won his first Academy Award for Best Original Score with it, and it is quite good. I think that he wanted to use the chase theme for some kind of release, but did not have the rights to use the original recording. Those would probably have been retained by the film company, so it may have been easier to just record a whole new version. I am not sure what he intended to do with that track, but I did a YouTube search and found both the original and the version I did. Mine was part of a compilation called *Synthesizer Greatest*. It turns out that the chase theme was a minor hit. The difference in sound quality is immediately obvious to me when I hear them both. It was funny to see comments about how it was just the best music ever, although it was really my version, not the original. I continue to be amazed at all the things I am learning about my own career in doing the research for this book.

All this work on movies had developed a strong relationship between the Moroder camp, Universal Pictures, and their record company, MCA. Oasis was conveniently located just down the street from Universal Studios, on Lankershim, a bit north of where Lankershim and Cahuenga intersect. MCA had recently signed Charlie Sexton, a talented sixteen year-old kid from Austin, Texas. He played guitar and sang, and had movie star good looks in a Matt Dillon kind of a way. They hired Keith Forsey to produce him, and Keith hired me. Charlie and I hit it off pretty well. I think it helped that we had a Texas connection. I had a long talk with Charlie one night in which he told me how eager he was to make a forward looking, modern album. Being from Texas and having learned guitar from Stevie Ray and Jimmy Vaughn, he felt a lot of Texas pressure to do the same old bluesy, rockabilly stuff that Austin is known for. It took some brass and foresight for him to want to go in a new direction. If anyone down in Texas ever thought that MCA pressured him into making a record he didn't want to make, they would be mistaken.

We got to work on Charlie's first album on January 5th at beautiful Conway studios in Hollywood. The next week we moved into Giorgio's Oasis studios. This project, which became Charlie's first full length album, *Pictures for Pleasure*, became pretty much my full time job for the next three weeks. I was proud of the work I did for Keith and Charlie, but in spite of considerable promotion by MCA, the album didn't do as well as expected. It reached #15 in the Billboard album chart, and the single from the album, "Beat's So Lonely" made it to #17 in the Hot 100. Not that bad, really, but less than hoped for. I'll get back to Charlie in a later chapter.

On the days I was not in the studio with Charlie, I was busy at my studio in Mar Vista on the minor remodeling and adaptation of the space into a studio. No major reconstruction was needed, so I was able to hire some friends to do the job. Among them was a slide guitar master, none other than Denny Wally himself. Thanks, Denny; the place is still standing. It was a lot of fun to shop for the equipment I needed for the studio. For the first time, I felt like I could afford to spend a little on some pro audio stuff. All this activity, along with a variety of sessions, kept me busy through January. The heady times continued.

I suppose this is as good a place as any to insert a few words about lifestyle in the recording scene at that time in L.A. The record companies seemed to have plenty of money to spend on making records and some productions could get pretty lavish. And being the 1980's, a lot of white powder was being shoved up a lot of noses. Though the record companies could get pretty stingy when it came to paying musicians, there seemed to be a bottomless well of dollars for equipment rentals. As luck would have it, there was a guy who had some gear to rent out who was also a coke dealer. He might charge $1000.00 a week to rent a piece of gear which was worth maybe $800.00, but it came with a gram of blow as a bonus. So the record company, which ultimately meant the artist if the album ever recouped, was providing the chemical entertainment. What a tidy little system.

Again, examining my datebook from this time reminds me of things I had forgotten, and even things that I have no recollection of whatsoever. Working on the song "Jealous" with Berlin falls into the latter category. I found an entry on February 11th, 1985 that says, "2: - 6: Phil Oakey, 6: - 5: Berlin - Jealous." This means I worked from 2 p.m. to 6 p.m. for Moroder, then 6 p.m. to 5 *a.m.* on a song called "Jealous" with Berlin. The title rang absolutely no bells, so I went to the web, and sure enough, there was a song by that title in a movie called *Just One of the Guys*. I listened to the track, and remembered the song right away and could tell immediately it was my kinds of sounds. I still, however, have no recollection of anything about doing it, though judging by the schedule, it must have been done at Oasis. Maybe I don't recall anything because it was one of those good old 15 hour work days, with the next 6 days being nearly identical in schedule; 14 and 13.5 hour days on the same two projects, and some work on a song for a singer Giorgio was trying to promote. That can fry your memory.

The Phil Oakey sessions grew out of the hit that he and Giorgio had with the soundtrack song "Together in Electric Dreams," from the movie *Electric Dreams*. It was the start of work on a duet album titled simply *Philip Oakey and Giorgio Moroder*. Giorgio conceived it as a continuous segue of songs without breaks, like a long medley, all to the same "four on the floor" disco drum beat. That was an unusual approach for us and not common at the time. Zito was less involved on this project, so I was left to my own devices more than usual, which I really enjoyed.

Because of Giorgio's citizenship situation, he had to leave the U.S. every so often. That time came in mid-February as we were deep into work on the Moroder/Oakey project. Giorgio did not want to stop the progress on it, so he flew engineer Brian Reeves and me to Europe to keep working on it there. On February 26th, we flew TWA to Zurich, where Giorgio was staying.

As I mentioned, Giorgio really knew how to live the rich guy lifestyle. The hotel where we stayed in Zurich was the Dolder Grand, a beautiful five star hotel on top of Adlisburg mountain, an absolutely gorgeous location. Apparently, Giorgio stayed there fairly often, because he kept a car parked in a garage at the hotel: a green Rolls Royce, complete with a driver for whenever he might be staying there! Talk about the lap of luxury, baby. We were in Zurich for just four days, recording at Powerplay studios, before heading for Munich. But while we were still in Zurich, Brian and I hit the town to celebrate my birthday. We had quite a bit to drink, and as we were walking down one of the cobblestone streets late at night, laughing and having fun, I gave Brian a good natured slap on the back. Unfortunately, it sent him crashing face down on the pavement, giving him a bloody face. He bled a lot, making it look far worse than it turned out to be. But still, I felt terrible. Giorgio got a good laugh out of it when he saw Brian as we crawled into the Rolls the next day. Sorry, Brian.

In Munich we worked at Musicland, the studio Giorgio had established in the late 1960's where numerous big stars had recorded, including Donna Summer, Queen, The Rolling Stones, Led Zeppelin, Elton John, and ELO, to name a few. The main engineer/producer there was Reinhold Mack. It was located in the basement of the Arabella high rise, which also housed the hotel where we stayed. It was interesting to see Moroder's original digs. It closed in the early 90's due to train noise from a new subway. We worked there only three days before heading home.

As for the Oakey/Moroder music itself, I always wondered whether Giorgio was really that into the project. He didn't supervise much, and seemed to just want to have it be finished as soon as possible. I never worked so fast in my life as on that album - we were cranking it out like sausage. I thought the songs were not up to Giorgio's usual standard. On top of that, the concept of having a lot of songs strung together with the same beat at the same tempo sounded like it could be a good idea, but after a while it gets to be wearing. Also, Phil's vocal style is so flat emotionally that it's hard to engage the listener for long. The whole idea of the project came from Virgin Records in an attempt to capitalize on the success of "Together in Electric Dreams." Unfortunately, the other singles from the album turned out to be duds. Nonetheless, I have had many people tell me they think the album is really great. I even met an engineer who used it to test studio listening systems because of how punchy it sounds. Like Zappa once told me, "There's no accounting for taste."

Giorgio stayed in Europe for a few more weeks, so there was no work with him for a while. My Mar Vista studio was functional by then, and the time off from Moroder gave me a chance to use it a bit. I had become good friends with Steve Schiff, who was flying high off his #1 hit song from *Breakfast Club,* "Don't You Forget About Me." He and I began writing songs together fairly often which helped me test out the studio and make sure everything was working properly.

One of the first clients at the studio was Peter Bergman of Firesign Theater fame. He was not there to do comedy, however. He had been hired to record his "serious" voice for some kind of automated phone answering system. We had to record every conceivable answer to questions that might be posed by a caller. It was tedious, but I was thrilled to meet and work with another one of my heroes. From the moment he opened his mouth, I was impressed by what a strong, professional voice he had. He had the training and experience to speak loudly, clearly, and articulately, so recording him was a piece of cake. There were many other fine artists who made their way to my studio over the years, and having Peter Bergman as one of the first felt like it got Lotek off to a good start.

In mid-March of 1985, I got a call from Michael Goldstone, who was the A&R (artists and repertoire) guy who signed Charlie Sexton to MCA records. Michael told me that Universal was going to re-release the 1954 film *The Glenn Miller Story*, and wanted to do some kind of modern remix of a Miller song to help promote the re-release. He thought I would be just the person who could do the project justice, and asked if I would be interested in helping him out. He indicated that he was under some pressure from "upstairs" to come up with something quick. At first, I was reluctant. It was hard for me to imagine how I might adapt a swing era sound to the 1980's dance sound he wanted, but of course, I said yes, mainly because Michael really seemed to need me to do it. It was left to me to choose which tune to do. I decided on the Glenn Miller hit "In The Mood." I had permission to sample anything I wanted to use, and was provided with a high quality tape copy of the original Miller recordings.

I did the prep work here at my studio, then recorded the master tracks on one of the still new 24-track Sony digital machines at Oasis Studio B, with the fabulous Dave Concors engineering. I decided to use a triplet feel with four on the floor similar to the 1979 version of "Knock on Wood" by Amii Stewart, or "Why Me" by Irene Cara that I had done with Moroder when I first started working with him. I used a combination of analog synths and samples from the original, and got Schifty to come down and lay down a smokin' crazy guitar solo. It turned out really great, and I have heard from people all over the world who love it, even though it didn't sell a lot of copies.

By the way, when I mixed, I used a little trick I learned from Giorgio, who was really very clever at times. We left two of the twenty-four tracks unused on the Sony digital multi-track recorder, then mixed onto those two tracks instead of mixing to a separate two-track machine. So instead of automating the mix, we simply started recording the mix at the beginning of the tune on the open tracks and mixed along until we wanted to change something, rewind, and then punched-in the whole stereo mix, continuing this process to the end of the song. You can't do that on an analog machine, because you get a sort of feedback screech sometimes bouncing to adjacent tracks, and the punch-ins are not as clean as on the digital machines which do little cross fades at punches. Once we were done mixing, we transferred it to a two-track and that was it. Of course, now that everything is done on computers, none of this information is of much use, but I am including it for the audiophiles who might enjoy knowing about how things were done back then.

Another technique that Moroder used that I thought was very cool was his twenty-four tracks of voices tape. He had created a 2" analog master tape that had twenty-four tracks of his voice on each of *its* twenty-four tracks, singing "ah," spanning two octaves and looped together to create a continuous "ah" chorus of voices. He would figure out what notes he needed to create the chords he wanted and assigned those tracks to "groups" on the console, meaning that all the tracks assigned to a given group would come up on a fader elsewhere on the mixing console. He could then "play" the lush sound of the voices by pushing up the group faders with the right chords at the right time. Pretty clever, I thought.

Donna Summer re-appeared on the Giorgio scene in May 1985, and I worked with her for a few days on some demos. Donna and Giorgio were going to try to work together again, but it never happened. It was a bit uncomfortable being with her, because she was an enthusiastic born-again Christian by then, and seemed pretty self-righteous about it. Maybe the project fell through because it was around that time that she allegedly made some anti-gay comments about AIDS being God's punishment for homosexuals. This took a big toll on her career and it never really recovered. She sure could sing, though.

I had heard a few stories about Donna from some of the guys who had worked with her back in her heyday with Giorgio. Being a writer/producer, Giorgio was very much in control of his projects from start to finish. All he needed from the singer was to record the vocals when the time came, and that was it – bye-bye, singer, you're done. That seemed to be a perfect match for Donna, because she apparently had very little patience in the recording studio. Lyricist Pete Bellotte told a story about the recording of the top ten hit "On the Radio." There is a verse in the song where she just sings "la-la" instead of lyrics. In fact, there were lyrics written for that verse. Supposedly, she simply had not turned the page in time to sing them. When Pete asked her to go back and sing the verse with the actual lyrics, she declined, saying she didn't have the time and had to go! They left it that way, and it was still a hit. Just goes to show you something, I guess. I know that she is credited for the lyrics, but that's the story Bellotte told me, I swear. This is pure speculation, but maybe Donna had written the first page of lyrics, and Pete had written the second. By "not having the time" to do the second page, it ensured that she would get all the lyric writing credit.

May of 1985 brought another Oakey/Moroder session, more sessions with The Motels, and an increasing amount of time spent writing with Steve Schiff. Schifty and I did come up with a few good songs, but we spent an awful lot of time fiddling with effects and other fun studio trickery. For the amount of time we spent in the studio, there was not a whole lot to show for it. This was about to change dramatically.

In June, Steve called me about a TV show he was working on for Universal called *Misfits of Science*, which would be aired on NBC. He had written a theme song for the show with film composer Basil Poledouris called "Science, Straight From the Heart." Universal was very happy with the theme song, and asked Steve and Basil to do the music for the 90 minute pilot episode. They got me involved in the writing, playing, and production, and in the process, I learned a lot about film and television scoring from Basil.

It was really a privilege to work with Basil, who was a "real" film composer, having written many orchestral scores for film and television, including The *Blue Lagoon*, *Conan the Barbarian*, and *Red Dawn*. He certainly knew what he was doing, and was very generous about sharing his vast knowledge. He taught me crucial things about how to calculate click tracks to make all the "hits" sync up to the picture the right way. That process was very complicated back then, unlike now when it is easy to use a computer to line things up. But certain basic principles will always be true, and have come in handy over the years, like the practice of never having the sound come before the visual when things are supposed to line up. If it has to be a bit off, the sound should always come a little late, not early.

Misfits was an hour long show about a group of young researchers who had various super powers. I thought it was a cute show, and the cast included the late Dean Paul Martin, the son of Dean Martin (and Dino of Dino, Desi, and Billy) and Courtney Cox in her first TV role. Dean was a really nice guy. We got to work with him in my studio where we were doing the music. He sang a few songs in the show, including "Hit the Road, Jack." The songs were recorded before the filming so the actors could lip sync to the pre-recorded music played through speakers on the set. Sadly, Dean, who was a pilot in the California Air National Guard, died in 1987 when his F-4 Phantom crashed into a hillside in a snow storm. Though I knew him only a little, I was shocked and saddened when I heard the news.

By July we were in full swing working on the pilot episode. The working habits of Steve and me had to change, and drastically. There was no more time for fiddling about, we had work to do, and tons of it. It was an exciting new challenge.

We soon got word that the show had been signed to do at least a few episodes. Basil, however, had other obligations, and after doing the pilot, he had to leave the project. Schifty and I were on our own, just a couple of rock musicians who had never given a thought to composing TV music doing a major network show. Luckily, we would not be doing *all* the music. It would be divided between us and Jeff Sturges, another North Texas guy, who was already an experienced up and coming TV composer.

But before we got started, I became involved with what turned out to be one of my favorite songs from the Moroder years. Zito had been hired to produce a song for a new movie called *9½ Weeks* starring Kim Basinger and Mickey Rourke. It was a Randy Newman song called "You Can Leave Your Hat On," and it was to be sung by Joe Cocker. I love Randy Newman, and this song ranks up there among my favorites of his. Zito had worked with Randy before as a guitar player, and said that Randy actually did not like to write music. Whereas most songwriters would write at least a dozen songs when they needed ten for an album, Randy would write exactly ten, and that was it. However he wrote, it sure worked for me. We did a killer arrangement of the song complete with a very cool sliding bass part I came up with. And of course, Joe did a great job on the vocals. I have to hand it to Zito for a top notch producing job on that track. I recall hearing it on the radio as I was driving down Sunset Boulevard one day, and was really stoked, as they say here in California. It made it to #35 on the Billboard Hot Mainstream Rock Tracks, and I have to admit, it's kind of fun to watch Kim Basinger strip to music I'm playing.

By the end of September, Schifty and I were in full panic work mode on *Misfits*. There was an incredible amount of work to be done, with rock hard deadlines. There is *no* turning in music late when you are doing a weekly TV show. Of course, the music was always the last thing to be done, so that didn't help. We would be given a VHS tape of the episode with instructions about which cues (pieces of music underscore) we were to do. For the first few episodes, we would sit down and watch the whole hour long tape to get the gist of the story before we started. Pretty soon we just skipped that step and bought a TV Guide magazine to read the synopsis, then get to work. That's how tight it was – we got the tape and the TV Guide on Monday, and it was aired that Friday!

In addition to the cues Steve and I did at my studio, I did *Misfits* sessions for Jeff Sturges over at Universal, because Jeff wanted my sounds in his cues to keep the consistency of sound between his music and ours. Unfortunately, his sessions were sometimes at 8:00 a.m., which sucked, because Steve and I often worked till 3 or 4 or 5 a.m.! I was beat when I got to the sessions, but I got through them all. I was pleasantly surprised to see Vinnie Colaiuta on one of them. It seemed that both of our careers were blossoming, and that felt good.

In October I somehow squeezed in a few other sessions. Among other things, Giorgio had written a song with Dean Pitchford for the Kevin Bacon movie *Quicksilver* called "Quicksilver Lightning," which was sung by Roger Daltry. I never got to meet Roger, I just worked on the tracks. Until I started doing the research for this book, I had completely forgotten about this song and "working with" Roger Daltry. It just goes to show how busy I was that I could forget about working on a song with one of The Who. It could also have been forgotten due to something else much more important and tragic that happened at that time, and surely pushed other events out of my memory.

On Wednesday, October 30, 1985, I was at Oasis working on the Quicksilver music for Giorgio, when my wife called, and told me to go to a private phone and sit down. I picked up the phone in the shop area; she told me that my brother Edward had just been killed in a motorcycle accident in San Antonio. It was like a knife in my heart, and I began to sob. He left behind a wife and two young sons. My mother was still alive to suffer this loss as well. I cancelled the sessions I had coming up and went to San Antonio for the funeral. It was the saddest moment of my life. I still miss him terribly. Fortunately, after some struggles and tough times, I am happy to say that both of my nephews Tommy and David, survived the tragedy intact and have grown up to be well adjusted, successful adults. R.I.P., Edward.

I flew back to L.A. on Sunday, November 3rd and went right back into my overloaded schedule on Monday. I think it was probably a good thing that I was so busy because it took my mind off of my brother. I worked seven days straight through, including rehearsals with Robby Krieger and a fundraising gig with him for Muscular Dystrophy at Calamigos Ranch on Sunday, the 10th. For the next month after that it would be all *Misfits* work, all the time.

In early December, I flew up to San Francisco to do some recording with Zito who was now producing Eddie Money. I was picked up at the airport by a nice young man from Eddie's management company. I admitted to him that other than "Two Tickets to Paradise," I was not familiar with Eddie's work. He gave me a classic reply, saying, "A lot of people don't realize it, but Eddie is a huge star," and he meant it sincerely! Richie's production career was now taking off, and this was a big deal for him. It turned out that there was some rock star behavior to put up with, though. I remember Money sitting in a studio lounge one day talking on a phone with a long enough coiled cable to reach across the room. When he was done talking, instead of getting up to hang up the phone, he just tossed the handset across the room in the general direction of the phone cradle. That is just one example. Oh well, I was getting paid, and one of the songs I did with him, "Take me Home Tonight," reached #4 on the Billboard Hot 100, and #1 on the Billboard Album Rock Tracks. Eddie claimed to hate the song, but Zito believed all along it had hit potential.

Basil Poledouris, the composer I'd worked with on the *Misfits of Science* pilot, liked my synth work and hired me to play on some real orchestra sessions for him including for the film *Iron Eagle,* and the TV show revival of *The Twilight Zone*. These sessions were pretty nerve wracking for me. There I was for the first time as a musician on a real, big time Hollywood film session, with a full orchestra comprised of the best players in town. I had a pretty complicated set up at that point. It included having to acquire a click track signal from the engineer patched over to my gear to sync up sequenced parts, which I would have to start on the fly at the right time, an iffy proposition at best. I had to find all the right sounds, and then sight read the sheet music, something that has never been a strong point for me. It didn't make it any easier that I felt a bit of coldness from the other musicians. They may have seen the coming wave of electronic sounds as a threat, which I personified. All in all, it was both an interesting challenge and a hairy experience, but I managed to do my parts, and I don't recall ruining a take with any screw ups. I also did a couple of sessions with fellow Texan Joe Ely, but other than that, it was full time *Misfits* TV music composing, arranging, performing, and engineering for the rest of 1985.

Chapter Fifteen

Misfits still was alive as 1986 began, but it was always just barely hanging on. Only a few episodes at a time were approved, but we plowed ahead. The ratings were never great, and they really went downhill once the show was competing with *Dallas* on CBS. In the middle of February, NBC decided to cancel "Misfits," and the last episode was never aired. We worked on a total of sixteen episodes.

I got to have a good time on January 8th. It was Robby Krieger's 40th birthday, and he had a big wingding at The Whisky a Go Go night club on the Sunset Strip where the Doors had played so many times in their heyday. There were musical instruments set up, and I had the privilege of playing bass on some Doors songs with Robby, Ray Manzarek, and John Densmore – all the remaining original Doors. I was standing next to Ray on stage and to my great surprise, he couldn't remember the chords to a lot of the songs. I found myself calling out the chord changes for "Lost Little Girl" to him as we played it there on stage at the Whisky! I learned later from Robby that Ray always had a hard time memorizing the songs, and even in recent years when Robby and Ray were frequently playing Doors songs together, he always had a little cheat sheet with the chords to some of the songs. I should hasten to add, however, that this in no way diminishes my respect and admiration for Mr. Manzarek. Sadly, Ray died on May 20th, 2013. His death is a great loss.

At the end of February, I did a Veterans of Foreign War (VFW) benefit with Krieger at the L.A. Forum in Inglewood. This is yet another event that I had completely forgotten about until I saw it in my 1986 datebook. Robby recalls doing the gig with drummer Bruce Gary from The Knack. I am starting to have some recollection of it so, I guess it really did happen.

I also got another call from Michael Goldstone at MCA Records around that time. Goldie, as he was known, had been very pleased with the work I had done on "In the Mood" and the Charlie Sexton album. He asked me if I would be interested in doing a 12" re-mix of one of Charlie's songs, "Impressed." Even though I did not consider myself a re-mix engineer, I was ready to take on the challenge, so of course I said yes. I booked Giorgio's studio, Oasis, and hired my favorite engineer, Dave Concors, to man the big SSL mixing console in studio A. We did a bunch of cool stuff with delays and other kinds of groovy "fairy dust" generators. I did not go the route of taking what is basically a rock song and putting a completely different dance beat to it, like so many mixers were prone to do. Instead, I extended and re-arranged the original version. I think it turned out well and is something I am proud of. Side two of the 45 rpm 12" was another re-mix of the same song by producer Steve Lilywhite.

    I'm sure glad I kept all these old datebooks, because they continue to amaze me about how many things I worked on that I forgot about. Here's another instance: I mentioned Amii Stewart's version of "Knock on Wood" as an example of the type of groove I used for my "In the Mood." I just saw in my 1986 datebook some sessions in March with her name, and found the invoices that matched. I did a bit of research on the internet, and sure enough, there is an album called *Amii* on which I played keyboards and bass. Half of the songs are produced by Giorgio, and Wikipedia lists Zito and me as musicians. Someone posted the songs on YouTube, and once I heard them I remembered playing on them. I actually liked a couple of the tracks, except that there is too much Yamaha DX7 digital synth bass used. (It was a new keyboard then and all the rage.) I am even featured playing some nice fretless bass licks. There is a song on the album called "Easy On My Love." It is a perfect example of one of Giorgio's latin-ish grooves I mentioned that is infused with the spirit of "Spooky" by the Classics IV. Usually, back in those days, if you played on a record, you got a free promotional copy of it, but in this case I never did. Maybe that's one of the reasons I forgot about it.

    March also brought another big movie Giorgio's way that would end up making him a ton of money; the Tom Cruise film *Top Gun*. I did not work on the score, but did play on Giorgio's songs. Not surprisingly, I didn't forget about these sessions. The movie soundtrack album was #1 for five weeks and sold more than ten million copies. I did arrangements and played keyboards on five of the songs. "Take My Breath Away," sung by Terri Nunn of Berlin, was a #1 single, winning the Academy Award and the Golden Globe for best original song in 1986. "Highway to the Danger Zone," sung by Kenny Loggins, made it to #2 in the charts. In addition to those songs, I also played on "Lead Me On" by Teena Marie, "Through the Fire" by Larry Greene, and "Destination Unknown" by Marietta Waters. Like the typical soundtrack album, I got no credit, of course. I have to admit that it pains me somewhat to know that my performance on the only #1 Oscar winning song I ever worked on is credited to Berlin, who had nothing to do with it except for Terri Nunn's voice. And that's not meant to take anything away from Terri who did a great job on the vocals.

It was an interesting experience working on "Take my Breath Away." Every instrument you hear on that recording is played by me except for guitar and drum machine, done by Zito. I used the DX7 for the imitation fretless bass sound, layers of analog synthesizers, and there is even a sample of my voice singing an "ah" sound in there. Everything was played by hand: there was no "sequencing" involved.

The fact that it was for a big budget movie is part of what made it interesting. First, Giorgio wrote the song, (Lyrics by Tom Whitlock, Giorgio's car mechanic and studio assistant. Lucky guy!) and we recorded it in a good key for the demo singer. The song then had to be submitted to the film studio for approval. Once approved, the search for the right singer was on. When a singer was being considered, an entirely new track would have to be created if the original key was not right for her. I recall doing about a half dozen versions of that song in different keys until it was finally decided that Terri Nunn would sing it for the film. I have never recorded a song in so many different keys! The process was the same for all the songs for the movie, though "Take My Breath Away" is the only one I recall doing in so many different keys. I once asked Zito about how it was decided who would be chosen to sing a given song, and he replied, "Basically, you start with The Beatles and you work your way down." Well put, Richie.

Like Giorgio, Richie had a good sense of humor. I recall one day working on a track with him when I came up with an idea that was perhaps a bit too adventurous for a pop song. Richie said, "Wow, that's a great idea! You should save it for your solo album."

At the same time the *Top Gun* sessions were going on, Steve Schiff got a call about doing some music for another TV show, a spin off of the teen movie *Fast Times at Ridgemont High* called *Fast*

Times. It was not a successful show, and we only worked on one or two episodes, but one of them featured none other than then budding actress Moon Unit Zappa in a big role. The Zappa coincidences just wouldn't stop.

I also did some Moroder work for the dystopian glam punk band Sigue Sigue Sputnik. Giorgio had produced a #3 song in the U.K. for them called "Love Missile F1-11," but there were some samples from the film *A Clockwork Orange* used in that version that did not have copyright clearance. It was my job to re-create those samples with new sounds for the U.S. release. We also did a 12" re-mix of the song. It was odd to be working on what is basically a U.S. military propaganda movie like *Top Gun* and this seemingly anti-American band at exactly the same time. I say seemingly, because I think they were just some shock-value oriented, misguided blokes who liked *A Clockwork Orange* a bit too much.

In April I got a call from MCA about doing another 12" re-mix, this time it would be an Oingo Boingo song called "Stay." It's a good song, but once again it was a rock song, not a dance song, and so was not a good candidate for a re-mix, in my opinion. But they asked me to do it, and I wasn't going to say no, so of course I said yes. I recall having one or two phone conversations with Danny Elfman, the main Boingo guy, about musical direction, but I was mostly left to my own ideas. I holed up in Oasis Studio A with engineer Dave Concors and we did justice to the song, I think. I seemed to be moving up in the world of producers, but not really in the direction of my strong suit. I am better at working on projects from the beginning, doing the music arrangement work, gladly letting someone else do the mixing chores.

In July, I started work as producer for a band called The Pink Fence. Herein lies a cautionary tale of the first order. They were naive young guys who were very much into the British pop sound of the day, and they had won a "Battle of the Bands" contest sponsored by MCA and local radio station KROQ. The winner was awarded a contract with MCA to record a five song EP album. The MCA guys called me to see if I would be interested in producing the EP and of course, I said yes. I was happy to have something sent my way that was more up my alley than doing 12" re-mixes, and I liked the band's songs.

We started pre-production in July at my studio, but we were not able to work full time because I was still busy with other sessions. After a couple of months of recording and mixing, we finished a very cool set of five songs, all very current sounding and yet innovative. Unfortunately, the guys at MCA who had made the agreement with KROQ had been fired, and as usual in the music business, their replacements didn't care about their predecessors' projects. The record never came out. I couldn't believe it. How could that be? They won a contest hosted by KROQ, a major L.A. radio station, to put out a record, for Christ's sake! But of course the contract favored the record label in every possible way, so the thing was never released. I think the label was able to get away with it because the winner of the contest got a recording contract, not a guarantee of a release. The label always retains the right to cancel a release, and when they do, it's *poof*, no record.

It turns out, this scenario happened all the time in the record business. There seemed to be a more or less fixed number of A&R people, each of whom might last for a short time at one label, get fired, then hired by another label, and around and around it went, like a game of musical chairs. The new A&R person didn't care about the artists signed by the previous A&R person, so too bad for the artists.

And so, the moral of this story is: don't enter a battle of the bands contest, and for heaven's sake, don't win one.

In October, another production gig came Zito's way and he hired me to play keyboards on the project. It was special to me, because it was for Gregg Rolie, who had been the singer and organ player in the original Santana, singing lead and playing the ultra-cool B3 solo on the band's first hit "Evil Ways" in 1969. Gregg seemed like a very nice guy, a real gentleman. I recall distinctly learning his B3 solo on my father's Hammond organ and trying to get just the right settings for that great sound. It felt odd to be doing the keyboards for a player whose work I had cut my teeth on. It seemed like an upside down world again, like when I was calling out the chords of Doors songs to Ray Manzarek. And, of course, it was another one of those funny coincidences since his big hit song "Evil Ways" was the basis for Zappa's "Variations on the Carlos Santana Secret Chord Progression." The tunes I worked on came out on Gregg's album *Gringo* in 1987, replete with Vinnie Colaiuta on several tracks. For some reason, I never got a copy of this album, either. I am listening to it on YouTube for the first time right now as I write this. Not too bad, I'd say. I think "One of These Days" is a good, strong, 80's pop song.

At the end of the year, I got a call from MCA again, this time from Steve Moir, an A&R guy. He had signed a band called Taxxi and asked me if I wanted to produce an album for them. Of course I said yes, and was glad to have another shot at producing. There was even a budget of $100,000 to work with. They were an English rock band with some really good songs, and by January 1987 we got to work, recording some of the tracks in my studio, and using bigger rooms for drums and other things. We ended up with a strong and solid rock album.

Taxxi provides another perfect example of record company stupidity. Even though we had a decent budget, MCA refused to pay the band members *anything* for recording the album. The band was based in the bay area at the time, and though MCA paid to get them down here and put them up at The Oakwood Apartments for several weeks, they wouldn't actually *pay* them directly for their work. The band asked me to see what I could do about it, and I ended up in an upstairs office at Universal with one of the money guys. This guy told me to have the band send in rental bills for their instruments and equipment, and MCA would pay them for that, no problem. I couldn't believe the guy in the business office was telling me to do this, as if it was no big deal. I wanted the band to get some money, so we went ahead and did it, giving the band barely enough money for food.

Alas, this poor band was yet another victim of the record company game of musical chairs. In a situation similar to the Battle of the Bands winners, Steve Moir, the A&R guy who signed Taxxi, was fired from MCA. His replacement didn't care about the band, so the album was never released. The band had always jokingly referred to MCA as "Music Cemetery of America," even before they were carted off to the mortuary.

The same thing happened with another MCA artist I was working with. It turns out that Max Gronenthal, the keyboard player I met in 1977 on the Swedish tour, was signed as an MCA artist, going by the stage name of Max Carl. We wrote some songs together, and co-produced an album together, even recruiting

Colaiuta for some drum tracks. We produced a really good album together when, *poof*, it was musical chairs again, and our work would never see the light of day. That made three in a row, not an encouraging start to my career as a producer.

Zito's production career was still zipping right along, though. I did a few sessions on some songs he was producing for Kenny Loggins at Village Recorders, the same studio where *Joe's Garage* was recorded. Back in those days, it was common to smoke in the studio control room, and Richie was a very heavy smoker. Kenny couldn't stand the smoke, so he had an oxygen mask sent to the studio. When I saw him, he was on a massage table getting rubbed by his personal masseuse with a plastic oxygen mask over his face. I don't recall anything else about him, but that image is seared into my brain. I played on "Tell Her" from the *Back to Avalon* album.

On February 5th, 1987, I went up to Frank's house for the first time in a while. I am not positive, but I'm pretty sure this was the time I brought my old friend Tom Brown with me, providing the hard-core Zappa fan with a dream come true experience. Frank was very polite to him, even including him in our conversation, I am happy to say. Frank had invited me up to the house to talk about hiring me for an exciting new project he was working on. He was on the verge of getting his own late night TV show, which he wanted to call *Nite School*. It was to be a humorous, politically oriented talk show, along the lines of what John Stewart eventually did. Frank wanted to have a house band, and wanted me to be the band leader and musical director. He also told me to start brushing up on current events, because he wanted the band to throw out questions to the guests. I was ecstatic about the idea. What could be more perfect? I would get to be working with Frank again, my true musical love, without having to be on the road all the time. A gig like that would have paid quite well, too. But like so many of Frank's great ideas, this one never came to be. My guess is that the TV execs got cold feet.

In June I received a call from Steve Moir, the A&R man who had recently been fired from MCA. He was the guy who hooked me up with the ill-fated Taxxi project. There was a trend in the music biz at that time of producers having managers just like artists did. There was some guy who was one of the first to start managing producers and engineers, and soon had a lot of the big names in his camp. Zito had signed with him, which was part of the reason his production career was going so well. Moir had decided not to try to get an A&R gig at another label, but instead would get into this new game and start his own producer/engineer management company. He wanted to know if I would be interested in signing with him as one of his first clients. I had always liked Steve. Compared with your average record company executive, he was seemed like one of the good guys, so I decided to sign with him and see what happened. He would be keeping a percentage of everything I earned, whether he found the gigs for me or not. This proved to work to his advantage when it came to my session work, since most of the money I earned while signed with him were recording gigs that he had not found for me. I would have had those sessions anyway, no manager needed. To his credit, he did find me a couple of low budget recording projects.

One gig he found for me was some mixing and producing with an all-girl band called The Pandoras. They had been signed to Elektra Records by a very nervous guy who had also signed a glam metal band called Jetboy. Probably the main reason he was so nervous was that he had made the mistake of becoming romantically involved with Paula Pierce, the lead singer and main songwriter of The Pandoras. Paula was quite talented and the band had some good songs. Sadly, she died of an aneurism at age 31 in 1991. She was obsessed with being thin, and exercised as much as she could. I was told she died on her exercycle.

My favorite Pandoras song was "Run Down Love Battery," which I thought was clever in a crude kind of way. Unfortunately, by the time the band got to me, they had almost no budget left, and we had to record at my studio. At the time, my place was good for synth work, but I did not have much of a microphone selection, and my main recorder was a half-inch 16-track Fostex, which is not really a good machine for drums or bass. Even so, the recordings came out pretty well. But once again, their A&R guy was fired before the album came out, so of course, The Pandoras and Jetboy were dumped by Elektra. Musical chairs again! It was the fourth time this had happened on a project I had worked on. Was I jinxed or something?

In August, I got a call about playing piano on a song or two with Charlie Sexton. MCA was not thrilled with the first Sexton album that Keith Forsey produced, and was considering having country songwriter Steve Earle produce Charlie's second album. We recorded at the famed Capitol Records studio, which was always a thrill. I played acoustic piano, and the song turned out all right, but I thought Earle was a very odd and poor choice of producer for Charlie. It just didn't make sense to me to have a country guy produce Charlie, who was decidedly not country. Steve seemed like a nice guy and we got along well, both being Texans and all that, but he did not end up producing Charlie.

Moir got me a gig doing some demos for a two man band from Dallas called DDT. Island Records was interested in them and provided a small budget to make some demos. These guys were into sampling and hip-hop using ugly, pulsating sounds. Neither one of them was a musician who played an actual instrument. One of their songs was titled "Turgid Noise" which was an apt description of their sound. One guy, Dave, did all the technical stuff with the noises and samples, and the other guy didn't seem to do much except be cool and romance the female A&R rep from Island who was "interested" in the band. Other than paying some bills, nothing good came of that project. Sadly, Dave later died of a drug overdose.

My new manager also hooked me up as producer for a local ska band called The Untouchables. They had been a very popular live band in the early 80's, and were one of the first U.S bands do adopt the ska sound. They were a great live band, but there were no strong songwriters or singers in the band. Jerry, the quintessential Untouchable, was more of a front man than a singer. They were not signed to a real label and had almost no budget; there was no choice but to record at my studio on the Fostex. So, we had no songs, no singer, and no chance of getting a first rate recording. The album did come out, barely, on their own label, Twist Records. Although I did the best I could under the circumstances, the album wasn't as good as it could have been and went nowhere.

Probably the best thing Moir did for me was to suggest that Charlie Sexton and I try to write some songs together. Things had not worked out with Steve Earle producing him, but Charlie was continuing to write and record some songs at his house in Hollywood. Goldie was still his A&R rep at MCA. He had shopped some of Charlie's new songs around to all the big name record producers, but based on what they heard of the songs, all of them passed on taking the job. Charlie and I had always gotten along, and he welcomed the opportunity to collaborate. We began to work together in October 1987 at my studio. We got off to a good start right away. I had an idea for a song with strong, strumming acoustic guitar part for the intro and verse. He dug it, so we worked on it and soon had a very cool song called "Save Yourself." We quickly recorded a killer demo version of it that really rocked. When Goldie heard it he just about went nuts, he loved it so much. We wrote a couple of other good songs that he liked, too, and gave him a tape with three songs we had written and I had produced: "Save Yourself," "For All We Know," and "Seems So Wrong." Goldie liked them all. This was great news for me.

But it was about to get even better. Goldie said he wanted me to produce Charlie's next album! This was just what I had been hoping for. Finally, something I could really sink my teeth into from the start of the project, collaborating with an artist I liked, and who showed a lot of promise. In addition to being an artist and a singer Charlie is a very good guitar player. (He went on to be Bob Dylan's guitar player for many years.) It could not have been more perfect from my point of view. I was ecstatic. It seemed almost too good to be true.

In the meantime, I did another mix for MCA in December of a song called "Let Her Fall" by a British band called Then Jericho. I did the mix at Conway with super engineer Mick Guzauski and even had Charlie come and add some new guitar parts to the song. 1987 ended on a high note.

Chapter Sixteen

As I said, getting the chance to produce Charlie Sexton seemed too good to be true. Turns out that it was. As I was continuing to write and do intense, unpaid pre-production work with Charlie through January 1988, Goldstone was cooking up a little surprise for me behind my back. He had made copies of the tape of the new songs Charlie and I had written and was sending them to all the big name producers again! Lo and behold, big shot producer Bob Clearmountain suddenly became interested after having passed on the project before hearing the new songs. Because Clearmountain is more of an engineer than a musician, a musical co-producer was still needed, but it was decided that I was not the right guy even for that. They chose Tony Berg for the job, a guy no more qualified or experienced than me. As if that wasn't bad enough, Berg and I had the same manager, Steve Moir! What a slap in the face. When I confronted Moir about what a huge conflict of interest I thought this was, he just shrugged. I was beginning to think that my "manager" had just needed some warm bodies to get his new career as a producer manager going, and I happened to be handy.

The up side was that the three songs Charlie and I wrote were going to be on the album, though two of them, "For All We Know" and "Seems So Wrong" ended up with a third co-writer, the new co-producer, Tony Berg, for changing a word or two without even asking me if I liked the alterations. The lyric changes were unnecessary and not an improvement over what Charlie and I had originally written. A few months later, Charlie came by the studio to play me the new versions of our songs. "Save Yourself," the best song of the batch, was a disaster. They had not captured any of the intended vibe and it was totally lifeless compared to our demo. Moir did redeem himself somewhat by finding me a publishing deal. I heard the final mixes of the songs I had written with Charlie before the album was released. Once I heard the botched production Clearmountain and Berg had done, I knew the album would stiff. I got a pretty good advance selling part of my publishing on those songs, and I have never regretted that. The publishing company will probably never recoup my advance. The album, *Charlie Sexton*, peaked at #104 in the Billboard 200 after its release in 1989.

In February Keith Forsey called me about doing some demo work at my studio with Malcolm McClaren, the British inventor of the Sex Pistols. Though I never liked punk rock, I did enjoy some of the solo records McClaren made in the 80's like "Living on the Road in Soweto" with producer Trevor Horn. I was looking forward to working with him. I hate to say it, but I think the project with Keith was rather ill-conceived. He wanted to do the old song "Bird in a Gilded Cage" dance style, interspersed with samples from a Strauss waltz. But worst of all, it turned out that McClaren seemed to think he was some kind musical deity. He acted like I was a servant and even called me "boy" until I got in his face and told him "I have a name, and it's not 'boy,' it's Arthur. Don't *ever* call me 'boy' again." When we went out to the Fatburger for lunch every day, not once did he offer to pick up the tiny tab, always letting Keith or me pay the bill. He tried to rip me off, too. When we were done with the work, I sent an invoice to his company, aptly called "Swindle Incorporated," but got nothing for weeks. I finally had to call Keith and have him raise hell to get me paid for the work I did. I shed no tears when I heard that McClaren had failed to swindle death.

By the spring of 1988, it had already been five years since I had begun working with the Moroder camp, and the always fickle music business was changing. The synth power pop style that we did had gone out of fashion, and new styles like rap and grunge were taking over. My session work as a synth player had almost completely dried up. Except for a 12" remix of a cover of "I Know" by Marcela for the movie *Salsa*, all I had going was the ultra low budget production of the Untouchables album, and another one for a band called Red River. The summer pages of my 1988 datebook look mostly empty, compared to the densely covered ones from the preceding years.

But my luck would hold out for a little longer. In September I got a call from Keith Forsey about doing a couple of sessions for the new Billy Idol album he was producing. Those couple of sessions turned into doing almost the entire *Charmed Life* album, including the hit single "Cradle of Love" which reached #2 on the U.S. Billboard Hot 100 chart. The album also has a very cool track called "Prodigal Blues" that I am very proud of. It was great to be working with Keith again, this time with his biggest artist. At that time, Billy had mega-superstar status, so working with him was quite a feather in my cap.

The first batch of sessions took up most of the month of September, which happened to be a time when the planet Mars was about as near to Earth as it ever gets, and was clearly visible to the naked eye. I had been checking it out each night as it got closer, and on September 22nd, the night of its closest approach, it was shining brightly overhead and could easily be seen from the parking lot of Track Record studio where we were recording. On a break, I asked Billy if he wanted to come out and have a look at the red planet. He said his eyes weren't too good, but he came out anyway to try to find it. Sure enough, he saw it readily, and said, "Oh wow, that's it, is it? It's so bright, why don't they use it for the north star or something?" Astronomy was not his strong suit. Billy has a bad boy image, some of it deserved, but the only times I saw Billy get weird were when he was drinking tequila. I recall sitting next to him one night after we were done working as he drank Cuervo Gold, and he started sort of snarling like a wild animal, I swear to God. That was when I looked at my watch and said, "Oh my, look at the time," said goodbye, and left.

I really enjoyed those sessions, and they were made all the better because my pal Dave Concors was the engineer. It was the only album I ever worked on that ran up over a million dollars in production costs. *Charmed Life* went platinum in 1990, and Billy was nice enough to insist that I receive a Platinum Record for it. I proudly have it hanging on my wall next to the Diana Ross Gold Record for *Swept Away*.

In November, Moir found a promising artist for me to possibly produce; Canadian Scott Merritt, for Duke Street Records. Scott and I saw eye to eye and Duke Street decided to hire me. I really liked his songs a lot, especially his lyrics. He is a very gifted artist. We recorded part of the album in Toronto and part of it here in L.A. We rented a 24-track analog machine and a high class vocal mic so we were able to do a lot of the recording at my studio, and then did drum tracks elsewhere. I thought Scott and I worked together very well, and I found the project artistically satisfying. The album is titled *Violet and Black* after a song by the same title. It is a gorgeous song. In retrospect, I think that Scott was the most talented and sensitive songwriter I have had the pleasure to work with, and a real gentleman as well. I think it is the best album I have produced for another artist.

As 1989 got underway, I went to Canada for about 10 days to begin the first Scott Merritt sessions. But before I left, I was in talks with the director of a low budget movie, a silly horror/comedy called *Beverly Hills Bodysnatchers*. It starred Vic Tayback, and I really thought it was funny and ridiculous in a good way. I took the gig composing music for it while also finishing mixing the Untouchables album. I was working a lot of hours, but I wanted to get those projects completed before Scott Merritt came to Los Angeles to begin his album in earnest. He got here in mid-February and we worked straight through to the end of April. Scott then returned to Canada and the plan was for me to join him there in May for a few more overdubs to complete the recording process and be ready for mixing. However, an unexpected medical situation arose in my family and I was not able to go at the appointed time. I asked if we could delay my arrival for a week or two, but the record company said no, citing the issue of studio availability. It was decided that Scott would oversee the final overdubs, which were mainly some organ tracks. I was not happy that I had been dumped from that part of the production, but I was still enthusiastic about the project and wanted to see it through. I was hearing feedback from the label that they were concerned that the album wasn't turning out to be as commercially viable as they hoped, so I wanted to do all I could to make it the success I believed it could be.

Sadly, things got ugly when it came time to mix. Without consulting me, the label decided to hire Joe Chicarelli to do the mixing in June at a studio in the valley called Master Control. I had known Joe since he was engineer on *Joe's Garage*, and we had always gotten along fairly well, although as Frank put it, he was one those "ambitious, career oriented guys," which I sensed, too. Still, he was a pretty good engineer. I mostly left him alone to work on the mixes and would come in the control room from time to time to make producer comments, which Joe did not seem very happy to hear. Finally, he was mixing a song in which Scott and I had decided there would be one section with no drums, something that was easy to do in the studio by simply muting the drum tracks. Chicarelli really bristled at this suggestion and said to me, "Look Arthur, the record company is not that happy about the way this album is turning out. They have hired me to try to save it, so I am in charge of the mixing and I will mix it as I see fit." I was furious, but I quietly packed up my stuff and left the mixing room. On the way out of the building I had a little talk with Scott. I said, "Remember how I always told you that one of the things I could do for you as producer was to be a buffer between you and the idiots at the record company? Well, sorry, but I'm afraid you just lost that buffer. Good luck." I said goodbye, and left the studio and the project, feeling rather badly about the whole thing. It was a shame, because it had been such a pleasure up until that point. Although I still feel the album was an artistic success, it was not a commercial one. The album was released, but went nowhere on the charts.

In July, Robby Krieger called again about doing a couple of gigs with him and Bruce Gary, the drummer from The Knack. We rehearsed a few days then played Bogart's in Long Beach, the Coach House in San Juan Capistrano, and the Wadsworth Theater in Westwood, on the grounds of the U.S. Department of Veteran Affairs. It's a lovely place built in 1939 and has a great vibe for something on military property. It felt really good to do some live gigs after all the unpleasantness I had been going through. Good old Robby just kept coming through for me year after year. Spoiler alert: there is no bad ending to the Krieger part of my tale.

In August, Keith Forsey hired me again for about a week on yet more Billy Idol sessions, for which I was also very grateful. Things slacked off for a while after that, so I took a trip to Texas to see my mother who was beginning to show early signs of dementia. It is an awful thing to watch; may you never have to go through it.

At my manager's suggestion, in early November I began writing songs with Martha Davis of The Motels at my studio. We did this for several months and came up with some good songs. But her manager didn't "hear a hit," so he never tried to shop any of our demos. I think we could have restarted her career with those new songs, but they were never even heard by any record labels, as far as I know.

In mid-November, Robby hired a video crew to shoot footage of our power trio with drummer Bruce Gary playing our instrumental version of "The End," with me doing a lot of the melody parts on the bass. It's a pretty cool version. It has since been released as part of a Doors Collection DVD put out by Universal.

In December, there were some more Billy Idol sessions, including the hit "Cradle of Love." Keith and Billy didn't really like the song much, and were getting a bit burned out after having worked on the album for more than a year by then. Keith gave me a cassette with a demo of the song and pretty much left it to me to arrange and program the main synthesizer tracks. I'm not that crazy about the song either, but like I said, it was a hit and made it to #2 in the Billboard Hot 100.

In January 1990 my studio was booked a lot of the time by an unusual cello player named David Coleman. He was the brother of Lisa Coleman from Prince's back-up band, Revolution, and had co-written and played on "Around the World in a Day." He was pretty amazing and did some very interesting things overdubbing multiple cello tracks. Unfortunately, I don't think anything he recorded here was ever released. Too bad, because it was some cool, out there stuff. By having Eric Westfall engineer, I could go out and do a few more Idol sessions while he and David continued recording at my studio without my needing to be there. Sadly, David died in 2004 at the age of 42.

There were more Krieger gigs around that time, too. One was near my home in Santa Monica at a club called At My Place on January 7th. I'm pretty sure that was the night that Eric Burdon of The Animals sat in with us and sang "Roadhouse Blues." He sounded great, but he confused the lyrics a bit, admonishing the listener to watch the wheel and keep his/her hands upon the road. What a great voice, though, one of the best.

In February, I got a very interesting call from Robby about a film that was being made, *The Doors,* by Oliver Stone. Stone needed to do a pre-record of some Doors songs for a scene in the Venice rehearsal space the Doors had in their early days. Stone was intent on using vintage equipment, the original engineer and producer, and the remaining Doors to re-record their parts for the movie. But there seemed to have been some kind of falling out between Ray Manzarek and Stone, and Ray was not asked to participate in this pre-record. Instead, I got the call to go to Cherokee studio and pretend to be Ray pretending to be himself! So the organ you hear in that rehearsal scene is actually played by me. That was fun. As it turns out, Stone starts the movie with a clip from "The Movie," the track I worked on for The Doors' *American Prayer* album, re-creating the scene of Morrison recording his poetry alone in the studio. So the very first sound you hear in the movie is me, too, on my little synthesizer rig from 1978.

A few days after that, Robby called again about a TV show gig. There is a local TV weatherman in L.A. named Fritz Coleman, who is a great weather guy and also has a good sense of humor. He had talked the local NBC channel into letting him do his own show with guests and some comedy. Robby, Bruce Gary, and I were hired to be the house band. The show didn't last long due to poor ratings, but I enjoyed the gig, and Fritz was a very nice cat. One thing that stands out in my mind was an appearance by a very perceptive and funny guest that I had never heard of before by the name of Bill Mahr. I could tell immediately that this guy was someone special, and I have been glad to see his career do so well. Go Bill, and thanks Fritz.

Generally speaking, I had a lighter workload in 1990 and so was able to have more time to work on my own music. I had the studio, all my musical equipment, and the time to spend there in my own little magical wonderland. Finally I had all I needed to create my own music geared toward what *I* wanted to compose and hear, as opposed to what some record company executive thought was good. Producing the Scott Merritt album gave me hope that I, too, might be able do an artistic album of my own. I wrote and recorded all the music for my first album and took a tape of it to my manager. He quickly reverted to A&R guy mode telling me that he would never be able to sell a label on music of that kind. He was probably right about that. He also let me know he wasn't even going to try because he was representing me as a producer only, not as an artist. Well, OK, then, thanks a lot. I decided to release my album independently. With my old friend Tom Brown and his friend Slev, we made copies of my first CD, *Music for Listening,* in 1991, and sold it using a mailing list that Tom had built up over the years. I think we sold a few hundred copies, which wasn't bad for an album that contained several avant-garde classical compositions and made no attempt to be commercial in any way.

Session work continued to slow down alarmingly. The synth power pop style I had been doing with Giorgio had run its course, and I felt the effects like the reverse engines and brakes on a jet plane that is dramatically slowing down after landing. Even though I had a manager, I decided I had better start to advertise in The Music Connection, the local music rag. This was something I had never had to resort to before. It can be a very dangerous thing to do if you have a studio full of equipment. I once met a guy who was tied up and robbed by some people who saw his ad and wanted to come over to "check out the studio." I have been lucky and never had any problems of that sort.

Months went by before doing another Idol session with Forsey in May, a song called "Star Crossed Man" for the movie *Days of Thunder*. I don't know if the song made it into the movie or not, but I doubt it, since it's not on the soundtrack album.

On May 7th, I parted ways with my manager Steve Moir. He had not found any production gigs for me in months. His company had grown larger with a roster of producers and engineers that were better known than Arthur Barrow. I was sure all the choice recommendations were going to them, and I still had a bitter taste in my mouth about the way the Charlie Sexton producer swap to another one of his clients had gone down. To make matters worse, he had been receiving his percentage from my session work, including those lucrative Billy Idol sessions that he had nothing to do with. I had been working for Keith long before I signed with Moir as manager. Those sessions generated far more money than the minor production gigs he had found me. When we parted, he had definitely gotten the better end of the deal.

Some time in the spring of 1990, I heard through the grapevine that Frank Zappa was ill with prostate cancer. On Saturday, May 12th, the day before Mother's Day, I went up to his Laurel Canyon home at 9:30 p.m. He looked a little down, but I think he was happy to see me. I told him that I had heard he was sick and asked him about it. He looked down and said briskly, "I don't want to talk about it." I replied, "I'm sorry, Frank, it's just that I'm so concerned." He said, "I understand, but it's just not my favorite subject." I didn't bring it up again. He did reveal that he had a tube coming out of his body and a bag attached to his leg to collect urine. The poor guy was already in bad shape.

Frank had been working on a lot of new music on the Synclavier, and was eager to play some tracks for me, a lot of tracks, really. I had brought a tape of some of my new music and we listened to that, too, which was something of a rarity, since he always had plenty of his music he wanted me to hear. He seemed to like my stuff and was very encouraging. I was doing some virtual orchestra music by then, and he said that I should try to get my pieces performed by a real orchestra. I still hope that day comes eventually, Frank.

We also talked about his recent trip to Czechoslovakia for a meeting with Vaclav Havel and members of the once banned and imprisoned band, the Plastic People of Prague, named after the Zappa song "Plastic People." I recall meeting them in the late 70's on one of the Zappa tours, and I still have the album they gave me at the time. When he got to Prague, Frank said he was greeted at the airport by throngs of fans, similar to when the Beatles came to America, only the Czechs were carrying giant posters of Frank's face, the way Iranians carry around huge pictures of their Ayatollahs! Frank said that some people there told him that they had been arrested and tortured for listening to Zappa music. The torturers said, "We will beat the Zappa out of you!" Frank said it was very disturbing to learn that someone had been tortured in his name. I can only imagine what that must have felt like.

It was a great visit, even though it was tinged with sadness. I stayed there until 1:30 in the morning - four hours, just Frank and me hanging out together with no interruptions. I didn't know it at the time, but it would be the last time I ever saw my hero.

* * *

It felt good when Charlie Sexton called me about doing a session in June. He had been asked to sing a song for a new movie called *Air America* and wanted me to play bass on it. We recorded a version of the old Hollies song "Long Cool Woman in a Black Dress" at The Complex, a state of the art studio. I enjoyed working with Charlie as always, and we laid down some great tracks.

I did get some new clients from my ad, but they were all from people who were spending their own money, never from a label or someone with financial backing. I worked with some very nice people, and although it was not as stimulating as some of the other work I had been doing, it paid the bills. The occasional "real" session drifted in once in a while, but nothing notable. I was writing quite a bit with Martha Davis, so there was some artistic satisfaction there. And good old Robby came up with a few gigs in August. I took a lot of meetings trying to drum up some work, but nothing panned out. Life had definitely been turned upside down in the crazy world of Arthur Barrow, and the winds of change in the music business were no longer favoring what I had to offer.

Chapter Seventeen

Some good things started happening again in 1991. As I mentioned, my first solo album was released, which was a milestone for me. I was proud of it, and to this day I still think parts of it hold up well. In April, I got the opportunity to write the score for a documentary film about the total solar eclipse seen from La Paz, Mexico in 1990 called *The Great Eclipse* for a director named Robert Amram. It could not have been more up my alley because I am a very big fan of anything having to do with astronomy. I really enjoyed the project. The film was shown on PBS in 1992. It was a thrill for me to watch it as it was aired. I found a review of it on the web where it was called "The *Woodstock* of eclipse films." I think the film is well done, and like the L.A. times said, it "…captures the essence of the whole experience." It was a proud moment for me to do an entire score on my own without a musical collaborator.

I wrote some music for another documentary around that time called *Saviors of the Forest* made by Hollywood camera guys Bill Day and Terry Schwartz. They had gone down to Ecuador to shoot footage about the destruction of the rain forest and the bad behavior of oil companies. They told the awful story with a sense of humor, which makes it entertaining and sad at the same time. The film was nominated for a Grand Jury prize at the Sundance Festival in 1993. It was a pleasure to be a part of their production.

I mentioned earlier that I had worked with Randy California and Spirit. In April 1991, on a recommendation from Bruce Gary, they came to do some recording at my studio in Mar Vista. Randy was already waiting when I arrived. I drove up and saw an old VW bus and a hippie-looking guy sitting under a palm tree strumming on an acoustic guitar. That was Randy. Ed Cassidy, the bald headed original Spirit drummer was here, too. It turns out they needed a bass player, and asked me to fill in. Of course I said yes. This was a guy who had been in a band with Hendrix, for Christ's sake! He would show me the basics of a song, not even bothering to play it all the way to the end, and say "Yeah, you got it, let's record." And so we did, with me following my instincts when we'd get to the end. We recorded and mixed the whole album in three days. It certainly wasn't a slick production, but he was happy with it. I was very sad to hear of his death in 1997. He died rescuing his son from a riptide in Hawaii. The son survived, but he did not. R.I.P., Randy.

In July, Steve Schiff called me about a score he was doing for a horror/comedy film called *Waxworks II: Lost in Time.* He wanted me to help out with the writing and the recording. I thought it was pretty funny, featuring a detached wax hand committing mayhem on the screen – very silly. By that time, Schifty had the first computer based (Atari) midi system that did music notation. It was called Notator and was made by a company named Emagic, which eventually became Logic Audio, the system I still use. When Steve showed me how I could play something on a music keyboard as he recorded me, then display in music notation what I had just played, I decided I had to have that capability. I bought my first dedicated music computer, an Atari with Notator. It worked great, too. It was so simple that it was nearly glitch free. I did a lot of music on that system, including many of my "imaginary orchestra" pieces.

As 1992 rolled in, I was finishing up work on *The Great Eclipse* and doing some recording and a gig at the NAMM (National Association of Music Manufacturers) show with Robby and Bruce Gary, as well as continuing to write with Martha Davis. I also had to make a trip to Texas due to my mother's deteriorating condition. Sadly, it was time to sell the family home in Alamo Heights and empty its contents. I could not bear to see my dad's Hammond organ be sold for pennies on the dollar, so I towed it all the way back to L.A. in a U-Haul trailer. I am very happy I made that decision. That organ gets a lot of use, and is a great asset to have in the studio. I have had clients tell me it is the best sounding Hammond in town.

It was at around this time that Zappa made a deal with Rhino records to issue some "bootlegs" in a series called *Beat the Boots*, seemingly designed to get back at bootleggers. Frank always had a bug up his ass about bootleggers ripping him off and wanted to even up the score somehow. The idea was to bootleg the bootleggers by re-releasing the bootlegged albums. But Frank wanted nothing to do with the project, not even selecting which bootlegs would be copied and released. My friend Tom Brown worked at Rhino at the time and it was left up to him to choose which of his many bootleg Zappa albums would be used. He told me that the series was going to come out as legitimate albums, and that everyone would be paid what they were due. Naturally, I encouraged Tom to submit bootlegs with me on them, which he did. The project was underway.

Happily expecting to get paid, I called the Rhino business office several times but got no response. Finally a secretary called back to tell me I needed to talk to Gail Zappa. I should have dropped the matter then and there, knowing Gail as I did. But no, I decided to call her. What a mistake. When I called on February 24th, she was very hostile and among other things talked about the difficulty of finding all these musicians to pay them. I said I didn't know about the others, but you don't have to look for me, I'm right here. After she started yelling at me, I said I would check with the union and see what the rules were for live recordings. With that, she totally flipped out, telling me that I had better get a team of lawyers, and that I was forbidden from ever calling the house or having any contact with Frank or anyone in their organization! I was blacklisted! I had been one of the most loyal, agreeable musicians Frank ever employed. I never made a fuss when he bent union rules to enable him to pay me less than he should have, or anything like that. I never asked for any kind of pay increase, and I was always completely reliable in every way. Now I was on the shit list just because I wanted to know if I was going to get paid for some records that were coming out? This was my reward? I did call the union, but it seemed there was nothing they could do. The series sold well, and with almost zero overhead (no recording or musician costs) the sales were nearly pure profit for Rhino and the Zappa family. I never saw a dime, and I don't think any of the other Zappa players did either.

In March, Robby called with a musical idea he had for us to do together. He had been listening to *Sketches of Spain* by Miles Davis with arranger and composer Gil Evans. He had heard some of the virtual orchestra music I had been composing and wanted to do something like *Sketches of Spain* with me as co-writer and arranger. Of course I said yes! We spent a lot of time on it, doing a mock-up version using my "virtual" orchestra sounds, with the idea that we could get some record company interest and raise the money to record it with a real orchestra. Unfortunately, we couldn't find a label that was interested. So, for years our "Russian Caravan" languished, unappreciated and alone.

Most of my time was filled with good creative things, writing with others and on my own, but with very little work that was generating actual income. Luckily, my engineer friend Dave Concors was working at Disney by then, and late in the year starting sending me some work having to do with music replacement. This involved re-creating music for the purpose of making foreign language versions of some of the older films that did not have separate music and dialogue tracks available. This was tedious work, but it paid well, and I was very grateful for it.

One of my writing partners at this time was Joe Faraci, the singer from The Pink Fence, the ill-fated Battle of the Bands winners. We had done some industrial sounding tracks and landed a record deal with a spin-off of Private Music called Maxbilt Records. A seven song CD called *Mona Lisa Overdrive* was released, but when it did not become an overnight success, the band was dropped. That was my one and only experience being a "signed" artist. Fortunately, we had received a small advance, so it was not a total waste of time. This activity took up the better part of 1993, along with some more music replacement work for me at Disney, and a session with Keith Forsey for Simple Minds in November.

December brought the sad news of the passing of Frank Zappa on Saturday the 4th. Even though I knew he was dying, it was still devastating. I immediately wanted to listen to the song "Joe's Garage" for the nostalgic and sentimental feelings I knew it would stir in me. When it got to the part about only getting one chance in life to play that song, I sobbed for a good while. Oh, how I miss you still, Frank. You were the most brilliant musician/composer I ever worked with, by far. The world is not the same without you.

A few months later, in March, 1994, I was asked to be a part of a group of former Zappa musicians that would go to Germany to perform in the Stuttgart Jazz Festival that summer. The name Band From Utopia (later changed to Banned from Utopia) jumped into my head and that's what we called it. I volunteered to be clonemeister. The other players agreed, so I ran the rehearsals. We did the first few rehearsals here at my studio, some more at a place in Hollywood, then a few more when we got to Germany. We played Stuttgart on July 1st and Koln on July 3rd. It was for this band that I resurrected the version of "Thirteen" that Frank was working on in early 1980, but abandoned until he used part of it in "Tink Walks Amok." I recalled what a cool version it was back in 1980, so I created a medley of the two and called it "Tink/Thirteen." There is a good version of it on the Banned From Utopia CD *So Ya Don't Like Modern Art*. In late November I went to Austin for a week to supervise the mix of the live concert in Stuttgart.

Given all the changes in the music business, the number of paying gigs I had continued to diminish, but at least that gave me more time to work on my own music. I was able to put together enough tracks for my second CD, *Eyebrow Razor*, which came out on Muffin Records in 1995. I was very happy to have Bruce, Walt, Steve, and Tom Fowler, and Kurt McGettrick playing on one of my favorite cuts, "The Ears Have it," as well as having Robby Krieger, Ike Willis, and Ray White performing on "Believe It."

Something promising came along late in 1994 in the form of the possibility of doing more music replacement work, this time for some vintage Warner Brothers cartoons. It was the same type of work I'd done at Disney. They wanted to create foreign language versions of the cartoons, but did not have separate music tracks without dialogue. Through my friend Larry Klimas, a great sax player who plays with Manhattan Transfer and Neil Diamond, among others, I met Pat Murphy who was an executive at Turner Entertainment. Turner had the distribution rights to the Warner cartoons. There were several hundred cartoons that needed this work done, so getting the gig would be a solid money making project. Pat knew Mark Mothersbaugh from Devo, who was doing cartoon music at the time, and Pat thought it would be wise if we submitted the work as a team with Mark for added credibility. A Daffy Duck cartoon was chosen as an audition piece, and we did a really slick job of music replacement; my recent work with Disney had been good preparation for this. We passed the audition, but the gig never happened. The Warner legal people said that as distributors, Turner had no right to alter the content in any way, and that the Warner music people would do it in-house with similar music already recorded that they could edit in. That was a big disappointment.

On December 7th, 1994 I did my last session with Keith Forsey for The Divinyls. I don't recall much about it except that they seemed very self-absorbed, and that I had a hard time getting paid. The change in the music business was now complete, and the kind of session work I had thrived on during the 80's had all but dried up.

As 1994 turned into 1995, I realized that it was time for me to try something radically different. I was offered a job at Turner

Entertainment by my new friend, Pat Murphy. It was an eight to five full time job, something I had never done since I moved to L.A., but I decided to do it. Except for that brief part-time stint at the Serge factory, I had never had a real "day job" since I moved to California to begin my music career. I recall the day I went to the Turner building where I would be working in Culver City. It was my 43rd birthday. As I sat in the tiny windowless office filling out the employee application form, I was so distressed that I actually began to feel faint, getting to the point of tunnel vision before coming back. How could things have changed so much that an experienced musician like myself could no longer survive doing music work?

Although I didn't like the hours, I did rather come to enjoy the work. I was now on the business side of the music replacement process for foreign dubbing work. My work was overseeing the music and effects tracks for the dubbing department. I learned a lot about the technical side of the film business and met a lot of good people there. It was a humbling, but worthwhile experience for me. There were also health insurance benefits, and I never once had to fight with anyone to get paid.

I had been working there for about a year and a half when it was announced that Warner Brothers would be taking over Turner in a merger, and that there would be layoffs. As I had recently negotiated a raise, I was among the first to be let go. I was given a check and sent on my way. I remember driving away from the workplace on my last day feeling elated and free. But it was also scary to be on my own again, with no regular paycheck and no benefits.

Fortunately, there would be another kind of benefit from having worked at Turner. One of the good things that happened was that I became friends with a great guy there named Craig Johnson. He is an expert in video mastering, which basically means transferring film to video. He was involved with mastering some old silent films, and had come across several that had no soundtracks at all. This mastering work was being done for the Turner Classic Movies channel. They wanted to air a Greta Garbo film called *The Torrent*, but it had no audio track. Since things at Turner were in a chaotic state due to the corporate takeover, it was left to Craig to figure out what to do about the music. He asked if I thought I could create a music score for this classic 1926 film. Of course I said yes!

The Torrent is a melodrama based on a book by Ibanez about a very poor young Spanish girl who becomes an opera star but never finds happiness. Garbo is fabulous in it of course, but it was kind of weird trying to figure out what to do with the music in the singing scenes. It made no sense to hire a singer for a silent film – if we can hear the character sing, why can't we hear her talk? I figured out ways to make it work, though, like doing piano practice exercises for the score during her lessons to emphasize that she was doing vocal studies.

Scoring a silent film is very different from doing a talkie in a fundamental way. In a normal modern movie with dialogue, sound effects and ambience, the music generally has to take a back seat to the dialogue and sound effects in terms of prominence in the mix. You don't want a strong melody going on at the same time as important dialogue, for example, because it would distract from the main focus, the story. In a movie that is loaded with sound effects, you don't want to spend too much time on music for the chase or shoot-out scenes, because the music will likely be overpowered by the sound effects in the final mix. In a silent film, there is no dialogue, effects, or any kind of sound other than the music, so the music has to help in every way possible to clarify and illuminate the story, and move it along. And, unlike a talkie, the music in a silent film never stops during the entire movie, except for brief pauses between scenes or musical pieces. Therefore, a lot more music is needed for a silent film, compared to a modern movie that will have a lot of scenes with no music. *The Torrent,* for example, is almost 90 minutes long, so that meant I had to compose about 90 minutes of music. That's a lot of music to compose. In vinyl terms, that's about 10 to 15 minutes longer than a typical *double* album.

Another big difference is that the directors, writers, and all the other creative people who worked on the original movie are all dead and gone. Normally, the composer of a film score works closely with the director, collaborating and finding agreement over where the music cues should begin and end, and what the character of the music should be when it occurs. But when I compose the silent scores, I am mostly on my own. Luckily, Craig Johnson, who hired me to do the work, was very helpful and encouraging, stopping by the studio several times to see how it was going, and to offer his opinion. His input was insightful and helpful.

To date, I have done three silent movie scores for TCM. The other two were *The Camera Man* starring Buster Keaton, about an aspiring Hollywood camera operator, and *The Boob,* a spoof on cowboy pictures starring George K. Arthur, with a brief appearance by a young Joan Crawford. All three are shown on TCM from time to time. I often get emails from people after *The Torrent* is shown telling me how much they enjoyed the music, which is very welcome. Doing one of these scores is a huge effort; it's a couple of months of full time work. But when it's done and delivered, (aside from Craig in my case) there is no applause or praise from the director or film company, and no celebration or anything like that. The result is there is a bit of a letdown when the work is finally done. So, when I hear from someone out of the blue that liked the music enough to write to me about it, I am very grateful.

On a beautiful spring day in Austin, my dear mother finally succumbed to the horrible Alzheimer's disease that she had been suffering from for many years. As painful as it was to lose her, it is such an awful illness that her passing was almost as much of a relief as it was a loss. One of my favorite smells, the blossoms of Texas Mountain Laurel, filled the air that day, as if to honor her and help me accept the fact that she was gone. It felt like the aroma had come to comfort me and let me know that her suffering was over, and that she was better off than she had been for a very long time. She was a lovely, kind woman, and I will always miss her.

Although the busy and lucrative times of the mid-eighties were never to be matched again, I have continued working on various types of projects in my studio. The good side of not working every minute of every day, year after year, is that I have had more time to work on my own original music. In 1999, I released my third CD, *AB3,* and my fourth, *On Time* in 2003.

But there was still one more big feather to put in my cap. I had the honor of working a couple of times with the late, great Keith Emerson. My old pal Will Alexander, the guy who had brought that Arp 2600 to my house all those years ago in San Antonio, had followed his dream to California like I did. He wound up working for his hero, Keith, for many years, so we have parallel stories in a way. In the late 1990's Will called me about doing some demo recordings with Keith and Zappa Vaultmeister Joe Travers on drums. I don't think anything was ever used from those recordings, but it is a thrill to be able to say I worked with Mr. Emerson. A few years later, Keith hired me to do a transcription and a chart of some music for him. When he and Will came over to my studio to pick up the chart I enjoyed showing Keith some of my keyboards. I wanted to demonstrate my Rodgers virtual pipe organ to him, and of course I was nervous playing in front of him. I said, "I'm going to say what I always say when I sit down to play keyboards for someone, which is, 'I'll do the best I can, but I'm no Keith Emerson.'" I think he got a kick out of that. I was deeply saddened when I heard of his untimely death.

In 1999, I received an email from an Argentinian named Marcelo Gasio. He asked if I would be interested in coming down there to do a Zappa concert. If I did it, I would be the first Zappa band member to perform his music south of the equator, so of course I said yes. We scheduled my trip for early December. Argentina is in *south* South America, so it is a very long way to go for just a few days. It's an eighteen hour trip including a stopover in Miami. The people down there were very friendly and accommodating, but there was no doubt that I was in the third world. The signs were everywhere, from the beggars on the street to the children who seemed to live in the subway selling gum and baseball cards. While I was there I did some rehearsals, a radio show, a clinic, and still had a little time to see some of beautiful Buenos Aires. There is something exotic and magical about the place. It is a different world from anything I had ever seen. Even the vegetation looked foreign to me.

The main focus was the music, of course, so we got right down to rehearsing as soon as I got there. The language barrier was pretty severe, however. Few of the musicians I worked with spoke much English, so I did my best to talk to them in my very broken Spanish. But we managed to communicate, and after some intense rehearsals, the concerts went well. Before I could blink an eye, I was on a plane for the flight home. My biggest disappointment was that the skies were cloudy every night I was there, so I never got a chance to see what the southern sky looked like.

In the early part of the 21st century I organized a lot of free-form improvisation sessions at my studio. That kind of jamming has always been my favorite, and the time was ripe to invite some of the great musicians I know over to see if we could create some magic and manage to get it recorded. The best incarnation of these sessions was a group of the best players I know. I called it The Mar Vista Philharmonic, or MVP for short. The players included Vinnie Colaiuta on drums, Bruce Fowler on trombone, Walt Fowler on trumpet, the late Kurt McGettrick on bass clarinet and flute, Tommy Mars on keys, and either Larry Klimas or Albert Wing on sax. When you have musicians of that caliber who are sensitive enough listeners to know what to do in a free improv, amazing things can happen.

In 2003, I got an email from a guy at BBC radio who wanted to interview me for a series of shows he was doing on Zappa and his relationship to jazz called "Make a Jazz Noise Here." I agreed, and he soon came to L.A. to interview me and several other Zappa band members for the upcoming BBC radio broadcast. While he was here, I gave him a copy of one of our free jams just because I thought he might enjoy it. I called it *No Forest Fire*, based on words that Tommy improvised in one of the jams. The BBC guy did like it, and soon after he returned to England he sent me an email asking if I thought I could get the MVP together to do a recording that would be broadcast as part of their Zappa series. Of course I said yes! He asked if we could come up with something related to Zappa, but wasn't specific about what he thought we should do. I decided that we should do very free versions of some of the classic Zappa jams, like "Treacherous Cretins," "Five-Five-Five," and the solo vamp from "Inca Roads." In response to the misguided, deadly invasion of Iraq by George W. Bush, part two was a sad, minor key version of the U.S. national anthem. We did the recording, then I mixed it and sent it off to the BBC. They loved it and aired it with the original series, and again some months later as a popularly requested encore. *No Forest Fire* was later released by my Norwegian friend Jon Larsen and is available on his Hot Club Records label.

Sometime in 2008, Robby called and said he wanted to go back to work on our ambitious composition "Russian Caravan." He wanted to record a scaled down version of it at my studio. It took quite a bit of technical trickery to transfer the information from the 1992 Atari Notator files into my 2008 Mac setup. Once that was done, we recorded the parts one or two instruments at a time. It's a pretty impressive line up: Vinnie Colaiuta, Tommy Mars, Sal Marquez, Bruce Fowler, Walt Fowler, Larry Klimas and others. It took quite a while to complete, but when we were done, we were pleased enough that we decided to write more tunes so that we could put together an album of music. The result was the 2010 release of the CD *Singularity* by Robby Krieger on Oglio Records, co-produced and co-written by Robby and me. *Singularity* was nominated for a Grammy for Best Pop Instrumental Album in 2010. We lost out to Larry Carlton, a worthy musician.

Shortly after *Singularity* came out, Robby and Ray Manzarek were contacted by a conductor named Brent Havens who had found a niche conducting the music of famous rock bands with arrangements he had written for full orchestra. He wanted to do a project with the band Robby and Ray had that was doing Doors material. Ray had recently heard the *Singularity* album and was so impressed with "Russian Caravan" that he suggested to Robby that they hire me to do special arrangements and orchestrations of some of their songs for the performances with Brent. Of course I said yes! They wanted me to hear their band live, so they flew me up to San Francisco for a day to see a show at the original Fillmore West. We talked before the show about the orchestra project, and they also invited me to come sit in with the band on bass for a song. When it was nearing the time for me to go on, I made my way to the side of the stage, and just so I could say that I did, while no one was looking, I danced a little. Now I can say that I danced at the Fillmore for real. Then I got up on stage and did "Roadhouse Blues" with The Doors. Sweet. I didn't see any wig stores, though, Frank.

This project turned out to be the kick I needed to get on board with the computerized music notation software that had become available. (I use Sibelius.) I did orchestrations of "Not to Touch the Earth," "Moonlight Drive," "Horse Latitudes," and "Wild Child." Robby and Ray encouraged me to be adventurous, and not just stick with orchestrating only the parts that were on the records, so I really went for it. I am very lucky to be friends with Bruce Fowler who is now a big time Hollywood orchestrator, and really knows what he is doing. He is very generous with his knowledge, and always seems to have time to answer my many questions. I could not have done it without him. The same thing goes for Liz Finch, a great professional music copyist who I got to know through Bruce. Her depth of knowledge is amazing. Unfortunately, I have not yet heard my orchestrations performed live, but by all accounts, they were well received.

With the release of *Singularity*, some offers for Robby to play live gigs began to come in. Robby and I put together a band that still exists as of this writing, with Tommy Mars on keys, Larry Klimas or Vince Denham on sax, and variously Chad Wackerman, Tom Brechtlein, or Joel Taylor on drums. Among other places, we have played the Clive Davis Theater in the Grammy Museum in Los Angeles, the Iridium Club on Broadway in New York, and gigs all across the north American continent from San Diego to Montreal. We are currently working on a new album at Robby's beautiful new studio in Glendale.

In 2014, I made the long trip to Europe twice to do music work. Banned From Utopia had been doing some gigs featuring Ray White, Ed Mann, and Robert Martin from the Zappa band, and the great Mike Miller on guitar. Mike was not going to be available for a spring tour they wanted to do, so they needed a guitar player. Ed had heard me play guitar before and thought they should get in touch with me to see if I wanted to do it. I was reluctant at first, since I don't play guitar much in public, but when I heard Chad Wackerman was going to play drums, I decided it was too good to pass up. I practiced guitar more than I had in decades, and managed to learn what I needed to. It was a very intense schedule, doing eleven gigs in ten days, all in different cites. I had a great time playing my Stratocaster with a whammy bar, and it was a treat to sing harmony parts along with Robert and Ray. They are both so good that it was easy for me to blend in with them and sound better than I really am.

I was invited to go to Norway in July of 2014 to participate in the Molde Jazz Festival. I played guitar and bass with my Norwegian friend Jon Larsen. He is a fabulous guitar player who specializes in Django Reinhardt style music, among other things. Molde is on the north coast of Norway, not too far from the artic circle. I was looking forward to a cool, peaceful time in a small coastal village. I was in for a big surprise. For one thing there was a heat wave going on, so it was hotter there than it was in Los Angeles! I stayed in a lovely old hotel with a room overlooking the fjord. Unfortunately, there was no air conditioning there, so it was pretty uncomfortable. But much worse than that, I was right across the street from a public park which had a huge P.A. set up. They fired it up every night at midnight and cranked throbbing disco until three o'clock in the morning! I had to give up on sleeping and go hang out somewhere till they shut down, then try to get some sleep, but I had to be sure to get up before ten A.M. or I would miss the complimentary hotel breakfast. Since Norway is so expensive, eating breakfast out would have set me back about $50. Still, I had a good time playing the music, as I always do. Thanks Jon.

    I am also happy to be moving towards doing more work in the academic realm. Thanks to Dr. Joseph Klein, the current chair of the composition department at my alma mater, The University of North Texas, I have done three residencies there. Dr. Klein is a brilliant composer and happens to be a Zappa aficionado. I found out some years ago that he was teaching the occasional class on Zappa, and he invited me to come to Denton in 2009 to give some lectures and do a performance of Frank's music. In 2012 he invited Tommy Mars and me to come and put on a much bigger concert in the beautifully refurbished Voertman Hall in the music building. It was the same hall where I used to give my organ juries in the early 70's. (Alas, the pipe organ is no longer there.) I did my third UNT residency and Zappa concert in April of 2015 in the same fabulous concert hall. I think the 2015 concert was the best one so far. I had some great student musicians to work with, and I have to say, they gave me hope in the new generation of people in our culture. They worked very hard on their parts and came through with the goods. They didn't even complain when I asked them to turn off their cell phones during rehearsal. I have also lectured at Chapman University and done a Zappa residency and concert at the University of South Dakota. I hope my future involves more such ventures into academia. I am talking to people at other music schools around the country about doing more of these projects. I think it is important to introduce Frank's music to new generations of musicians by performing it, not just hoping they hear about it somehow. There is no one like Zappa – no one who has incorporated the rock, jazz, avant-garde, and classical idioms the way Frank did. This is music that is worth studying and playing.

Coda

I was born in 1952. The world has changed enormously since then. In 1952 there had not yet been a detonation of a hydrogen bomb. No man or man-made device had ever gone into space, much less to the moon. It was thought that there might be planets orbiting around other stars, but there was no proof. Now we know of dozens of exoplanets. Black and white TV was still in its infancy; color TV was non-existent. Stereo FM radio did not exist, only mono AM. There were telephones, but no answering machines, no cell phones, and no Internet. To go overseas, most people traveled by sea instead of air. Igor Stravinsky and Joseph Stalin were still alive. At our house, we had a milkman who delivered fresh milk to our back door. Where I lived in Alamo Heights, it was a safe and fun world, at least if you were a white middle class male like me. It seems like ages ago.

The changes in music and recording are also staggering. In 1952 analog magnetic tape recording was a fairly new thing in the states. (The Germans invented it and used it during World War II to broadcast speeches by Hitler.) All records at that time were mono; stereo came along later. In the studio, all the music and the vocals had to be done live to disc or tape. Getting a good mix balance was done by moving closer to or further away from the one microphone. Gradually, multi-track recording became available, first with two tracks, then three, four, eight, sixteen, twenty-four, and there was even a forty-track machine made by Stephens. Synchronizers were invented to enable locking up two or more machines to operate together, providing as many tracks as needed if you had the gear and the patience to wait while the machines got up to speed and eventually locked. Improvements were always being made in tape quality and noise reduction. Analog tape adds noise called "hiss" to the sound that really starts to build up when playing back a lot of tracks.

Just getting ready to make an analog recording required many adjustments to the machines, which could take an hour or more depending on the set-up. Every type of tape was a little different, so an engineer had to set up the machine for the kind of tape that was going to be used. First, a test tape with standardized tones would be used to set the playback levels and frequency response, then tones had to be recorded to set the levels and frequency curves, and an adjustment had to be made to something called "bias." If a noise reduction system like Dolby was being used, that had to be set up and tweaked as well. It was an ordeal, but when it was operating properly, it sounded great. I am going into this much detail only to emphasize how complicated the process was and how much knowledge was needed to make it work.

Recording to analog tape remained the standard until the mid 1980's when digital recording came along. The first ones were reel to reel, then there were formats that used video cassette tape for storage, and finally the computer recording formats such as Pro Tools or Logic Audio that are in use today. These are very easy to use and provide plenty of tracks, great built-in effects and instruments, all delivered in high quality, noise free audio.

My first analog recorder was a two-track Ampex. Later I got a two-track Sony, a two-track Revox, a four-track Teac, an eight-track Otari and a sixteen-track Fostex. I put a lot of miles on those decks. My first digital machine was a stereo DAT recorder which used a small cassette for storage, then I got four eight-track digital ADATs that used VHS tape. These machines could be locked together to get up to thirty-two tracks. All of that equipment became obsolete when I got a computer and started using Logic Audio, which is what I use now. It is a bit depressing to realize that a lot of the knowledge I acquired over the years is now basically useless.

When I first started playing electric guitar things were very different from the way they are now. For one thing, almost all electronics back then used good old vacuum tubes, even the one-watt Kent amp that was my first. Tube amps are still preferred by most guitar players because of their warm tone and the way they distort at higher volume levels, but just about everything else is solid-state. Another important difference is that there were few effects available outside of the built-in spring reverbs and tremolos that came on the better amps. Tape based echo devices such as the Echoplex became available in the early 1960's, but they were pricey. The most important effect ever for the electric guitar was distortion, or "fuzz." When Keith Richards used a Maestro Fuzz-Tone on "Satisfaction," the electric guitar changed forever. Other distortion boxes soon emerged, such as the Mosrite Fuzzrite, one of which I had for a while, and the Arbiter Fuzz Face which Jimi Hendrix used. I still have one of those, a blue one. There are dozens of kinds of distortion devices available now.

The next big thing to come along was the Vox Wah-Wah pedal, which had a resonant filter hooked up to a pedal to create a radical effect on the sound. A good example is "Up From The Skies" by Hendrix. The first time I heard a Wah-Wah was when I heard Jimi use one live in San Antonio. He played "Voodoo Child" long before the song was released. I couldn't believe my ears. I told my friends, "He made the guitar *talk*, man!" It was amazing.

In the 1970's more effects pedals emerged such as phase shifters, flangers, and choruses. These were similar to each other and generally made a sound that sort of sparkled up the tone, sometimes making a sound like two guitars were playing together. By the late 70's, a company called Eventide came out with a device called a Harmonizer. It was an early digital device which could shift the pitch of a sound, but it was pretty "grainy" sounding, and very expensive. Digital echo boxes appeared as well.

The world of keyboard instruments was rife with change, too. For one thing, the Hammond organ, which was invented in the 1930's and greatly enhanced by the invention of the Leslie rotating speaker system in the 1940's, made quite a comeback in the 1960's. Bands like Steppenwolf (on "Magic Carpet Ride") and Procol Harum (on "Whiter Shade of Pale") used them to great effect, recording them in a way that emphasized the effect of the Leslie and sometimes driving it into distortion for that "psychedelic" sound. Small combo organs like the Vox and the Gibson were being widely used, too. Ray Manzarek of The Doors used them to create a very big part of that band's sound. Electric pianos such as the Rhodes and the Wurlitzer were invented. They are cool instruments, but don't really sound anything like a piano. I have a primo Rhodes Mark I Stage Piano which still gets a lot of use. An electric clavichord called a Clavinet was invented by Hohner. As I mentioned, I own a lovely, very funky Clavinet C.

The biggest explosion was the invention of the synthesizer, of course, most notably the Moog. A whole new palette of sounds opened up to those who had access to these machines. I was enthralled from the first time I heard the sound of the Moog on the album *Switched on Bach* by (then) Walter Carlos. Soon, many manufacturers got into the synthesizer game, like EMU, Roland, Arp, Korg, and others. My first was an Electrocomp EML 101. I now have a classic Roland Jupiter 8, an Oberheim Xpander, and a very obscure system called a Serge Modular as well. I still love them all and use them from time to time.

The invention of MIDI was very important. It is a digital protocol which enables synthesizers to talk to sequencers or computers, allowing the instrument to be programmed as well as played manually. It took a lot of know-how to get the early synthesizers to make the tones you wanted, and there was an awful lot of fun to be had in inventing new ways of hooking things up to make a wide variety of novel sounds. Nowadays you can buy an inexpensive machine full of wonderful sounds to be had at the push of a button. That's a great thing and saves a lot of time, but it is not nearly as much fun as doing it from scratch in analog land.

Another big innovation was the concept of sampling, or digitally recording audio that can be played back at the touch of a key. The first widely used system with sampling capability was the Fairlight, followed soon after that by the Synclavier, which also produced sound through a means called FM synthesis, something too arcane to try to explain here. These systems were very expensive, in the six figure range. I am glad I never invested in either of them, because soon much less expensive samplers and FM synthesis gear became available. Sampling of other artists' music has become a huge part of some genres, though it never appealed much to me. I prefer to create music from out of my own head, not use the work of someone else. I have incorporated sampling in some of my work, but not from recordings by other artists, with the exception of my version of "In the Mood," which was a special case.

Today, any guitar effects box, computer synth sounds, or computer effects are mostly imitations of the innovations I have just described. Other than the dreadful auto-tune, nothing much new has been invented, though there have been many excellent refinements in what can be done. For example, I have a new guitar effects box that does some incredible things including harmonizing a single note part into a chord and pitch-bending the sound by a full octave up or down. And of course, the editing capabilities of computer recording are light years ahead of what could be done in the days of analog recording.

I get a strange, sad feeling sometimes when I look at an instrument or a piece of equipment that I was so excited about when it was new, but is now obsolete. How could something that was so important to me at the time I bought it be so worthless now? Some things change too quickly for me to digest, I guess. On the other hand, I have a deep feeling of satisfaction and warmth when I play my still fabulous 1965 Stratocaster I've had since I was a sophomore in high school, or when I sit down at the console of the mighty 1959 Hammond RT3 organ that I inherited from my father. So maybe things balance out in a way.

I now find myself in a musical world where so much technological progress has been made that for a fairly small amount of money, you can buy a computer with some music software and basically have a studio in a box. What a wonderful thing. Now just about anyone can make a recorded music product. But this technological progress has also brought us to a point where so much music is stolen from musicians, or they are paid so little for streaming their music, that these new musical recordings have little way of being monetized. I think that may be a bit of actual irony. I am sad to say I don't see that the technology has enhanced creativity. Where are the Beatles, Hendrix, Doors, or Zappa of today?

I considered using *A Cautionary Tale for Would-Be Musicians* as a subtitle for this book, but any word of caution is also obsolete by now. The music scene I was part of in the 70's and 80's no longer exists in any recognizable form, so a lot of things that happened to me would not apply to musicians trying to function in the current state of the music business. The music industry is now nothing more than a shell of the enterprise it once was. It seems that musicians are really getting the short end of the information highway stick. I think the record companies really blew it when they rushed to jump on the digital bandwagon without first addressing how easy it was to make digital copies of CD's. They screwed themselves and the poor innocent musicians. Except for the few at the very top, it is now nearly impossible to make a living selling recorded music. Maybe things will get better, but it's hard right now to see how that might happen. Time will tell.

Perhaps my cautionary attitude does have some value in that it is surely even harder to have a career in music now than it was when I came to Los Angeles in 1975. Then, there was at least a pretty good chance you could get into the recording session work scene, or at the very least make some kind of a living in a top 40 or wedding band, but there isn't even much of that any more. DJ's have taken over most of that work.

I do regret the fact that there is no longer a figure with the stature of Frank Zappa around, one who made you practice harder and play better than you ever thought possible. His intense presence in the world of music always held out the possibility for young musicians that with enough hard work and good luck, you might get to play in his band and share the incredible, mind expanding experience that entailed. Words cannot describe how glorious that was. I wish something like that was still possible for today's young players and singers.

All in all, though, I have been very lucky to have been able to be a professional musician for almost all of my working life. I am especially lucky to have worked with my all time musical hero, Frank Zappa. I am perhaps even luckier to have hooked up early on with another one of my heroes, Doors guitarist Robby Krieger. The thing that has stood out to me the most as I have been digging through my history is that from the time I met him, shortly after moving to L.A., usually not more than a couple of months went by without a call from Robby about some gig, or a project, or an offer of some sort. I consider it a very high honor to have collaborated with the guy who wrote "Light My Fire" and all those other great songs. I have no rip-off stories to tell about Robby, no humiliations, no insults, no bad endings. Thank you Robby Krieger. If only all aspiring musicians could be so lucky as to have Kriegers in their lives.

I don't want to sound discouraging if you are an aspiring musician and a virtuoso player like Vinnie Colaiuta on the drums, Jaco Pastorius on the bass, John Coltrane on the sax, or an amazing composer like Zappa, or a genius songwriter like Dylan. If that's really the case, then by all means go for it, but don't assume you will be guaranteed success. The emphasis in music now is more focused on sexy looks, dancing, and stage spectacles than on musicianship. You might even seem to reach the pinnacle of your career only to have the fickle music buying public turn their backs on you and go stampeding towards the next new fad.

As for the rest of you, love music, play music, support music, but maybe don't quit your day job.

All that said, I have little regret about becoming a professional musician, and I still believe that, aside from love, music is the best gift that life has to offer. It is the closest thing to magic that humans have. I am glad that when the right opportunities came along, of course I said yes!

The book is now done, time for me to get back to music.

So now I say, "OK, ready? From the top! 1, 2, 3, 4!"

THE END

Recordings with Arthur Barrow that charted in the top 40 somewhere:

Singles:

TITLE	ARTIST	POSITION/CHART	YEAR
"I Don't Wanna Get Drafted"	Frank Zappa	#3 Sweden	1980
"Why Me?"	Irene Cara	#8 Hot 100 #7 US Dance	1983
"The Dream"	Irene Cara	#37 Hot 100 #26 US Dance	1983
"New York/N.Y."	Nina Hagen	#9 US Dance	1983
"Over My Head"	Tony Basil	#4 US Dance	1983
"Rush, Rush"	Debby Harry	#28 US Dance	1983
"Breakdance"	Irene Cara	#8 Hot 100 #13 US Dance	1984
"No More Words"	Berlin	#23 Hot 100	1984
"Reach Out"	Paul Engemann	#1 Germ. Singles	1984
"Never Ending Story"	Limahl	#1 Japan, Norway, Spain, Sweden Top 10 - Austria, Fr., It., Germ., Ire., Sw., UK #17 US Hot 100, #10 Dance Club Play	1984
"Together in Electric Dreams"	Phil Oakey	#3 UK Singles	1984

Song	Artist	Chart	Year
"Touch by Touch"	Diana Ross	#18 NLD	1984
"Special Girl"	America	#15 US Adult Cont.	1984
"Beat so Lonely"	Charlie Sexton	#17 Hot 100 #24 Mainstream Rock	1985
"Edge of a Dream"	Joe Cocker	#31 US Adult Cont.	1985
"Leave Your Hat On"	Joe Cocker	#35 Mainstream Rock	1986
"Take Me Home Tonight"	Eddie Money	#4 Hot 100, #15 Canada #1 Billboard Rock Tracks	1986
"Take My Breath Away"	Berlin	#1 Hot 100 US, UK, Belg. Can., Ire., NLD Top 10 all of Europe	1986
"Danger Zone"	Kenny Loggins	#2 Hot 100 #7 Can #10 Germ., #6 Switz.	1986
"Cradle of Love"	Billy Idol	#2 Hot 100, #34 UK	1990
"L.A. Woman"	Billy Idol	#18 Mainstream Rock	1990
"Prodigal Blues"	Billy Idol	#35 Mainstream Rock	1991

Albums:

Joe's Garage Act I	Frank Zappa	#27 US, #1 Nor., #2 Swed.	1979
Joe's Garage Acts II&III	Frank Zappa	#3 Nor., #4 Swed.	1979
Tinsel Town Rebellion	Frank Zappa	#13 Nor., #8 Swed.	1981
You Are What You Is	Frank Zappa	#12 Nor., #26 Swed.	1981
Ship Arriving Too Late	Frank Zappa	#23 US, #20 Nor., #26 Swed.	1982
Man From Utopia	Frank Zappa	#23 Swed.	1983
Them Or Us	Frank Zappa	#22 Swed.	1983
What a Feelin'	Irene Cara	#29 Germ., #8 Switz.	1983
Love Life	Berlin	#28 US, #3 New Zealand	1984
Swept Away	Diana Ross	#26 US, #7 US R&B #37 Can., #10 NLD	1984
Dream Street	Janet Jackson	#19 US R&B	1984
The Breakfast Club	Various Artists	#17 US	1985
Shock	The Motels	#36 US, #23 AU	1985
Pictures for Pleasure	Charlie Sexton	#15 US	1985
Top Gun (Soundtrack)	Various Artists	#1 US	1986
Policy	Martha Davis	#28 AU	1987
Charmed Life	Billy Idol	#11 US	1990

Film music with Arthur Barrow:

Scarface (1983)	Musician, Arr., Lyricist
D.C. Cab (1983)	Musician, Arr.
Electric Dreams (1984)	Musician, Arr.
The Never Ending Story (1984)	Musician, Arr.
Teachers (1984)	Musician, Arr.
Metropolis (1927/1984)	Musician, Arr.
The Breakfast Club (1985)	Musician
The Twilight Zone (1985)	Musician
Top Gun (1986)	Musician, Arr.
Quicksilver (1986)	Musician
Iron Eagle (1986)	Musician
9 1/2 Weeks (1986)	Musician, Arr.
The Doors (1991)	Musician

Film and Television with music composed, performed and arranged by Arthur Barrow:

The Torrent (1926/1997) silent with Greta Garbo
The Boob (1926/2001) silent with George K. Arthur
The Cameraman (1928/2004) silent with Buster Keaton
Heavenly Bodies (1984)
Misfits of Science (1985–1986)
Fast Times (1986)
Beverly Hills Body Snatchers (1989)
Waxworks II (1992)
The Great Eclipse (1992)
Saviors of the Forest (1993)

Made in the USA
Columbia, SC
05 April 2019